THE REVELS PLAYS

Former editors
Clifford Leech 1958–71
F. David Hoeniger 1970–85

General editors
David Bevington, E. A. Honigmann, J. R. Mulryne
and Eugene M. Waith

THE MAGNETIC LADY

THE REVELS PLAYS

THE REVELS PLAYS

THE
MAGNETIC LADY

BEN JONSON

edited by Peter Happé

MANCHESTER
UNIVERSITY PRESS
Manchester and New York

Introduction, critical apparatus, etc. copyright © Peter Happé 2000

The right of Peter Happé to be identified as the editor of this work has been asserted by him in accordance with the Copyright, Designs and Patents Act 1988.

Published by Manchester University Press
Oxford Road, Manchester M13 9NR, UK
and Room 400, 175 Fifth Avenue, New York, NY 10010, USA
www.manchesteruniversitypress.co.uk

Distributed exclusively in the USA by
Palgrave, 175 Fifth Avenue, New York NY 10010, USA

Distributed exclusively in Canada by
UBC Press, University of British Columbia, 2029 West Mall,
Vancouver, BC, Canada V6T 1Z2

British Library Cataloguing-in-Publication Data
A catalogue record for this book is available from the British Library

Library of Congress Cataloging-in-Publication Data
A catalog record for this book is available from the Library of Congress

ISBN 13: 978 0 7190 8040 1

First published in hardback 2000 by Manchester University Press
This paperback edition first published 2009

Printed by Lightning Source

Contents

Illustrations

1 and 2: With thanks to Brian Woolland and by kind permission of
Lib Taylor, photographer. 3 and 4: Keynes D.6.23 by kind permission of the Cambridge University Library.

General Editors' Preface

Clifford Leech conceived of the Revels Plays as a series in the mid-1950s, modelling the project on the New Arden Shakespeare. The aim, as he wrote in 1958, was 'to apply to Shakespeare's predecessors, contemporaries and successors the methods that are now used in Shakespeare's editing'. The plays chosen were to include well-known works from the early Tudor period to about 1700, as well as others less familiar but of literary and theatrical merit: 'the plays included', Leech wrote, 'should be such as to deserve and indeed demand performance'. We owe it to Clifford Leech that the idea became reality. He set the high standards of the series, ensuring that editors of individual volumes produced work of lasting merit, equally useful for teachers and students, theatre directors and actors. Clifford Leech remained General Editor until 1971, and was succeeded by F. David Hoeniger, who retired in 1985.

The Revels Plays are now under the direction of four General Editors, David Bevington, E. A. J. Honigmann, J. R. Mulryne and E. M. Waith. Published originally by Methuen, the series is now published by Manchester University Press, embodying essentially the same format, scholarly character and high editorial standards of the series as first conceived. The series concentrates on plays from the period 1558–1642, and includes a small number of non-dramatic works of interest to students of drama. Some slight changes have been made: for example, in editions from 1978, notes to the introduction are placed together at the end, not at the foot of the page. Collation and commentary notes continue, however, to appear on the relevant pages.

The text of each Revels play, in accordance with established practice in the series, is edited afresh from the original text of best authority (in a few instances, texts), but spelling and punctuation are modernised and speech headings are silently made consistent. Elisions in the original are also silently regularised, except where metre would be affected by the change; since 1968 the '-ed' form is used for non-syllabic terminations in past tenses and past participles ('-'d' earlier), and '-èd' for syllabic ('-ed' earlier). The editor emends, as distinct from modernises, the original only in instances where error is patent, or at least very probable, and correction persuasive. Act divisions are given only if they appear in the original or if the structure of the play clearly points to them. Those act and scene divisions not in the original are provided in small type. Square brackets are also used for any other additions to or changes in the stage directions of the original.

Revels Plays do not provide a variorum collation, but only those variants which require the critical attention of serious textual students. All departures of substance from 'copy-text' are listed, including any relineation and those changes in punctuation which involve to any degree a decision between alternative interpretations; but not such accidentals as turned letters, nor necessary additions to stage directions whose editorial nature is already made clear by the use of brackets. Press corrections in the 'copy-text' are likewise collated. Of later emendations of the text, only those are given which as alternative readings still deserve attention.

One of the hallmarks of the Revels Plays is the thoroughness of their annotations. Besides explaining the meaning of difficult words and passages, the editor provides comments on customs or usage, text or stage-business—indeed, on anything judged pertinent and helpful. Each volume contains an Index to the Commentary, in which particular attention is drawn to meanings for words not listed in *OED*, and (starting in 1996) an indexing of proper names and topics in the Introduction and Commentary.

The introduction to a Revels play assesses the authority of the 'copy-text' on which it is based, and discusses the editorial methods employed in dealing with it; the editor also considers the play's date and (where relevant) sources, together with its place in the work of the author and in the theatre of its time. Stage history is offered, and in the case of a play by an author not previously represented in the series a brief biography is given.

It is our hope that plays edited in this fashion will promote further scholarly and theatrical investigation of one of the richest periods in theatrical history.

DAVID BEVINGTON
E. A. J. HONIGMANN
J. R. MULRYNE
E. M. WAITH

Editor's acknowledgements

It is a great pleasure to thank all those who, in diverse ways, have helped me along the way, especially Mark Bland, Martin Butler, Sarah Davies, Peter Glazebrook, Olga Horner, Alastair MacDonald, John McGavin, Bella Millett, Brian Murdoch, Oliver Padel, Alison Samuels, Julie Sanders, Anna Trussler, Meg Twycross, Melanie Wisner, Chris Woolgar, and Brian Woolland. I am much indebted to staff at the Alexander Turnbull Library, Wellington, the Bodleian Library (especially in Duke Humphrey), Boston Public Library, Cambridge University Library (especially in the Rare Books Room), the Folger Shakespeare Library, Washington, D.C., the Harry Ransom Center, Austin, Texas, the Hartley Library at Southampton University, the Houghton Library, Harvard, the Huntington Library, the New York Public Library, the Pierpont Morgan Library, New York, and to the Librarians at Christ's, Gonville and Caius, King's, Newnham, and Trinity Colleges in Cambridge, and at All Souls, Oxford. I have benefited more than I can say from the advice and learning of my General Editor, Ernst Honigmann, who has always borne a wary eye.

PETER HAPPÉ

Abbreviations

JONSON

Alc.　*The Alchemist.*
Augurs　*The Masque of Augurs.*
BF　*Bartholomew Fair.*
Cat.　*Catiline.*
Conv.　*Conversations with Drummond.*
CR　*Cynthia's Revels.*
DA　*The Devil is an Ass.*
Disc.　*Discoveries.*
E. Blackfriars　*An Entertainment at the Blackfriars.*
EH　*Eastward Ho.*
EMI　*Every Man in his Humour.*
EMO　*Every Man out of his Humour.*
Ep.　*Epigrams.*
Forest　*The Forest.*
Fort. Isles　*The Fortunate Isles, and their Union.*
Love's Welcome　*Love's Welcome at Bolsover.*
Misc.　*Miscellaneous Poems.*
ML　*The Magnetic Lady.*
Nept. Tr.　*Neptune's Triumph for the Return of Albion.*
NI　*The New Inn.*
Poet.　*Poetaster.*
Staple　*The Staple of News.*
Sej.　*Sejanus.*
SW　*The Silent Woman.*
SS　*The Sad Shepherd.*
T of T　*The Tale of a Tub.*
Und.　*The Underwood.*
Volp.　*Volpone.*

Editions

F　*The Works of Benjamin Jonson.* [The Third Volume] (London, 1641).
F3　*The Works of Ben Jonson* (London, 1692).
Fc　*F* corrected.
Fu　*F* uncorrected.
G　*The Works of Ben Jonson,* ed. William Gifford. 9 vols (London, 1816).
H&S　*Ben Jonson,* ed. C. H. Herford and P. and E. Simpson, 11 vols (Oxford, 1925–52).
Peck　*The Magnetick Lady,* ed. W. H. Peck (New Haven, 1914).
Wha　*The Works of Ben Jonson,* ed. Peter Whalley, 7 vols (London, 1756).
Wi　*The Complete Plays of Ben Jonson,* ed. G. A. Wilkes, 4 vols (Oxford, 1982).

SHAKESPEARE

Cor.   Coriolanus.
Cym.   Cymbeline.
Gent.   Two Gentlemen of Verona.
Ham.   Hamlet.
2H4   King Henry IV, Part 2.
H8   King Henry VIII.
Lear   King Lear.
LLL   Love's Labour's Lost.
Mac.   Macbeth.
MerVen.   The Merchant of Venice.
MND   A Midsummer Night's Dream.
MWW   The Merry Wives of Windsor.
Oth.   Othello.
R2   King Richard II.
RJ   Romeo and Juliet.
Shrew   The Taming of the Shrew
TwN   Twelfth Night.
Act, scene and line references are to the Arden Shakespeare.

OTHER

Apology   Sir Philip Sidney, *An Apology for Poetry*, ed. Geoffrey Shepherd (Manchester, 1973).
Barton   Anne Barton, *Ben Jonson, Dramatist* (Cambridge, 1984).
Bentley   G. E. Bentley, *The Jacobean and Caroline Stage*, 7 vols (Oxford, 1941–68).
BJJ   *The Ben Jonson Journal.*
Burton, Anatomy   Robert Burton, *The Anatomy of Melancholy* (1521), ed. N. K. Kiessling, T. C. Faulkner and R. L. Blair, (Oxford, 1990–   ).
Celebration   W. Blisset, J. Patrick and R. W. Van Fossen (eds), *A Celebration of Ben Jonson* (Toronto, 1973).
Chalfant   F. C. Chalfant, *Ben Jonson's London: A Jacobean Placename Dictionary* (Athens, Ga, 1978).
Chambers   E. K. Chambers, *The Elizabethan Stage*, 4 vols (Oxford, 1923).
Chaucer   *The Riverside Chaucer*, ed. L. D. Benson (Oxford, 1987).
Cotgrave   Randle Cotgrave, *A Dictionarie of the French and English Tongues* (London, 1611).
cw   catchword (textual notes).
Dent   R. W. Dent, *Proverbial Language in English Drama Exclusive of Shakespeare, 1485–1616* (Berkeley and Los Angeles, 1984).
DNB   *The Dictionary of National Biography*, ed. Lesley Stephen and Sidney Lee (London, 1908–9).
Donaldson   Ian Donaldson, *Jonson's Magic Houses* (Oxford, 1997).
Earle, *Microcosmographie*   J. Earle, *Microcosmographie* (London, 1628), ed. E. Arber (London, 1869).
EETS   Early English Text Society.
Gen. Prol.   Geoffrey Chaucer, *General Prologue to the Canterbury Tales.*

Greg   W. W. Greg, *A Bibliography of English Printed Drama to the Restoration*, 5 vols (London, 1939–59).
Heywood, John, *Dial. Provs John Heywood's Dialogue of Proverbs*, ed. R. E. Habernicht (Berkeley and Los Angeles, 1963).
Heywood, John   *The Plays of John Heywood*, ed. Richard Axton and Peter Happé (Cambridge, 1991).
JAB   The Jonson Allusion Book, ed. J. F. Bradley and J. Q. Adams (New Haven, 1927).
Johnson, *Architecture*   A. W. Johnson, *Ben Jonson: Poetry and Architecture* (Oxford, 1994).
Kay   W. David Kay, *Ben Jonson: A Literary Life* (Basingstoke, 1995).
Lyly   *The Complete Works of John Lyly*, ed. R. Warwick Bond, 3 vols (Oxford, 1902).
Middleton, *Trick*   Thomas Middleton, *A Trick to Catch the Old One* in *The Works of Thomas Middleton*, ed. A. H. Bullen, 8 vols (London 1885–6).
MP   Modern Philology.
OED   Oxford English Dictionary.
ODEP   F. P. Wilson, *The Oxford Dictionary of English Proverbs*, 3rd edition (Oxford, 1970).
Partridge   E. Partridge, *Shakespeare's Bawdy*, revised edition (London, 1955).
Plautus   *Plays*, ed. and trans. P. Nixon, Loeb edition, 5 vols (London, 1950).
RES   The Review of English Studies.
Riggs   D. Riggs, *Ben Jonson: A Life* (Cambridge, Mass., 1989).
SB   Studies in Bibliography.
SEL   Studies in English Literature (Houston).
SP   Studies in Philology.
STC   A Short-Title Catalogue of Books Printed in England, Scotland and Ireland, and of English Books Printed Abroad, 2nd edition, ed. W. A. Jackson, F. J. Ferguson and K. F. Panzer, 3 vols (London, 1976–91).
Stevenson   Burton Stevenson, *The Home Book of Proverbs, Maxims and Familiar Phrases* (New York, 1948).
Stubbes, *Abuses*   Phillip Stubbes, *The Anatomie of Abuses* (1583), ed. F. J. Furnivall (London, 1877–9).
Terence   *Terence*, ed. and trans. John Sargeant, Loeb edition, 2 vols (Cambridge, Mass., 1912).
Tilley   M. P. Tilley, *A Dictionary of the Proverbs in England in the Sixteenth and Seventeenth Centuries* (Ann Arbor, 1950).
TLS   The Times Literary Supplement.

Introduction

Biography

When the Master of the Revels licensed *The Magnetic Lady* on 12 October 1632,[1] Jonson was well into the difficult last phase of his life, which had begun with the stroke he suffered about four years earlier. As a result of this affliction he was now confined to his chamber in Westminster, being looked after by a woman about whom very little is known. Though there is evidence that some friends visited him from time to time, he now lived a relatively solitary life in which he gradually became forgotten by those who inhabited the worlds of the stage, the social life of the taverns and the Court, in all of which he had been so successful. On 20 September 1632, John Pory, a not necessarily hostile purveyor of news, noting the imminent appearance of *The Magnetic Lady* remarked that it was by 'Ben Jonson, who I thought had been dead'.[2]

Nevertheless Jonson remained remarkably productive up to his death on 16 August 1637.[3] We should recognise that in terms of the quantity of projects he undertook his output compares favourably with his earlier years. Even at his most successful he was reputedly slow in composition. In this period of physical disability, besides *The Magnetic Lady*, he wrote *The New Inn* (1629), *The Tale of a Tub* (1633), and four Acts of *The Sad Shepherd* (1635), as well as planning and outlining *Mortimer, His Fall*. He wrote two Court masques: *Love's Triumph through Callipolis* for Twelfth Night 1631, and *Chloridia* for Shrovetide (performed 22 February, a few weeks later). Both these works went to the printer in the same year. In response to the Earl of Newcastle's patronage, he wrote *The King's Entertainment at Welbeck*, performed in Nottinghamshire (31 May 1633) for King Charles I as he journeyed north to be crowned in Scotland; and Jonson celebrated the King's return on 30 July of the following year with *Love's Welcome at Bolsover*. He also wrote a formidable number of occasional poems in these years, and it seems certain that he was still at work on *Discoveries*. He was arranging for the abortive publication of Volume Two of his *Works* in 1631 (containing *Bartholomew Fair*, *The Staple of News* and *The Devil is an Ass*, and demanding close editorial attention), for the printing of *The New Inn* independently in 1631, and preparing many other items for publication after his death, in what was eventually to become Volume Three of the *Works* (1641).[4] We shall see later that *The Magnetic Lady* was one of these, and, like several of them, the text that we have is almost certainly the product of his own careful transcription. A number of the extant prose works such as *The English Grammar* and *Horace his Art of Poetry* were also in preparation at this time. Thus it seems that Jonson was not impaired mentally by his illness. The great variety of moods and settings in the plays he wrote at this time suggests that he remained highly inventive and was still prepared to innovate, though innovation was now often blended with retrospect.

Concurrently Jonson also suffered from some financial difficulty.[5] This had come about initially following the death of James I in 1625: from the latter, Jonson, as unofficial Poet Laureate, had derived many favours, including an income for writing Court masques practically every year for over twenty years. There were many changes initiated by King Charles, as we shall see, but there is an overriding impression that Jonson did not fit in so well with him, since he was of a more reserved and fastidious temperament than his father. Jonson now had to be active in the search for income, even though there was still some support from the new King to whom he remained persistently loyal. The financial difficulties may well have been why *The Staple of News* (1626) was his first completed and performed drama for ten years, and why he sustained his attempts to write the later plays and masques, and, in spite of frustrations, to have them printed. It is likely, however, that his motives were not simply financial: Jonson's attention to posthumous publication and his appointment of Sir Kenelm Digby as a literary executor suggests that fame was still a spur, and also that until the end of his life he tended to value the printed book above the stage performance, however brilliant.

In the Induction to *The Magnetic Lady* Jonson makes an indirect personal appearance. In this case he is referred to specifically by his own name, whereas we shall see that the characters of Compass and Ironside, following the precedents in other plays, represent complementary aspects of his own personality in the plot. John Trygust, the Boy at the Blackfriars who offers hospitality to Mr Probee and Mr Damplay, explains that the real Jonson is absent from the playhouse

(Ind.12–14) and goes on to give two insights into Jonson's thinking about this play. The first is that he is in a retrospective mode, with the approach of the end of his life, 'the shutting up of his circle'.[6] The reference is to Jonson's *impresa*, which he acknowledged to Drummond in 1619 in *Conversations* (578–9). It had the motto '*Deest quod duceret orbem*' ('That is missing which should control the circle'), and it comprised a compass with one leg broken, signifying his persistent sense that he had not quite the control over his work he might have wished.[7] The Boy shows that the idea of the 'Magnetic Mistress' is a 'fantasy' arising from this state. He leaves us to discover the link that the leading character of the play is called Compass, who directs most of the events of the story by manipulating the humours of the characters. This line of thought is explicitly connected to a retrospect concerning two humour plays from the beginning of Jonson's career, *Every Man in his Humour* and *Every Man out of his Humour*. Jonson now proposes a play which reconciles humours, neatly drawing upon what had once been well known, but giving a new twist to the outcome in line with the rather more tolerant and less acerbic satire which now pleased him. Much of Jonson's writing at this time shares this retrospective intent, as in the revival of Robin Hood in *The Sad Shepherd*, and in the recall of Elizabethan comedy in the fantastic adventures of *The New Inn* and the countrified ways portrayed in *A Tale of a Tub*.[8] Jonson may also have been responding to the popular kind of comedy now being performed on the Caroline stage.[9]

The second outstanding point made by Trygust is that Jonson will not write a Prologue, because 'he has lost too much that way already, he says'. He claims that the players had wanted Jonson to write one to explain that the current disorders in the state might be related to the conflict of humours, but Jonson had declined. This delightful but pointed fiction is extended by Trygust's comment: 'and he himself, it seems, less cares'. There are several undercurrents here. One is that Jonson, through many of the plays, had kept up a dialogue with his audiences in the Prologues and Epilogues, and that he had also sought to dramatise his relationship with them by such devices as the contract enacted in the Prologue of *Bartholomew Fair* (1616), and the presence onstage of an audience of commenting 'gossips' in the Intermeans of *The Staple of News*. Another recurring aspect is that Jonson from time to time had shown some impatience with his audiences, in spite of having sought with meticulous and unstinting effort both to please and to instruct them. Even at this late stage of his life this fascinating enigma remains a feature of his plays. It is important not to reduce it just to resentment over some failures, even though Jonson was certainly disappointed at times, as he was to be with the response to *The Magnetic Lady* itself. It is perhaps wiser to see this recurring metatheatrical discourse as part of Jonson's dramatic code: a salient and attractive feature of his way of influencing and entertaining.[10] Hence Trygust observes, 'he will not woo the gentle ignorance so much' and that he is confident the play 'shall super-please judicious spectators'. In all probability Jonson's sense of his audience had two distinct parts which he emphasised at different times and in different circumstances—his dissatisfaction with public taste, and his genuine concern to grapple with improving it—but the whole issue is cleverly surrounded in irony in which Jonson's words cannot be taken at their face value. Probee and Damplay, come to judge the play, explicitly refer to their mandate from the people (Ind. 24). We can be certain, however, that Jonson always considered the audience worth his attention, and that he could not, and would not, create his plays without thinking of them. As he put it in *Poetaster*: 'If I prove the pleasure but of one, / So he judicious be, he shall b'alone / A theatre unto me' (Apol. Dial.213–15).

One may conclude from this discussion that Jonson was still, as always, deeply conscious of the impact of his plays, and also very resourceful in bringing this about. Thus he turns to advantage the retrospective mood, and we can also see from this dialogue between Trygust and the two observers that, if what he has to say has contemporary political implications by way of allegory, the process will be very well hidden. Nevertheless we must also consider the political and religious contexts of the play and how these were reflected in his other writings at this time. Jonson was always aware of the political world even though he habitually played a cautious hand when it came to portraying and influencing it.

Public contexts

King Charles's dissolution of Parliament in 1629 initiated the period of personal rule leading ultimately to the outbreak of the Civil War, which Jonson himself did not live to see. The Court became an object of much criticism from Puritan opponents, but recent historical writing has suggested that Charles did much to remove abuses and excesses of behaviour which had characterised some of the Jacobean entertainments.[11] One of the most positive aspects of the new regime at Court is that both the King and the Queen became active participants in the masques. Admittedly the enormous expenditure was a target of criticism, but Charles probably intended that the idealism displayed in these masques should be part of the moral improvement. Though he held himself to be above debate, he saw it as a duty to promote them and to take part in them himself on a ceremonial basis. He took his role seriously enough to practise assiduously on a daily basis.[12] Possibly Charles was still reacting to the scandals of his father's reign such as the Overbury affair in 1616 in which the King was tarnished by the criminal excesses over the marriage of his favourite, Robert Carr, Earl of Somerset, to Lady Frances Howard, Countess of Essex. Jonson had been bold enough to pinpoint this outrage in *The Devil is an Ass* in 1616, but he handled the vindication of justice more circumspectly in the Whitehall masque *The Golden Age Restored* in the same year.[13] Especially from about 1630 King Charles's regime sought to promote obedience and political stability within the framework of the royal prerogative. As for the corruption, there was also a preoccupation to protect the country from it, and to do this Charles revived the pressure exerted by his father to ensure that the aristocracy exercised its responsibilities in country areas away from London.[14]

The authoritarianism of his government was echoed by the policies of William Laud, who became Bishop of London in 1627, and Archbishop of Canterbury in 1633. A much stronger emphasis upon ceremonial was now expected of the churches at parish level. This derived in part from the influence of James Arminius, the Dutch theologian (d. 1609). He was an object of much vilification from the extreme Protestant wing because his English followers, who many thought were papists in disguise, were hostile to the fundamental Protestant doctrine of predestination. Even James I had favoured those who thought Calvinism subversive, and Charles followed him in fearing Protestant unrest.[15] From the beginning of the new reign, Church and government worked closely together to promote a political objective which comprised a spiritual mystery at the heart of the state. This programme included architecture, and painting as well as the masques to which Jonson made his two contributions in 1631.

Though politics and religion could hardly be separated in most of the seventeenth century, there are two strands in Jonson's life which bear upon these issues in the 1630s. His religious history shows him in conflict with the authorities on a number of occasions. The most notable was that, having become a Catholic while in prison in October 1598, he was questioned in the aftermath of the Gunpowder Plot in 1605. However, Jonson sought to turn this to his advantage by demonstrating his loyalty to the new king who had so fortunately escaped destruction.[16] A year later he had to answer in the Consistory Court in London for not attending church as he was legally required to do. The upshot was that he was ordered to submit to religious instruction with a view to persuading him to return to the Anglican communion. He remained outside for several more years, perhaps until 1612. He commented to Drummond 'at his first communion in token of true reconciliation, he drank out the full cup of wine'.[17] The gesture and the memory of it suggest that religion ran deep in Jonson and that he had great difficulty in deciding his response to its challenges. Nevertheless it remained an active part of his imagination, especially in the mockery of the behaviour of some religious people on the stage. His satire of the worldliness of some Puritans occurred in the portrait of Zeal-of-the-Land Busy in *Bartholomew Fair*, where he might well have been called Lust-for-the-Land instead. More direct reference to his personal sense of religion is the assertion to Drummond that he would have liked to be a preacher: 'He hath a mind to be a churchman, and so he might have favour to make one sermon to the king'.[18] Perhaps that he would have felt more at home with the aspirations of Laud's conservative Anglicanism, but he was always courtier enough to avoid extreme manifestations of religious zeal. There are places in *The Magnetic Lady* where Laudian practices are at least pointed out, if not satirised, as in Polish's comments at 1.5.10–23. One has the sense that with Jonson religion was an essentially private matter. In an age where extreme opinions could be dangerous, Jonson's restraint is still remarkable.[19]

On the other hand he departed from the gloomy expectations of the Puritan concept of human beings, in his faith that, in spite of the corruption of society which he pilloried in his many portraits of avarice and self-seeking, people could be persuaded to improve. This optimism informs many of his later plays, and it may well be that one of the turning points was his portrayal of Wittipol in *The Devil is an Ass* (1616), where philandering turns to genuine sympathy for the unfortunate and likely to be impoverished Mrs Fitzdottrel. Though follies are mocked in *The Magnetic Lady*, the end of the comedy—the reconciliation indeed—is cheerful, and once again the financial rights of a woman are secured. In both plays justice is done by exposure and not by vindictive punishment.

The strand of political intentions is firmly tied to his loyalty to the King. He may rebuke the Court for being dilatory in paying him his dues,[20] but there is in the poetry a persistent strain of praise and respect for the monarchy. Jonson himself admits to being anxious about overplaying the praise of his superiors:

> Though I confess (as every muse hath erred,
> And mine not least) I have too oft preferred
> Men past their terms, and praised some names too much
> But 'twas with purpose to have made them such.
>
> (*Und.*, 14.19–22)

Yet he wrote a sensitive poem of sympathy to Henrietta Maria (who was a Roman Catholic) on the loss of her infant son in 1629, urging reassertion of faith:

> But thank His greatness and His goodness too;
> And think all still the best that He will do.
>
> (*Und.*, 63.9–10)

This may well be a moving recall and reflection of his own sense of loss on the death of young Benjamin Jonson at the age of seven in 1603 (*Ep.*, 40). There are many other interventions into the lives of the King and Queen which sustain this sense of proper respect and support. It may well be that the assassination of Buckingham in 1628 removed an influence on the King about which Jonson was suspicious, and that he was attracted by the happy prospect of the developing royal marriage.

Jonson also extended his interest and support to the aristocracy, but, if this might seem to be self-seeking, it too is often graced with tender feelings. This may best be seen in his poem entitled 'To the Immortal Memory and Friendship of that Noble Pair, Sir Lucius Cary and Sir H. Morison' (*Und.*, 70). The consolation for Cary on Morison's death in 1629 is that the latter died at his best, not feeling the decay of age, and that their friendship is not divided: 'Two names of friendship, but one star' (l. 98). The poetic complexity of this work suggests that Jonson was deeply interested in the close links between the two young heroes, and that he had to evolve adequate ways of reflecting this.

In the year of *The Magnetic Lady* Jonson wrote *An Epithalamion: or, a Song*, celebrating the marriage of Jerome Weston, son of the

Lord Treasurer, and Lady Frances Stuart.[21] It is a poem of similar complexity to the Cory–Morison Ode, and its genre as a wedding poem offered a number of poetic conventions which Jonson happily accepted and exploited. Its importance for our purposes lies in the emotional intensity, which it shares with the Ode. This time the celebration is for appropriate sexual discovery and fulfilment in marriage. It evidences the sensitivity of Jonson's sexual perception, which still includes a touch of bawdy humour. Nevertheless there is a palpable context of the patronage of the Treasurer, and the King and Queen, who were both present at the wedding (ll. 73–112). There is even an ambiguity at one point over which couple Jonson has in mind: the bride and groom, or the King and Queen.[22] Jonson's delicacy envisages pleasure and propagation, and hopes for lasting love. Of the bridal bed he says:

> That when you both are old,
>   You find no cold
>   There; but, renewèd, say,
> (After the last child born); this is our wedding day.

(ll. 165–8)

Although both these poems are not about Jonson's personal life at this time they reflect his ability to experience and to represent sensitively the feelings of others. Further examples are to be found in the 'Elegy on the Lady Jane Pawlet' who died in childbed in 1631 (*Und.*, 83), and 'Eupheme' (*Und.*, 74), the sequence he wrote in 1633 in memory of Lady Venetia Digby, beloved wife of Sir Kenelm Digby, his literary executor. These poems suggest that Jonson was not psychologically damaged by his misfortunes, and I propose that we should look at the late plays in the light of this. Alongside satirical discourse he introduces emotional elements which do not sentimentalise human relationships. His solitariness may have been the result not only of his illness: he had lost both his wife and his children by the time of its onset. It is hard to dispel the impression that Jonson's emotional life was still vigorous, even though he externalised it chiefly in the lives, and the rites of passage, of others.

The two Court masques and two entertainments for the Earl of Newcastle which Jonson composed in the 1630s show how much he was committed to the idealisation of the monarchy and of the royal marriage. Neoplatonic concepts of kingship were used to celebrate the purity and chastity of the Court, and of the King and Queen at its centre. In *Chloridia* there is a saturnalian underworld which threatens rebellion as a manifestation of unbridled passion.[23] The antimasque shows the effects of a rebellion by Cupid, who thought he had not been sufficiently noticed. With the help of scenery by Inigo Jones, the dancers from hell show the disturbance on earth, which can only be calmed by Chloris, goddess of flowers, danced by the Queen herself.

In general there is a willingness to make political statements in these Caroline masques even though Jonson had reason to be cautious because of his own declining position, and also because his feud with Inigo Jones was leading him into a more hostile environment.[24] There is a close link between the qualities of love and chastity perceived and portrayed in the royal marriage and Jonson's support for a stable monarchy. But, loyal though he was, Jonson was never one to allow himself to be silenced, and in any case his views did certainly support the monarchy, and his religious attitudes were more or less in line with some of the Laudian principles. It has been pointed out that the entertainments given to King Charles at Welbeck and Bolsover were remarkable in that they allowed Jonson to speak in his own voice even though the main point of such events was to draw attention to the interests of the aristocratic host rather than the individual interests of the poet, his servant for the event, who was normally required to remain in the background.[25] Perhaps one of the most intriguing aspects is the way Jonson now limited the effect of the antimasque. Instead of allowing it to be a challenge to the intention of the main subject, there is a sense that the device was now to contain and even suppress the contrary impulses. In *Love's Welcome at Bolsover* Inigo Jones is ridiculed in the figure of Coronel Vitruvius and the dance of his Mechanics. But the King and Queen are represented as the rose and the lily, and by two Cupids who complement one another in celebrating the 'School-Divinity of Love' (l. 162). Jonson's work in these four pieces, which are roughly contemporary with *The Magnetic Lady*, shows him adjusting sensitively to the changes at Court in spite of his personal isolation; and although he expressed elsewhere his resentment at the growing importance of the visual aspects of the masques manifested in the contribution by Inigo Jones,[26] Jonson was still highly inventive and adaptable, and his creative work here shows sensitivity to the theatrical context for which it was intended. As it is in the plays, the issue of the audience's awareness of what Jonson meant for them is apparent here in the two masques. The ephemerality of one night's experiences was turned into printed form, and *Love's Triumph through Callipolis* begins with a statement which must by definition have been addressed to a readership rather than to an audience about the objective 'to carry a mixture of profit with them, no less than delight' under a heading: 'To make the spectators understanders'.

JONSON'S THEATRE: THEORY AND PRACTICE

Time and place

Like most of Jonson's plays from *The Devil is an Ass* onwards, *The Magnetic Lady* was performed by the King's Men at the Blackfriars.[27] There is very little in the text to suggest that Jonson demanded much from the physical circumstances of this theatre, which was small in size and tended to have an elite audience because of its relatively high admission charge, referred to by Damplay (2 Chor.61–2). Jonson's tendency to use a relatively plain stage for most of his plays was presumably a deliberate choice, since he disliked stage machinery which, he thought, distracted from the all-important spoken word.[28] In this play Jonson followed the unities of time and place quite closely. As to time, the action lasts from the morning, before dinner, through the afternoon. Palate is reluctant to marry Compass and Pleasance in the afternoon (4.6.33). Needle is to have a pill 'afore supper' (5.7.73); and in the last scene it is said that the stars have been retrograde since six o'clock (5.10.12–14).

The place is treated with similar simplicity. Most of the action occurs in a room in Lady Loadstone's house. It is not given a particular designation, but when Sir Moth is brought in, in shock on a chair, he has to be moved 'into the air' (3.5.1), suggesting there is a window or an outside door. The First Act, however, is played in the street outside the house. This is a deliberate revival of the practice in classical comedy where most of the action is often in a street with doors into houses from which characters can enter. The Boy's comment makes clear that Jonson saw the plain stage as linked with the classical precedents of the market place: 'Sir, all our work is done without a portal—or Vitruvius. *In foro* as a true comedy should be' (Ind.76–7).[29] Lady Loadstone apparently meets her guests at her door and briefly converses with them there. Compass slips into the house unobserved (1.2.48), and subsequently comes out again at the beginning of 1.5, to speak of Sir Moth, Loadstone's brother who is within (1.6.31). Once inside, everything is played in the room itself, occasionally, as in 2.4, with two groups of characters onstage who are not directly communicating with each other. This arrangement is reminiscent of that used for *The Alchemist*, where the clients are received in turn in the workshop and yet there are scenes outside the house in the street framing the main action. In both cases the neutral central space acts as a magnet for the various visitors who come to exploit what is on offer within.

The use of this space is made more complex however by two devices. One is the creation of imaginary spaces around the actual stage in which various actions and moods can be described or suggested. The most important is the scene in the dining room, which is concurrent with Act 3, scene 1. The seating plan is described and, after an offstage uproar, the consequences of Ironside's throwing a glass of wine at Sir Diaphanous are first related, and then revealed in snatches as the characters emerge from the scene in various states of surprise. The dramatic technique here involves a narrative of what has happened, which appears in scattered details, as well as the making of a theatrical analysis of the consequences. The characters are presented one by one, each with a tale to tell, except for Placentia who is carried across the stage unable to speak because, as it turns out, the shock of the assault at dinner has put her into labour (Act 3, scenes 2–5). Dryden made the following comment on this particular sequence, explaining that its purpose was:

> to save the undecent appearing of them on the stage and to abbreviate the story: and this in express imitation of Terence who had done the same thing before him in his *Eunuch*, where Pythias makes the relation of what happened within at the soldiers' entertainment.[30]

A set piece of similar kind occurs in Act 5 when Sir Moth, in offstage pursuit of treasure, has to be pulled out of a well in the garden. Further imaginary spaces are the room or cupboard in which Polish locks up Pleasance (5.2.10), Lady Loadstone's private chamber where she seeks consolation (3.3.31–2), and, outside the house, the church behind the old Exchange (4.6.10–11), and the ward (or local district of London, 5.6.17). This sense of offstage space is found in classical drama, but it was also much developed in the Tudor theatre.[31]

The second spatial device is the framing of the Chorus or commentary between the Boy and Probee and Damplay, who have come to see *The Magnetic Lady* in performance at the Blackfriars. This has a few distinctive physical aspects as the Boy welcomes them, seats them prominently near him, presumably on the stage somewhere with a good view of the action, and offers them wine.[32] There are hints that these two represent the upper social echelons as they are knights' brothers and knights' friends (Ind.62–3), but the Boy, no doubt echoing his master, declares he is more interested in understanding than in clothes (Ind.47–8). Jonson does not allow these observers to interrupt the action, confining them to a choric role between the Acts. Nevertheless they are there watching the play and giving voice to some of the objections to Jonson's decisions as a dramatist. In this way they give an extra perspective to Jonson's art, not least as they bring out an aggressive response from the Boy. Because they are outside the plot they give emphasis to other metatheatrical moments within it. As it happened, a remarkable irony developed at one early performance which can hardly have been anticipated by Jonson. The character of Damplay is a satirical hit at Inigo Jones (See Ind.72–3n). In the event Jones himself was present at one of the early performances and did indeed ridicule the play.[33]

The theoretical framework

For many years Jonson had made a practice of discussing his theatrical methods with his audiences in Prologues; he had also dramatised his theoretical preoccupations in a number of ways. *The Magnetic Lady* takes this process even further in that he makes specific and detailed reference to neoclassical theories of comedy. Indeed the play has probably been noticed by critics and historians more for his presentation of this topic than for any other reason. Jonson's motivation may not have simply been to assure his audience that his play was correctly constructed. His commitment to a specific exposition may have been part of his feud with Inigo Jones, and it may also have related to a shift in subject matter as Jonson strove to write a different kind of comedy from that of the so-called citizen comedies of his earlier years satirising London life, and yet to remain within classical precedents. The plot of *The Magnetic Lady*, as we have noted, ends in reconciliation, and there are three marriages in view at the last. Moreover it turns upon some rather unlikely plot conventions such as the exchange of the infants by Mistress Polish, as well as the elaborate recollection of the loving marriage of Mr and Mrs Steele, the parents of true Placentia. Jonson had adopted similar features in the complex story of the Frampul

family in *The New Inn*, and that play had not been well received on
the stage: it led to Jonson's irascible *Ode to Himself* (first printed in
the 1631 octavo edition) turning his back upon the stage—but not
for long. This change of plotting style was no doubt a reflection of
changes in Jonson's psychological outlook at this time, something a
bit mellower than previously. But it also moved him nearer to the
popular stage of the Caroline period in which romance became
part of popular expectation. Jonson ridiculed such things with
their miraculous and juggling elements in a passage reminiscent of
Sidney's mockery in the previous generation,[34] and the purpose of
the classical exposition was probably to show that, even if he had
moved towards a more romantic kind of drama, his work was still
properly plotted and controlled within the rules which he would
have traced back to Terence and to the theoretical exposition of Aristotle's *Poetics* and the commentators on it.[35]

Jonson separates emphatically the discourse about theory between
the Boy, Probee and Damplay from the rest of the action: the Boy
says that the poet has affirmed that the play needs no 'interpreter'
(Ind.140). As we have seen, the Boy expressly forbids them to
interrupt, whereas long before, in *Every Man out of his Humour*,
Mitis and Cordatus had been encouraged to do so (Ind.154–6).
This decision suggests that Jonson attached great importance to
the framing discussion, and in this play he has succeeded in making it a very lively affair. It is perhaps an extension of the Argument which he supplied for *The New Inn* when it was printed,
but that, of course, was expressly for the book form, whereas
here the material is dramatised. To do so he invented the characters
of the two critics come from the people, and the Boy who is probably based in part on his dramatic apprentice Richard Brome,
and partly upon himself. According to the fiction he invents, both
had received their learning at Westminster School, where an
introduction to the plays of Terence would have been part of the
curriculum.[36]

In response to critical comment, particularly from Damplay,
the Boy responds with two main concerns: the structure, and the
process of interpretation by the audience. The play must be arranged
in five Acts, the salient divisions being the *protasis* or setting forth
of the situation, the *epitasis* which complicates the situation, the *catastasis* in which there is a surprise development after a false resolution, and the *catastrophe*, which need not be a disaster but which
resolves the plot. In spite of the romantic events noted above, Jonson

sticks carefully to this. The First Act is the *protasis*. The *epitasis* is begun by the negotiations for a husband for Placentia and reaches a climax in Ironside's throwing the glass of wine at Sir Diaphanous, leading to the complication of the revelation of Placentia's pregnancy. The *catastasis* occurs through Compass's discovery of the swapping of the infants in 4.4, whereupon he promptly marries Pleasance, who, he now knows, is the true heiress. Finally the *catastrophe* is brought about in the exposure and defeat of the avaricious Sir Moth and the marriage of Lady Loadstone and Ironside. The Boy's exposition of the structure in 2 Chorus is supported by a further response to Damplay's criticism in 3 Chorus, after the *epitasis*, that it was 'a pitiful poor shift o' your poet' to make the principal woman pregnant in order to turn events. The reply is that the event was properly hinted in advance—he means by Rut's mistaken diagnosis of a tympany—and again Jonson is concerned to justify the classical purity of his plotting.

The Boy's second defence is the need to avoid specific identification of satirical elements with actual people. This is in response to Damplay's challenge at the beginning of 2 Chorus as to whether Bias has a real life counterpart. Probee energetically supports the Boy, defending the 'innocence and candour of the author' against calumny. The argument is sustained by the need to attack vices in general according to the precedents of Plautus and Terence (2 Chor.12–17), and again it is interesting that the importance Jonson attaches to this is sufficient to have Probee, rather than the Boy, cite this evidence.[37] Perhaps Jonson is protesting too much, for Inigo Jones is a recurring object of satire in this play, as well as in some of Jonson's other works of the time. It is thus ironical—and rather amusing—that Damplay, whose bad Latin is itself a hit at Jones (Ind.72–3n), is the one who raises the problem of specific identification.

In 4 Chorus, the last in the printed text, the discussion is also about controlling the response of the audience. Damplay, again the initiator, complains of the complexity of the plot. In some ways he is right, and his complaint may well be Jonson's own recognition that he did deliberately set about evolving complicated plot lines, here and elsewhere, especially in the second half of his plays, after the *epitasis*. However Damplay is advised by Probee to be patient and see how things turn out. The latter includes a telling phrase about the plays 'as they are made' (4 Chor.14–15) to strengthen the suggestion that audiences must respond to the author's intention.

This is a reprise of the Boy's point in the Induction, for which, significantly, he cites the authority of Jonson himself:

> For, I must tell you, not out of mine own dictamen but the author's, a good play is like a skein of silk: which, if you take by the right end, you may wind off at pleasure on the bottom or card of your discourse in a tale or so, how you will: but if you light on the wrong end, you will pull all into a knot, or elf-lock, which nothing but the shears or a candle will undo or separate. (Ind.128–35).

In these Choruses Jonson was using the ambiguities of dialogue and the ways by which the author's voice could be buried in it as a means of expressing his attitude to the play. The classical doctrine is certainly there, with its emphasis upon humane learning and proper decorum, and these are made explicit, but the underlying motivation is not so distinctive, and the play of irony in these framing scenes adds much to the entertainment of their dramatisation. This intriguing dramatic tension is enhanced by his own indirect presence in these scenes, especially where the Boy specifically refers to Jonson's authority; but the real-life, directing dramatist remains separate from the intermittent appearances of the *persona* of Jonson-in-the-play.

Theatrical qualities

As we shall see from the performance history of *The Magnetic Lady* (below, pp. 21–9) there is very little to be said which can be based upon practical experience of the play on the stage. What follows is an attempt to bring out some features which might be important in production by examining the text itself, and to an extent by considering how other more frequently performed plays by Jonson may illuminate this one. I shall deal with the plot, and some features of dialogue, scene and character.[38]

The initial exposition is a leisurely affair in which the suitors for the hand of Placentia, the heiress, are reviewed and characterised. In fact their arrivals and their descriptions by Compass, the manipulator and hero, follow a Chaucerian model, and once his view is established in Act 1 we see them again from the point of view of some of the women characters in Act 2, scene 1. These sequences are really a procession of 'humours' which, in accordance with Jonson's subtitle, it is the ultimate business of the play to 'reconcile'. The acceleration of the plot from Act 3 onwards, following

Ironside's assault at the dinner table, depends upon a skilful inter-weaving of two lines of narrative. On the one hand Placentia is deliv-ered of a child, as the audience is clearly informed, not least by the fact that the pretentious Dr Rut is egregiously and ridiculously wrong in failing to spot the pregnancy. It becomes a factor that this birth has to be concealed in order to sustain the issue of Placentia's marriage portion which is in the possession of her uncle.

But the second plot line is the revelation in Act 4, scene 4, at a very effective *late* moment in the play, to the audience and to Compass that Placentia was exchanged in her cradle for the real niece, Pleasance, by Mistress Polish, her true mother, for financial benefit.[39] This piece of information is carefully managed by Jonson so that the audience know it instantly: but some characters are kept either in complete ignorance, or at least in some doubt as to whether the exchange really did occur; or thirdly, some try to pretend that it was not so. Compass proceeds to manipulate the circumstances so that he marries Pleasance, the real heiress, while he frustrates Sir Moth Interest, the avaricious uncle who seeks to keep the portion for himself. But the unfolding of these events is deliberately made hard to follow by Jonson, not only to the characters but also to the audience, perhaps in accordance with the motivation noted above. The resolution is ultimately achieved by a clever interaction of the two narrative elements whereby the search for the very real baby is made the means by which the cradle exchange a generation ago is acknowledged by all. It is significant that when Pleasance confirms that she definitely did hold the new-born baby in her arms, and that it was alive, Compass comments, 'I ha' the right thread now, and I will keep it' (5.10.81). This picks up on the passage quoted above concerning the skein of silk (Ind.128–35).

In approaching the dialogue of this play I should like to look at the kinds of scene the play offers. There is for example, very little in the way of monologue or soliloquy: just the briefest aside by Compass as he thinks how to make the most of his chance discovery of the child-changing. But much of the play is conversation, and a good deal of that, in the first half at least, concerns the exposition of character. This occurs directly, so to speak when Compass gives a 'character' to Parson Palate in couplets, and another to Doctor Rut in blank verse. He draws attention to the verse form in the dialogue, and acknowledges that the verses were written by 'a great clerk' called Ben Jonson (1.2.33–4). This is a deliberately unrealistic speech in which Jonson is relying for its theatrical effect upon the skill and flair with which it is delivered: in this way the dialogue is also a contribution to the characterisation of Compass, who as we have seen has a special function as a kind of congenial presenter and manipulator of the action. There is also here an example of the self-deprecating joke, for Jonson's 'great' refers to his own twenty stones. It is a technique he shares with the bashful Chaucer of *The Canterbury Tales*.[40]

On the other hand Jonson sets out at times to write dialogue in which a large number of characters participate on quasi-realistic terms so that the changes in emotion which accompany changes in circumstances and fortune are portrayed, and we find ourselves carried forward by the momentum of the speeches. This can best be seen at the beginning of Act 3 in a sequence of short scenes. Off-stage, dinner is being served in Lady Loadstone's house. In the first scene Needle welcomes Item, the apothecary, who comes with news for Rut, at present seated within at the dinner table. He is encouraged to go in by Needle who gives a description of the assembled diners, but this is interrupted by a noise within and the panicky entrance of Pleasance who needs help for Placentia now frightened because weapons have been drawn at table. The entrance of Compass, seeking to calm down the enraged and indignant Ironside, is marked in the text, in Jonson's classical mode, as a new scene, but the action is clearly continuous. It turns out that Ironside took offence because Sir Diaphanous Silkworm, a courtier, insisted on drinking his wine 'with three parts water', a proceeding so effeminate that the aggressive Ironside threw a glass of wine in his face. The dialogue reaches a higher pitch of excitement however when Placentia overwhelmed by the shock at the dinner table, is carried over the stage by Dr Rut, Mistress Polish, Nurse Keep, Pleasance and Lady Loadstone accompanied by the following—

Lady. Good gossip, look to her.
Polish.   How do you, sweet charge?
Keep. She's in a sweat.
Polish.   Ay, and a faint sweat, marry.
Rut. Let her alone to Tim: he has directions.
    I 'll hear your news, Tim Item, when you ha' done.

                      [*Exeunt* ITEM, POLISH, KEEP *and*
                      PLEASANCE, *with* PLACENTIA.]

Lady. Was ever such a guest brought to my table?
Rut. These boisterous soldiers ha' no better breeding.

                     [*Enter* COMPASS.]

Here Master Compass comes. Where's your captain,
Rudhudibras de Ironside?
Compass.   Gone out of doors.
Lady. Would he had ne'er come in them, I may wish.

(3.3.4–12)

Even in this short passage of rapid exchanges from different points
in the stage space, we can see glimpses of character in Rut's bos-
siness, and Lady Loadstone's tentative sense of propriety. The
humours are thus embodied in the dialogue.

This discussion of some of the varieties of dialogue also points to
the versatility in the construction of individual scenes. For example,
the crisis noted above leads directly to a sequence in Act 3 concerning duelling. Diaphanous is so offended by Ironside's action
that he decides to challenge Ironside; but he is so incompetent that
Compass has to intervene to manage the situation. When Ironside
proves much fiercer than is comfortable—Jonson was always
interested in the stage possibilities of physical violence and
rage—Compass has to intervene to stiffen up the challenge by the
pusillanimous Diaphanous. His contribution however leads in
several different directions. One is to reveal the lack of true valour
in Diaphanous; another is to show how the crafty, court-based self-
interest of Master Bias, the 'politique', prevents him carrying the
challenge for fear of his political masters: 'I will not hazard my lord's
favour so . . . I have to commend me / Naught but his lordship's
good opinion' (3.6.8–11).

We should put this exploitation of the frightened duellist motif
alongside a variety of other types of scenes. There is Rut's ignorant
diagnosis of Placentia's fainting fit in which he gives a learned disquisition on several kinds of 'tympanies', except the correct one.
Jonson pursues avarice in another kind of scene in which Sir Moth
Interest, the greedy uncle, gives eight reasons to justify his view that
the love of money is not the root of all evil—or at least as far
as princes are concerned, with whom it may be a positive benefit
(2.6.41–101). In contrast to these two scenes, where there is a sense
that the verbal and rhetorical devices dominate the action, we have
the instant improvisation of Compass who moves events along at a
breakneck pace in the second half of the play—first he orders the
coach to go to the church and wait; then as his own marriage plan
develops rapidly he has it brought back. He manages also to give
an amorous hint or two to Pleasance on the way. This process is

undoubtedly stepped up by Jonson's confining events of the plot to the extent of one day.

The range of scenes is enhanced by Needle's performance of demonic possession in Act 5. Prompted by Item's desire to restore Rut's reputation by giving him something that he *can* cure, Item suggests that Needle pretend to have a fit in which he reveals hidden treasure in the garden. This takes in Sir Moth, who ends up falling into the well and having to be pulled out by means of a rope. The result of Item's scheme is reported from offstage, with much confusion. The device works successfully here because it acts as a distraction as Sir Moth tries to evade paying up the marriage portion, which is due on the recognition of the child-changing and the marriage of Compass and Pleasance. In short the plot management and the establishment of a variety of scene presentations are carefully integrated. One of the effects of this deliberate variation is that our sense of the artificiality of the events portrayed is enlarged. Though Jonson hardly pursued a comparable ideological and political polemic, there is no doubt that, like Brecht, he was prepared to exploit and juxtapose different processes of engaging the audience. That in itself increases the ways the audience can be induced to enjoy what they see, provided that they are not tied to 'realism': but it also means that the performance can be used to point up the evaluation of the moral issues which are at the heart of Jonson's poetic art. Performance is thus a servant of his intentions, and the text of this play gives us plenty of material which is entertaining, depending upon acting skills, and yet modulated in different ways.

In turning to character we should first note that the treatment of Mistress Polish, the mother of Placentia, works quite differently from the 'Chaucerian' character noted above. She is self-opinionated and over-solicitous, and, when it suits her, shows an excessive complaisance to her betters. But her main characteristic is her garrulousness, extending to malapropisms. These are carefully pointed up by Rut, who scorns them, and by Compass, who exploits them comically by deliberately misunderstanding. Such features come close to Jonson's fundamental interest in the purity of language, and it is noticeable that this is demonstrated dynamically and not by description. Indeed the hyperactivity of language is an effective performance feature. Experience showed Jonson, and should tell us, that bristlingly complicated language works well on stage. Here it has additional irony in that Polish's action in changing the babies may well have been justified. We shall return to the ambiguities of what she actually says below.

The characterisation in general shows a similar distancing to that noted in the plot. We are not really invited here to enter the emotional lives of the characters. Intimacy with the audience is not about emotions but about moral judgements and about the theatrical intentions which are necessary to mould the plot and direct the argument. In the marriage of Compass and Pleasance there are a few hints which give us the developing courtship, but really no sense that Compass, who on the whole is one of Jonson's admirable so-called 'gallants', is really in love with Pleasance. The contrast with Wittipol in *The Devil is an Ass* is striking. There the gallant sets out to seduce Mrs Fitzdottrel, but when it comes to the point he is moved more by compassion than lust and sets about giving her practical help—through plotting which is not unlike the dénouement of *The Magnetic Lady* in its complexity. In general the latter follows a discernible trend in Jonson's characterisation: that characters like Compass may be very active and ingenious, but we are not exactly being asked to like them. Nevertheless the performance opportunities arise because such characters have power and authority over the audience.

But if the characters are not given emotional depth their treatment in moral terms is purposeful. The follies of the professionals—the lawyer, the courtier, the doctor, the priest and the 'politique'—are ruthlessly exposed, and it is done, as I hope I have shown, using a variety of techniques. These humours characters exist only in their professional postures and posturing. Hence it does not really matter if they are not punished. Indeed what happens to them at the end is not retribution but exposure. Such an emphasis is in line with the ending of several others of Jonson's plays, including *The Alchemist* and *The Devil is an Ass*. Giving the characters signifying names is a further elaboration of this. The central attraction of the play, noted in the Induction, is Lady Loadstone, who draws characters around her. She is guided by Compass, and is eventually married to (capped by, see 5.10.145–6) Ironside, whom she trusts. Such metaphorical manipulation which is both verbal and performative is paralleled by a wealth of other detail such as the play on the child-changed girls' names, Pleasance/Placentia, and the exposure of humours, as in the gluttonous Parson Palate. Virtually all the names in *The Magnetic Lady* carry a symbolic or metaphorical reference.

It is desirable that a performance of *The Magnetic Lady* should take account of the non-realistic elements identified here. The text reveals, explicitly and implicitly, a very active consideration of how the structure and design of the play can operate to make of the audience 'true understanders'. In this way Jonson is firmly in line with the humanist blend of pleasure and instruction—an objective he always set himself, even at the risk of alienating the courtly audience and participants of the masques. But there is a creative uncertainty which is generated in performance. One specially interesting feature is that performance allows one to perceive the relative importance of different elements within a given play, and indeed it is a way of adjusting such emphases.

Performance history

We can but assume that the play has been rarely performed. I have been able to trace only three separate productions: the few occasions after its first appearance in 1632; a radio adaptation by Peter Barnes in 1987; and a staging at the Bridges Theatre, Bulmershe Court, University of Reading on 4–7 December 1996 (see figs 1, 2). There is in addition a limited amount of reference to the play in the seventeenth century which may suggest that it was known to some, but all these things indicate that historically very little time and effort has been spent by people of the theatre exploring the play. There has been no development of a performance culture around it, such as has been generated around the more well-known Jonson successes like *Volpone*, and directors undertaking a new production would have very little to follow or to react against. We may be able to glean a little from the three productions mentioned, but we have in *The Magnetic Lady* a play whose general critical reputation has not been high. Such a reputation is based on arbitrary factors, especially in relation to the 1632 production, and it may well be that the accidents surrounding that occasion have weighed too heavily on the fate of the play over the centuries. Stage reputation is notoriously fickle: it would seem that *The Devil is an Ass* suffered a very similar fate in and after 1616. Dryden's stigmatisation of the late plays as 'dotages' did not help.[41] The whole group has been more or less ignored by stage professionals and by literary critics for most of their time since their composition. Only within the last few years has the Royal Shakespeare Company attempted *The Devil is an Ass* (1995–6) and *The New Inn* (1987). With a dramatist of Jonson's stature, however, we may find that there is still a great deal to be discovered, were these plays performed more regularly.

1 Keep (Miriam Smith), Polish (Rosemary Hughes) and Chair (Margaret Tully) in the 1996 Reading University production

2 Diaphanous (Edwin Wills) negotiates with Bias (Darren Lee) in the
1996 Reading University production

The way was cleared for the first performance by the payment on
12 October 1632 of a fee of £2 by Knight, the book-keeper at the
Blackfriars, to the Master of the Revels: 'Received of Knight for
allowing of Ben Johnson's play called Humours Reconcil'd or the
Magnetic Lady to be acted'.[42] In broad terms there are three significant factors concerning the first performances. The first is that the
final Chorus, as printed in the Folio, is 'changed into an Epilogue to
the King', which implies that there was a performance at the Blackfriars and that there may have been at least an intention to present
the play at Court. The change may of course have been wishful thinking on Jonson's part, and no corroborative evidence from Court
records has come to light. But the implication of the Epilogue is that
the King's judgement is expected upon the play, whatever the present
'Gentlemen' may think. Whether these are Damplay and Probee,
who have no valedictory speech or action at their last appearance at
the end of Act 4, is not clear. It seems likely that there would have
been some parting shot from or about them in an original final
Chorus which the present ending superseded. As we shall see below
in discussing the text, the evidence surrounding it, especially the
spelling and punctuation, suggests that the copy for the printer was
a Jonson autograph, and there is no reason from either sense or presentation to doubt that the Epilogue is Jonson's own.

To judge from Alexander Gill's lampoon, there were at least
three performances at the Blackfriars in 1632, as he refers to 'three
shameful foils' (l. 23). But it is likely that the enterprise as a whole
never recovered from the uproarious behaviour by Inigo Jones and
Nathaniel Butter himself, who set about ridiculing the play off the
stage. The feud with Jones was now well advanced, and Jonson had
mocked both Gill's father in the masque *Time Vindicated to Himself
and to his Honours* and Butter in *The Staple of News*.[43] The disrup-
tive intention was supported by Gill's poem which suggested that
bricklaying, the trade to which Jonson had been apprenticed by his
stepfather, was a more fitting occupation for him than playwriting.
It reveals something of the atmosphere of a social occasion at the
Blackfriars in 'silks and plush, and all the wits . . . called to see' (ll.
9–10), and it shows how the mockery was conducted:

> O how thy friend Nat Butter 'gan to melt,
> Whenas the poorness of thy plot he smelt;
> And Inigo with laughter there grew fat
> That there was nothing worth the laughing at.

(ll. 15–18)

Jonson's annihilating reply follows precedents in some of Martial's *Epigrams*, but there is no disguising that he was affected by the ridicule, even though he makes a clever poem out of his anger.

Gill's poem gives us the names of two actors, John Lowen and Joseph Taylor, who were both King's Men and had appeared in *The New Inn*. Though this may just be a conventional reference to the two most important players of the company at the time, the kinds of parts they are thought to have played may help us to envisage aspects of the original performance. If Lowen was large in stature and played bluff parts he would fit Ironside well. Taylor, more commonly a romantic lead, but also playing ingenious parts, would do well as Compass.[44] There is also the strong possibility that Jonson knew these actors personally, and that when he wrote plays he was still able to design his characterisations accordingly.

The third event in the early circumstances of the play was a further entry by the Master of the Revels:

> Upon a second petition of the players to the High Commission court, wherein they did mee right in my care to purge their plays of all offense, my Lord's Grace of Canterbury bestowed many words upon mee, and discharged me of any blame, and layd the whole fault of their play called *The Magnetic Lady* upon the players. This happened the 24 of Octob., 1633, at Lambeth. In their first petition they would have excused themselves on me and the poet.[45]

Herford and the Simpsons assumed that the reason for the unease here, and the intervention of Archbishop Laud, was occasioned by the excessive use of oaths inserted by the players, but it should be noted that the quotation does not specifically refer to this. Martin Butler has pointed out that the censorship issue had actually been raised nearly a year earlier in a letter by Sir John Pory, dated 17 November 1632:

> The Players of the Blackfriars were on Thursday called before the High Commission at Lambeth, and were bound over to answer such articles as should be objected against them. And it is said to be for uttering some profane speeches in abuse of Scripture and holy ['wholly' in the original] things, which they found penned, for them to act and play, in Ben Jonson's new comedy called *The Magnetic Lady*.[46]

Again the cause of intervention is not actually oaths. The proposal by Butler that the real issue was the reference to Arminianism (1.5.10–23), the right-of-centre doctrines favoured by Bishop Laud, is more attractive, though it should be pointed out that Laud did not become Archbishop until 1633, being Bishop of London from 1627.[47] It seems likely that Polish's critical jibe may have attracted attention from a rather sensitive ecclesiastical quarter, and that as the players were ultimately held responsible there would have been some business or verbal embellishment in their playing which added to the uneasiness caused by Jonson's words. It is remarkable, however, that the issue and the playing were held to be important enough to be still active a year after the first performances. As Laud had in fact become the Archbishop by then, and the Master of Revels makes it clear that this was a direct personal intervention by him, it is possible that the matter was freshly important to him as he exerted his new authority.[48] The whole question emphasises that the theatre could be a matter of concern in high places, and it may help to explain why Jonson was very circumspect in these last years. If however there was continued disquiet about this aspect of the play it may have contributed to the failure of the play to become established in public esteem.

Ian Cotterell's Radio 3 production on 18 September 1987, to mark 350 years since Jonson's death, was adapted by Peter Barnes, and slightly shortened to a performing time of an hour and three-quarters. There were many minor changes in the wording in the interest of accessibility to a modern listening audience, but the essentials of the play were preserved unchanged. However successful, there are bound to be some limits upon what such a production can tell us since radio drama inevitably lacks the stimulus of audience response. Naturally a great deal depended upon the quality and blend of the voices, and in fact this brought out many aspects of the characterisation effectively. The garrulousness of Polish (Dilys Laye) as a loquacious busybody was wonderful to hear. Peter Bayliss gave to Sir Moth Interest a deliberate imperturbability which suggested that he was not going to be moved by anything except his own avarice. Peter Woodthorpe (Rut) and Tim Bateson (Palate) brought out the foibles of pretentiousness and crafty uncertainty, and all three of these actors managed to impart a decaying senility consonant with their humours.[49] Dinsdale Landen's Compass was fast and light, but there was an undertone of determination which was a valuable reading of this character. The blend of voices for the Induction and Choruses was very engaging: Andrew Branch gave a country burr to Trygust, while Edward de Souza's suave but rather malicious Damplay contrasted well with an optimistic and cheerful Probee played by Peter Howell.

In a generally favourable review David Nokes found the drama self-conscious and self-referential.[50] In contrast to the discussion of Act 5 above, he thought the plot rather episodic, though he did suggest that Jonson was interested in deliberately exposing the arbitrariness of narrative. Thus the radio version certainly gave the sense that Jonson was working hard on the nature of his art, almost to the point of experimentation. Indeed the review by Nokes seems very pertinent to Jonson's use of and challenge to many stage conventions. However the performance was a memorable one and it was well served by the streamlining of Barnes's adaptation for the medium of sound only. That Jonson's work should be so effective on the radio is largely a reflection of his plotting, and also of his ability to write closely integrated dialogue between distinctive voices.[51]

The production of *The Magnetic Lady* by Brian Woolland at Reading University allows us to add some practical responses to the text in performance.[52] The staging of this production was essentially simple. The director opted for an open stage with few properties and little furniture. The action flowed freely in this undetermined space, which bears out the discussion above of Jonson's conception of the dramatic space. The costumes, however, were felt to contribute much to the impact of the characters. Perhaps the most significant is that in playing the text was much more alive than it may seem on the page. A comic tone was quickly established as the audience responded to apparently static episodes like the Induction and the character descriptions in the first part of the play. Following the points made above about Jonson-in-the-play it is notable that jokes using this elicited a good response. In the programme note the Director drew attention to the relationship, which may indeed be a struggle, between the characters and the economic circumstances in which they find themselves. The emphasis upon theatricality and 'performance', which is apparent in the text, especially the Induction and the Choruses, gives a means for members of the audience to see themselves mirrored in the play. Such a view has strong attractions for a modern audience, as the interest in finance and greed has proved an abiding one. Practice's mental arithmetic about the gains made by Sir Moth Interest is highly actable (2.6.24–36). In the responses of the theatre critics to the Royal Shakespeare Company's production of *The Devil is an Ass* nearly all of them commented on the treatment of money and its acquisition.[53]

Exploring the play in rehearsal and performance brought out the congenial nature of Compass as he dominates the unfolding of the action. Perhaps less expected was the strength of the writing for the women's parts. It is clear that Jonson was giving generous stage time and space to them and allowing the presentation of their concerns, and also of their explicitly female predicament. There is a cross-reference here to the economic matter noted above. Polish is very determined to do the best for her daughter, and in spite of the mockery of her language by the other characters, she has to be listened to, and the playing of her part showed that she is theatrically effective in more ways than one. There is also a marked contrast with the silence of Placentia, which proved powerful in this production. The action could be made to pass around her silence and yet to highlight it. The effect is a striking one, and it may well be compared with Jonson's exploitation of the equally theatrical silence of Epicoene in *The Silent Woman*. The Director found that with some characters, notably Polish and Ironside, there was also room for some reference to the style of characterisation of the *commedia dell'arte*. Jonson had exploited this in *Volpone*, and it seems that here the presentation of a clear but grotesque exterior for some characters drew attention to performance in a way similar to that found in the Italian mode. There is more than one hint of Harlequin in Compass's manipulation of the other characters, and in his wry comments on them. The play is certainly late enough for such conventions to have some effect on performers and audiences alike.[54]

In the intervening years between the affair of the High Commission (1633) and Cotterell's radio production there is very little to relate of performance history, though there are a few hints that the play was known in the seventeenth century. One of these is John Cleveland's *The Antiplatonick*. The bawdy undertones of this witty poem draw attention to the potential sexuality of the encounter between the magnetic girl and the iron lover in the form of a soldier. It may have circulated in manuscript as some of Cleveland's poems did, but the earliest known publication was in T. Jordan's *Clarophil and Clarinda* in about 1650.[55]

Perhaps the most palpable imitation is that by William Cavendish, the Earl of Newcastle, whose support we have noted for Jonson over the entertainments for Charles I. His play *The Variety* was performed by the King's Men in 1641, and it is in parts deliberately modelled on *The Magnetic Lady*. Lady Beaufield, the heroine, is named as a 'magnetick widdow', and she attracts a miscellaneous group of suitors. Among these is Master Manly (the name probably from Manly in *The Devil is an Ass*), who throws a fit of rage, upsetting the assembled company, and draws his sword. Anne Barton points out that he embodies Elizabethan virtues which challenge the effeminacy of the Caroline Court,[56] but there is also reason to suppose that Newcastle himself found many aspects of Court life unpalatable in spite of his attempts to promote himself in royal favour. He described himself as out of sorts with the Court.[57] The process noted here however may be a reciprocating one, as Jonson probably alluded to Newcastle's courageous manhood in the character of Lovel in *The New Inn*. Newcastle's use of material from *The Magnetic Lady* is thus a part of a complex relationship between himself and Jonson, which also has expression in Jonson's praise of Newcastle as a master of swordsmanship in *Underwood*, 59. It may well be that the incapacitated Jonson had reason to admire the vigorous physical prowess of Newcastle as well as being drawn by his rather traditional outlook. Newcastle's theatrical adaptation reflects at least an awareness of the force of attraction of Lady Loadstone which we shall see has a certain allegorical force, based partly upon sexual attraction. It is notable that Richard Brome also supported Newcastle's venture with a poem.[58]

SOURCES AND ANALOGUES

For the central ideas of most of his plays Jonson was a highly original writer, and *The Magnetic Lady* is no exception. There are plays in which he develops narrative segments in the plot deriving from other writers, as in the Boccaccio element in *The Devil is an Ass*;[59] but even where these occur, Jonson tends to digest his borrowings thoroughly. He thought that to borrow skilfully from the works of others was the mark of a good writer (*Disc.*, 2466–9). Some substantial elements in the plot of *The Magnetic Lady* have not been traced to the specific work of other authors. The story of the child-changing by Polish and the consequences of its discovery could come from almost any romantic story. The Boy's comments at 1 Chor.15–24 suggest that Jonson deliberately chose it because it is typical of popular theatre. The triumph of Compass's manipulations, based upon overhearing the truth of the exchange by chance, fits in with the narrative style, but it is so short and simple a component that Jonson would hardly have had to go elsewhere for it. It is true that the exploitation of the joke about the unwilling and naive duellist in Sir Diaphanous might just owe something to the plight of Sir Andrew Aguecheek in Shakespeare's *Twelfth Night* (3.4), but, for his own reasons, Jonson matches his character with the awesome and ferocious Ironside rather than the equally unwilling Viola-as-Cesario. In some instances the plot constituents in Jonson's play are the direct result of the 'humour' of the characters, as in Sir Moth's unwillingness to see Placentia married off for fear of his having to surrender the dowry. His subsequent windfall when her pregnancy makes her unsuitable for marriage is naturally a cause of rejoicing to him, however unworthy.

If Jonson is more or less independent over matters of plot, there are still many things in the play which relate to the writings of others. Some of them are direct sources, as for example in the information on compasses and magnetism, for which he acknowledges the authorities he has used. But there is a good deal of lesser material in the play for which the more useful enquiry may well be to ask why he uses it rather than simply where it comes from. Jonson sought to use the fruits of his voracious reading (and memory) to establish the status of his text. The recognition of his scholarship is one of the strongest themes in the posthumous tribute to him by his friends in *Jonsonus Virbius*.[60] It has often been thought that his psychological need to establish his own position in contemporary society was a powerful motivating force, especially as he came from relatively humble beginnings, and was in many respects self-educated. Along with this goes his sense of the authority of his work when in printed form, something he sought tirelessly to establish. But he did in fact make himself a position among the intelligentsia of his time, especially when he was nominated in 1618 for the proposed 'Academ Roial', an association of thinkers under King James which anticipated the formation of the Royal Society after the Restoration.[61] It is not surprising therefore that his plays show the influence of this intellectual milieu. His connection with Gresham College, where he was an assistant lecturer in rhetoric for a time, is another aspect of this intellectual aspiration and achievement.[62] There are hints of Jonson's interest in mathematics in the references to logarithms, which were invented in 1614 (1.6.35), and parallax (1.6.39). Throughout his life he showed a capacity for intensive study of areas of knowledge which particularly interested him in connection with his writings, as in witchcraft for *The Masque of Queens*, alchemy for *The Alchemist* and magnetism for *The Magnetic Lady*.

The topic of Vitruvian architecture is closely associated with this, and Jonson was impressed by its emphasis upon proportion.[63] By

1632, however, the quarrel with Inigo Jones had become intense, and Jonson uses the architectural concept of framing to attack his enemy. He shifts the dramatic emphasis away from illusionistic framing and perspective implicit in Jones's set designs towards the staging practices of Plautus and Terence. The latter in fact are the chief debt, and Jonson both acknowledges their importance to him at this time and makes several minor allusions to them. As we have seen, Jonson makes the most of this debt in the Induction and Choruses, where he seeks to lay out a classical theoretical structure for this apparently romantic play. The minor references indicate that Jonson had the dramatic conventions of these dramatists continually in mind, and was measuring the nature of his own play against features of theirs. In 3 Chorus the debate between the Boy and the two visitors becomes vigorous, and allusion is made to six characters from these dramatists.[64]

The strong classical interest embedded in the editorial work of Herford and the Simpsons enables us to pinpoint a number of other classical references, such as the detail about wedge-shaped seats in the Roman auditoria (Ind.31n). There are details from Archilochus (2.5.45n), Pliny (4.4.7n), Cicero (2 Chor.36–8, 3.6.179), Horace (2 Chor.40–1, 3.4.114, 3 Chor.32–3) and Homer (3.6.164, 5.7.67). Martial played an important role in Jonson's intellectual development, and many poems, especially in the *Epigrams*, are written with his vigorous attack in mind. One of the references here is concerned with Jonson's sense of the misinterpretation of authorial intention which implies a fellow-feeling (2 Chor.44–7). Jonson's extensive interest in proverbs is strongly represented. Some of these derive from classical sources, such as Aesop (4.4.47), and some from the Bible (4.7.11). But many can be traced to native sources such as John Heywood's sixteenth-century collections.[65] The attraction is the vigour of demotic speech which fits in well with Jonson's sense that speaking is fundamental to the revelation of character.[66]

For some details Jonson turned to other English writers. Chaucer is an abiding presence in this play. The style of the 'characters' given by Compass in 1.2 is modelled upon the portraits in Chaucer's *General Prologue*. There are some satirical hits which seem to follow Chaucer's lead as in 1.2.39–40, 42; 2.2.51; 3.3.19; and 3.5.23.[67] Jonson's own presence in the play in spirit is rather like Chaucer's use of his own *persona*, a motif which is intensified by Jonson's occasional jokes against himself, as in the pun made by Compass over the 'great clerk' (1.2.33). Jonson also seems to have been influenced by the character studies in John Earle's *Microcosmography* (1628), and he is thought to have possessed a copy of Burton's *Anatomy of Melancholy* (1621). Both Chaucer and Burton may have contributed to Jonson's interest in medical matters. Both writers sum up much well-known medical information: we find a number of parallels between Jonson's text and Burton's, as at 3.5.44, and 3 Chor.24. The ancient and medieval theory of humours was employed by Jonson from his earliest-known plays onwards. In recalling it here he would have been able to refer to Chaucer and Burton, among others.[68] Rut's elaborate and pompous mystification of Placentia's 'swelling' has been traced to *Lanfranke of Mylayne*, translated by John Halle in 1565.[69] Jonson's attitude to these 'smock matters' may well reflect ridicule of the profession of midwife which was a commonplace. But here Jonson uses the various attributes of Mother Chair to help expose what is going on in the plot. As more and more men were becoming midwives at this time, it is interesting that he does not promote the idea, however, in spite of his connection with the New Science.[70]

Jonson himself provides some specific sources for the allegory of magnetism on the title-page and in Polish's allusion at 1.4.5–6, though it will be seen from what follows that he again digests his subject matter thoroughly, and uses it in an original manner. On the title-page he quotes from Claudian's *Magnes*.[71] This poem turns on the paradox that the plain, dull loadstone has more power than precious stones. It recruits its power from iron, and will die without it. The loadstone is identified with the feminine power of Venus who attracts spontaneously (*sponte*, Lat.) her beloved Mars, who is seen as iron. Claudian is impressed by the harmony between the two substances, and shows that Venus holds the fiery, wrathful Mars in check. The poem then shifts to Cupid's power which is so great that it stirs the passions of rocks and iron (as exemplified in the play's epigraph). The linking of their contrasted powers, equated with love, is a key theme in the play which leads up to the power of love to reconcile opposites, including the humours.

These ideas were enlarged by Jonson through his acquaintance with the works on magnetism by William Gilbert (1540–1603), William Barlow (d. 1625) and Mark Ridley (1560–1624). Gilbert in *De magnete magneticisque* (1600) notes the power of the loadstone to attract iron, citing Plato, and he adds that it 'expels gross humours', and enhances the power of iron (p. 19). He discusses the contribution of the mariner's compass:

In a round wooden box, having its top covered over with glass, a fly-card (*versorium*) rests upon a pretty long pin fixed in the middle . . . [This] is circular, made of light material, as pasteboard, to the underside of which is attached the magnetised iron or needle. (p. 83)

One of the properties he notes is that the compass is somewhat variable.[72]

The works of Barlow and Ridley depend upon Gilbert's. Barlow, who was Archdeacon of Salisbury, sees spiritual significance in the physical phenomena. God would 'make mutual amity between people and people though never so far separated'.[73] The fly has two wires which have to be made magnetic by the touch of the load-stone, and 'ought to be polished' (A1v) to make them more effective. In his later work, *Magneticall Advertisement* (1616), he discusses the repair and maintenance of sailing compasses, and declares that iron is better for capping loadstones than steel is (K4v), but the compass ought to be pure steel, 'For most assuredly steel will take at the least ten times more virtue than iron can do, but especially if it hath his right temper'.

Ridley's *A Short Treatise* (1613) is more scientific in its approach and contains excellent diagrams and a good deal of geometry. He refers to Mr Brigges, the Reader in Geometry at Gresham College who helped with a diagram (p. 130).[74] He discusses both magnet-ism, including its attractive power and the effect upon iron and steel (pp. 9, 84), and the working of the compass, with much attention to its variation (pp. 104–20). It seems likely that Jonson found sugges-tions for Polish's reference at 2.2.25–30, and for the episode in the garden sparked off at 5.7.47 in the following: 'Caelius Calcaginus saith that if the Magnet be preserved in the salt of the Sea-lampron or Remora, that is thought to stay a ship under sail, that the magnet will draw up gold that is fallen in the deepest well (a2)'. There may also have been a hint for the emphasis upon values in: 'The appre-hension of magnetical bodies is a strong tension, cleaving and stick-ing them together that they will hardly be severed, being strongly retained by the virtue and love magneticall' (p. 85).

Jonson's allegorising of the material provides him with a series of images about the attraction of opposites, and about reconciliation: these he integrates with his theory of humours. But the allegory is selective (as most allegories are), and we should remember Jonson's stated reluctance about interpretations which are too specific (2 Chor.21–3). Thus it is not clear that Compass is 'steel', though he was an associate of Master Steele (1.5.2), and his brotherhood with

Ironside is only a declared one (3.4.50). The character of Needle may be suggested by a compass needle, but Jonson makes more use of him for jokes relating to tailors and to pricking (bawdily).

Another intriguing resonance not strictly determined by the allegory but cognate with it is the figurative use of the loadstone as a metaphor for the womb: 'The womb is that field of nature into which the seed of man and woman is cast, and it hath also an attractive faculty to draw in a magnetic quality, as the loadstone draweth iron, or fire the light of the candle.' This passage from Jane Sharp's *The Midwives Book* (1671) appeared after Jonson's death, but she was in practice for at least thirty years before, and may well have been drawing upon a commonplace image.[75] Possibly Jonson's connections with intellectual circles may have brought such matters into question, though it is likely that many there would have upheld the patriarchal system. Jonson's presentation of the nature and role of midwives should not be seen as derogatory in a play which is generally sympathetic to the predicaments and difficulties of women. He creates an environment in which the male medical practitioners, Rut and Item, hardly inspire confidence in a corrupt and avaricious world. The implications of such an interpretation may be considerable upon the casting and playing styles for the women's parts, in a play which is remarkable for the number of women who are present. Jonson's work has indeed given rise to some very careful evaluations with regard to the position of women, and *The Magnetic Lady* cannot be seen as simply an endorsement of the prevailing sexist ideology of the period.[76]

CRITICAL APPRECIATION

Jonson's character comes down to us as prickly, irascible and contentious. He made enemies, and he had to exploit the business, literally, of patronage in order to live. He was seen as successful by his contemporaries in the middle of his career, but by its end many doubted him, and he possibly doubted himself. Nevertheless he still had patrons, friends and followers, as the publication of *Jonsonus Virbius* witnesses. We may see aspects of his character and circumstances in *The Magnetic Lady*, and yet the play has today to stand by itself in relationship with its audiences. Here we can point to some strong qualities which may help to suggest ways in which it might be valued or re-valued.

The general impression is that the play was written with a purposeful intensity, and that it shows a concentration of many of Jonson's most outstanding abilities. It is the work of a highly intelligent and skilled playwright who knows what he is doing, and sets about achieving his ends in a professional and emphatic manner. It is self-consistent and well sustained throughout, and it has a remarkable increasing tempo as it unfolds. The world he presents is still the same as that of his earlier plays. We have noted his intense religious feelings, even though he is not usually explicit about them. He believed that although society was redolent with vice, and people were corrupt—he assiduously, even obsessively, gathered examples—the universe is truthful, just and consistent, and that this metaphysical truth necessitated practical correction.[77] The conclusions of his plays recognised a better arrangement: in this case, the humours are reconciled. In this brief critical account of the play we shall consider the range of the characters, the nature of the plot, some moral and ethical issues, and the value and interest of the framing device.

It has been well established that Jonson's choice of names is a direct reflection of the nature of the characters, and usually of his own attitude to them, or rather of the attitude which he would like the audience to adopt towards them.[78] Thus there is not likely to be much sympathy for a doctor named Rut; and a courtier with a portmanteau name such as Sir Diaphanous Silkworm suggests idleness, transparency, luxury, together with something unattractive and mean as a worm. The impressions which play around many of the characters are indeed sometimes made significant as well as amusing by the word play in the dialogue: 'Good—Needle and noddle' (5.1.26). This pointed naming echoes Jonson's larger purpose in his selection of characters in *The Magnetic Lady*. He has assembled a range of people who have distinctive professional or occupational characteristics, and his manipulation of them is usually in terms of overriding moral and ethical criteria rather than consistency and verisimilitude: an allegorical way of thinking is never very far away. In many ways these characters are their profession.[79] To some extent the particular avocations are backed up by circumstantial details within the development of the plot, which is used as a means of activating or revealing leading traits of character.[80] These humours characters are all abusers of language in their different ways.

For example, there is a great deal in the play on the workings of the law. Practice, the lawyer's name, gives us the idea of being in practice, at the service of the public, but it also has connotations of craftiness and devious activities. When Placentia is discussing him as a possible husband, Polish draws attention to the elevated status of lawyers. The lack of personal loyalty of lawyers is noted by Compass (2.5.55), and Practice feels compelled to defend the law against the politician who may think it is 'but a dead heap / Of civil institutions' (1.7.17–18). Compass, whom we may suspect, at least in part, of articulating Jonson's own views, has a sharp exchange with Practice drawing attention to the law's invulnerability: even another Armada would not disturb the lawyers with their distinctive garb implying solidarity and complacency (1.6.14–23). As the plot works out, Practice contributes advice to Sir Diaphanous about seeking damages from Ironside (3.4.3–4); he obtains the marriage licence (4.2.54); he instigates the dreadful process of choke-bail which forces Sir Moth to come to heel (5.3.33); and he confirms the law which threatens those who make babies disappear (5.10.74–6). Originally he was favoured by Lady Loadstone as a suitor to Placentia, but by the end he is content to relinquish his claim to Pleasance whom he had really preferred, and in a struck bargain is prepared to settle for the reversion of the post which Compass had inherited. Thus the law is expressly used by Jonson to develop the plot, in virtually neutral ways, but the law itself is seen as avaricious, and Practice himself as self-seeking, and he is one of the contributors to the mechanism of 'bargain and sale' which controls the fate of young women.[81] His search for a wife is seen entirely in these terms: there is no question of love.

The details and activities of Dr Rut, and Parson Palate similarly show the mechanisms of their professions: how they acquire income and exercise control over other people. Both are given unattractive traits: Rut being most pretentious in his excessive verbosity about his own learning, and Palate, with a name suggesting gluttony, presiding avariciously over the rites of passage of his parishioners. Interestingly both prove themselves turncoats when it comes to the pursuit of their own interests, not unlike Practice. Rut has some setpiece diagnoses: he is egregiously wrong over Placentia's tympany; he treats the shocked Sir Moth by pinching him and boxing his ears; and when the latter is nearly drowned Rut offers retrospective astrological advice. Neither he nor Palate receives benefit at the end, and Jonson seems quite content to allow the demonstration of their folly to be sufficient punishment. Like the other humours characters Rut is an abuser of language, and his wordy diagnoses echo Jonson's translation from Vives: 'The vicious language is vast and gaping, swelling and irregular; when it contends to be high full of rock, mountain and pointedness; as it affects to be low it is abject and creeps, full of bogs and holes.'[82]

Bias and Sir Diaphanous are both figures from Court. The former epitomises the calculation of the politician who makes sure that everything he does strengthens, or at least does not weaken, his position of influence. Bias would have taken Placentia, at a cutprice rate offered by Sir Moth, but when her indiscretion is apparent he quickly backs off, and leaves her and Needle to the generosity of Ironside. Sir Diaphanous contributes a good deal to the ideas in the play by his disquisition upon valour, a quality which he lacks when confronted by Ironside. He is characteristically fastidious over his clothes, and is probably significant as a reflection of Jonson's criticism of courtly extravagance. He has an important role in exciting the wrath of Ironside, at a critical moment in the plot, but he is left as one of the few loose ends in the last Act.

These opportunists are supported by the discourse of mercantile prosperity which pervades the play. Lady Loadstone, of herself a rather sombre figure, lives on the fortune made by her late husband in foreign enterprises as Governor of the East India Company (2.5.71–4). Sir Moth Interest, her brother, defends his profit on the dowry, and sophistically justifies his love of money:

My moneys are my blood, my parents, kindred:
And he that loves not those, he is unnatural.

He goes on to contend, at some length, that the love of money 'Is not a virtue only in a subject, But might befit a prince' (2.6.39–43). Jonson's interest here is twofold, for he does not exactly reject the mercantile system and its concomitant wealth, but he is clearly uneasy at the scale of Sir Moth's undeserved profit. Moth boldly excuses himself to Practice; 'That's my industry; / As it might be your reading, study and counsel' (2.6.13–14). This extensive rhetoric occurs just after Sir Diaphanous has given Palate £500, and sent Polish a diamond of £60, and Rut an emerald, all of which he produces from his pocket (2.4.21–9).

But perhaps the most influential characters are Ironside and Compass. The former is something of a humours character in that his rage is an expression of his refusal to tolerate fools, and it is remarkable that Jonson chooses to reward him at the end of the play.[83] We have noted how rage is part of Jonson's own character, and it may well be that this reflects Jonson's toleration of it in himself, especially when it is directed to a just cause: there could be something productive in rage. There is a close link in that Compass calls him brother, especially as Compass himself points to his own authority in relation to the author, and he too is rewarded with a wife and fortune. In this Compass follows other Jonsonian characters like Horace in *Poetaster*, exercising caustic judgement on the rest. In the first half of the play his activities in connection with the plot are chiefly perception and comment, whereas after the crisis in Act 3 Compass becomes the author's principal means of developing the plot—it is Compass who overhears the vital disclosure by Polish in 4.4.[84] Barish has pointed out that in *The Masque of Beauty* the allegorical figure of Perfectio has 'in her hand a compass of gold drawing a circle'; but in *The Magnetic Lady*, the conception of a compass is somewhat more critical and it may be linked to the limitations implied in the *impresa*.[85]

McCanles, in his fruitful study of Jonson's management of parallel and contrast, suggests that after 1630 Jonson's role as explorer of moral ambiguities had changed into that of apologist for the state of things as they were.[86] The pursuit of wealth by Compass, and the opportunism he shares with Ironside to some extent undermine their moral position as they confront the Polish–Sir-Moth axis. Though Polish herself is constantly attacked by characters within the play, and almost uniformly by critics ever since, her defence of her daughter, as well as her appreciation of the qualities of the Steeles, and her perception of theological balance are positive attributes. By comparison little can be said in Sir Moth's defence.

It seems a distinct possibility that Ironside and Compass represent complementary aspects of Jonson's perception of himself. Both follow precedents in his plays which suggest that Jonson was preoccupied with his own aggression, as well as with his interest in the management of external affairs. The elaborate links with the allegory of magnetism, discussed in *Sources and Analogues* above, give some support to this, but we should at the same time beware of placing too literal an explanation at the heart of Jonson's theatrical dynamic. Caution is thus necessary in considering Larry Champion's interpretation of an explicit allegory in which he identifies Compass as the poet entertainer, and Ironside as the poet moralist.[87] The main objection to this is that the whole of the play should be seen as a moral essay, and that to confine moral truth to one character seriously limits the subtlety of Jonson's moral perception, which lies at the heart of his poetic aspiration. The means of judging the action is usually provided in Jonson's plays, though this is not necessarily by means of a single character.[88] As to Compass's management, it has been rightly pointed out that his achievement is carefully limited by his ironic and indirect methods which may well owe something to those he confronts.[89]

In considering the plot, it is notable that much of this material about wealth is concentrated in Act 2 where Jonson is still theoretically concerned with the *protasis*, substantially the laying out of the circumstances of the play before the action begins. It is complementary to the Chaucer-like portraits of Act 1. The exposition of characters is a major concern, dramatic in itself, and Jonson makes the most of his opportunity of blending and contrasting them in the first part of the play. The marriageability of Placentia, and her aunt's interest in it, are the means by which the range of people are drawn to the dinner which is the feature of Act 3. There is of course a very close link between the issue of wealth and the mercantile use of marriage as a means of increasing it, but this relationship leaves open the possibilities of the emotional aspects of love and marriage to which we shall return below, as well as Jonson's persistent concern with the social and personal predicament of women.[90]

Once dinner-time arrives the pace of the play quickens remarkably. Jonson's interest in this type of structure can be seen in other plays, as in the ring intrigue of *The Devil is an Ass*. Most striking in the latter part of the play is the ingenuity with which the plot lines are deliberately entwined. With characteristic intellectual brilliance Jonson here challenges the audience to follow him, and he cleverly has Damplay quickly fall by the wayside as the pace hots up: this rather obstinate onlooker wants to be able to interpret for himself, and he wants to impose his own requirements on a plot which has a dynamism he cannot grasp. Perhaps Jonson wanted to induce the audience to feel superior to Damplay and this was a means of encouraging them to keep a good grip on things. Compass's comment on 'the right thread' also promotes this.

The main intention is the reconciliation of the humours, but Jonson's handling of the plot shows that, like one who writes a detective story, or composes a crossword, he is determined to pursue a logical course, and yet pepper it with distractions which require to be disregarded, such as the visionary fit of Needle, and Sir Moth's (offstage) predicament in the well. Richard Cave has usefully noted that in the second half of the play there is a pattern of flouting the apparent expectation of events, citing the reconciliation which finishes the duel, Practice's withdrawal from the marriage and the reappearance of Placentia.[91]

The pursuit of a reasonable compromise, and the emergence of a solution are symptomatic of Jonson's overriding humanist ideology. The moral and religious values involve the exposure of excessive behaviour, whether determined by avarice or by the exigencies of professional bigotry and ineptitude. Even where he has a particular personal edge or grudge, as is perhaps the case with his mockery of Palate, or his ill-disguised thrusts at Inigo Jones, the underlying purposes are rationally related to his moral concerns to teach the possibility of improvement, and to do so in ways which provide entertainment for the discerning reader or playgoer.

This affects his presentation of emotional matters. Love is kept to a limited role here, perhaps because Jonson wanted to hold up to scrutiny the whole question of using women and marriage as a process of bargain and sale: he pointedly uses the phrase twice.[92] Nevertheless we see hints of growing affection for Compass from Pleasance (2.7.12–13, and 4.5.17), and we are presented with an ideal of 'turtles' in Polish's description of the loving marriage of the Steeles, the parents of Pleasance. The employment of two common elements of romance, the exchange of the infants and the ultimate recognition of their true identity, suggests that, while remaining within the discipline of classical comedy, Jonson wanted to give some scope to affection.[93] But his restraint, even reticence, here may be a response to the criticism he received for the rather fuller emotional events of *The New Inn*, or perhaps in his own emotional life, which seems to have been subject to some disappointment and also to stoical restraint, a feature which might have been exacerbated by his physical predicament after 1628. Such a restraint might explain why he puts the description of the marital happiness of the Steeles into the mouth of Polish, the ridiculously loquacious but loyal mother. One should perhaps hear her ample voice in affairs as an important complement to the rather astringent though perceptive Compass who manages affairs with such a cool hand. If we consider that it is also in her voice, backed up by her strange erudition, that we hear the critique of Arminianism, as well as her spirited defence of her own action in promoting the interests of her daughter, it is clear that Jonson has created in her not only an amusing stage character but also some intriguing ambiguity about how she is to be read: she defies the dismissals of both Rut and Compass. In this use of the indirectness of dramatic character we may find an important key to Jonson's art as a dramatist. In the plays his personal tensions are often buried in the ambiguities of the characters. This may be what attracted Jonson to write in dramatic form.[94]

When, finally, we turn to the metatheatrical framework of the discussions concerning the processes of the play, we see that their purpose is to insulate Jonson's views, even his prejudices and anxieties, within the art of playwriting. He must defend his art against his critics, real and imagined, in order to preserve the vehicle of comment and criticism of the society in which he lived. Primarily it is not about preserving the purity of his art, though that is important too: it is a question of how far the dramatic poet can carry out his function of pleasing and instructing his audience. To do this he must have a reliable means of delivery as well as a sense of the civilised values which Jonson pursued with all his mental vigour, even at this late stage in his life.

THE TEXT

Publication

The publication of Jonson's later works has proved to be a complex and in some respects unfathomable affair. After he conceived and completed his Folio edition of *The Works* in 1616, for which he selected, edited and rewrote many different pieces from his earlier output, he does not seem to have wanted to publish a further substantial volume until after the onset of his illness in 1628. By 1631 he had prepared and partially supervised what he must have thought of as Volume Two of his *Works*, comprising *Bartholomew Fair, The Staple of News* and *The Devil is an Ass*. His quarrel with John Beale, the printer, and John Allot, the bookseller or publisher, caused the suspension of the project even though Jonson may have intended to add other works to it.[95] Though these plays were undoubtedly printed by 1631, they were not released, and they became part of a complex trade dispute which was temporarily ended when Philip Chetwin, who had acquired the rights over these plays through his marriage with Allot's widow, published them in 1640. As he was not a Stationer himself he did this under the protection of a title-page which said they were printed for Richard Meighen, a former associate of Allot.[96]

Before his death in 1637 Jonson seems to have wanted to continue

THE
MAGNETICK
LADY:

OR,

HVMORS
RECONCILD.

A COMEDY compoſed

By

BEN: IOHNSON.

Iam lapides ſuus ardor agit ferrumq; tenetur,
Illecebris.——— Claud. de Magnet.

LONDON,
Printed M. CD. XL.

3 Title-page of the Folio, corrected

Act II. Scene III.

Rut. Polish, Lady, Keepe. Placentia.

Rut. Whence? what's hee call'd? *Pol.* Doctor, doe all you can,
I pray you, and befeech you, for my charge, here.
Lad. She's my tendring Goffip, loves my Neice.
Pol. I know you can doe all things, what you pleafe, Sir,
For a young Damfel, my good Ladies Neice, here!
You can doe what you lift. *Rut.* Peace *Tiffany.*
Pol. Efpecially in this new cafe, o' the Dropfie.
The Gentlewoman (I doe feare) is leven'd.
Rut. Leven'd? what's that? *Pol.* Puft, blowne, and 't pleafe your worfhip.
Rut. What! Darke, by darker? What is blowne? puff'd? fpeake
Englifh—*Pol.* Tainted (and 't pleafe you) fome doe call it.
She fwels, and fwels fo with it.—*Rut.* Give her vent;
If fhee doe fwell. A Gimblet muft be had:
It is a *Tympanites* fhe is troubled with,
There are three kinds: The firft is *Ana-farca*
Vnder the Flefh, a Tumor: that's not hers.
The fecond is *Afcites*, or *Aquofus,*
A watry humour: that's not hers neither.
But *Tympanites* (which we call the Drum)
A wind bombes in her belly, muft be unb-tac'd,
And with a Faucet, or a Peg, let out,
And fhe'll doe well: get her a husband. *Pol.* Yes,
I fay fo Mr. *Doctor,* and betimes too. *Lad.* As
Soone as wee can: let her beare up to day,
Laugh, and keepe company, at Gleeke, or Crimpe.
Pol. Your Ladifhip fayes right, Crimpe, fure, will cure her.
Rut. Yes, and Gleeke too; peace Goffip *Tittle-Tattle,*
Shee muft to morrow, downe into the Countrey,
Some twenty mile; A Coach, and fix brave Horfes:
Take the frefh aire, a moneth there, or five weekes:
And then returne a Bride, up to the Towne,
For any husband i'the *Hemifphere,*
To chuck at, when fhe has dropt her *Timpane.*
Pol. Muft fhe then drop it? *Rut.* Thence, 'tis call'd a Dropfie.
The *Timpanites* is one fpice of it,
A toy, a thing of nothing, a meere vapour,
He blow 't away. *Lad.* Needle, get you the Coach
Ready, againft to morrow morning. *Nee.* Yes Madam.
Lad. He downe with her my felfe, and thanke the Doctor.
Pol. Wee all fhall thanke him. But, deare Madam, thinke,
Refolve upon a man, this day. *Lad.* I ha' done't.
To tell you true, (fweet Goffip,) here is none
But Mafter *Doctor,* hee fhall be o' the Counfell:
The man I have defign'd her to, indeed,
Is Mafter *Practife* : he's a neat young man,

Forward

to prepare his unpublished work for the press. He brought out *The New Inn* in octavo in 1631, printed by Thomas Harper for Thomas Alchorne. The two Caroline masques, *Love's Triumph through Callipolis* (1630) and *Chloridia* (1631), were printed for Thomas Walkley, who was to play an important part in the posthumous publication of Jonson's remaining works.[97] It was Walkley who bought Jonson's papers for £40 in 1637 from Sir Kenelm Digby, Jonson's literary executor and patron, and he seems to have intended to produce a comprehensive edition. However, he was partly forestalled by Chetwin's Volume Two of 1640 noted above, as well as by John Benson's duodecimo edition of some of the non-dramatic works.[98] In his attempt to develop control, Walkley reveals in his bill of 1640 to the Keeper of the Great Seal a distinct possibility that some or all of the texts he had bought, which were eventually to make up Volume Three, and included *The Magnetic Lady*, were actually in Jonson's autograph:

> To whose care and trust the said Benjamin left the publishing and printing of them and delivered him true and perfect Copies for his better and more effectual doing thereof . . . the said Sir Kenelm Digby . . . delivered the same copies to your Orator [i.e. Walkley himself] to have them published and printed according to the intention of the said Benjamin Johnson. (*H&S*, 9.98)

This strongly suggests that Jonson, during his last years, certainly did want his works published, and in his retired and confined state he set about revising them with a view to publication. However the pieces to be included were in various states, and may not have been 'true and perfect Copies' as claimed. Greg offered the following account:

> Some of the masques were printed from manuscript, others from earlier quartos, but some of the latter bear signs of revision, and they may, therefore, have come from Jonson's library. The manuscripts were probably of various kinds, but they were certainly not autograph.[99]

It is reasonable to assume, from the evidence of the printing and format of the plays in Volume Two that Jonson would have liked the presentation of these later publications to match as far as possible the prestigious Volume One of the Works in the 1616 Folio printed by William Stansby.

Thomas Walkley was a publisher and bookseller rather than a printer. Volume Three was printed for him by John Dawson (the son) who was active 1637–48, though his address is not known. The *STC* reveals that Dawson's output included many religious works, and official publications for Parliament. He printed works on wine, horsemanship, sword play and needlecraft. His more literary output included Ovid, Cervantes and Hooker, as well as poems by Cowley and Carew, and dramatic pieces by Shirley and Nabbes.

When Volumes Two and Three appeared in 1640–1 they did not, after all, match the ambitious presentation of Volume One. Volume Two had the Meighen title-page which was noticeably less ornate than that for Volume One, with no decoration other than the printer's emblem. It appears that Walkley had such difficulties establishing his control that he could not enter the new works in the Stationers' Register, or legally create his own title-page, and none has come to light;[100] nor has any other preparatory matter, such as dedicatory verses, for either Volume Two or Volume Three. Indeed the contents of Volume Three appeared with different sequences of page-numbering and bound in variously differing orders. Sometimes *The Magnetic Lady* is first, as though to continue the sequence of plays from Volume Two; sometimes the masques begin the volume.[101] Commonly copies of Volumes Two and Three are bound together with the Meighen title-page which lists only the three 1631 plays: a practice which has proved misleading to cataloguers ever since.[102] *The Magnetic Lady* collates {2°: sigs A-H4; A1v, A2v, A4v blank; pp. 1–64; p. 50 misnumbered 52 in some copies}. It is normally followed in sequence by *A Tale of a Tub* and *The Sad Shepherd* numbered pp. 1–155 consecutively.

Perhaps because of the tortuous history of publication, the play does not appear in the Stationers' Register until 17 September 1658 when it is listed for Walkley under the *Third Volume* along with other individual works. By then Walkley had obtained control, and the point of the entry was to transfer ownership to Humphrey Moseley, which he did on 20 November 1658. Moseley advertised the Third Volume including *The Magnetic Lady* in 1660.[103]

The printing

The layout of the pages in *The Magnetic Lady* is less impressive than that of the plays in Volume Two. The pages of the latter were enclosed in a ruled box, with double margin on the outer edge. For *The Magnetic Lady* there is a running head and page number with rules above and below, but no more. Decorated devices were used in Volume

Two for each new Act, but in Volume Three the practice is simply to put in one rule below the last line of the previous Act, and slightly to increase the size of the type for the heading of the new Act and scene. Small capitals are not used for speech prefixes, and their use in general is much more restricted than it had been in the previous Volumes where Jonson himself was directly an influence.

In spite of Greg's caution noted above, there are several internal indications that the text of *The Magnetic Lady* was set from a Jonson autograph: these are some aspects of the spelling, the abbreviations used in the text and the layout of the scenes. It is difficult to be certain about spelling considered on its own, especially in a time when individual writers, including Jonson himself, often show inconsistencies within a very short space. Printers did not necessarily follow the orthography of the copy-text, though mercifully, from the point of view of this enquiry, the printers themselves were inconsistent in their attempt to normalise spelling either to uniformity within individual documents or to the imposed requirement of the style of a given printing house. The idiosyncrasies of the author almost always show through. In the case of Jonson we have enough evidence from other printed works, especially those which he changed in proof with meticulous care for Volume One, and from surviving holographs, to be fairly certain that the printer was working here from Jonson's own 'true and perfect Copies' or, at the very least, from a reasonably faithful transcript which manifested unmistakable Jonsonian characteristics. Furthermore though some of the masques in Volume Three, such as *Chloridia*, could be set from an earlier printed copy, there is no reason to suppose that one was available for *The Magnetic Lady*: the probability must be that the only text available was an autograph.

The spelling of the following words seems to be normal for Jonson: *vertuous, moneth, souldiers, inough*, and other words beginning *en-* in modern usage, such as *intangled, indure, intire*, as well as several words ending in -ick for modern -ic, as *magnetick, mechanick, comick, cholerick, artick*, and -ll for modern -l, as *civill, liberall, bountifull, immortall, faithfull. Niece* is spelt *Neice* throughout, a usage found elsewhere at the time (*OED*), but perhaps Jonson's choice was determined by the possible derivation from *nepta* (Latin). Beyond this there are a number of words which appear to be part of Jonson's classicising intention such as: *sillabes, Poët, phant'sie, merkat* (market), and possibly *malitious* and *pernitious*, as well as the digraphs in *Comœdy, Idœas, œconomick, Prœsto* and *Prœcipice*. Fredson Bowers noted that in general as a proof reader Jonson was prepared to tolerate inconsistency in spelling, but gave special attention to the words which did reflect the classical authority he thought desirable for his printed work as texts.[104] There is of course no possibility that Jonson saw proofs, but it is most likely that his attention to his own autographs would follow similar methods to his proof reading. This may be detected in some compound words which are meticulously hyphenated: *gentle-man, states-man.*[105]

Some of the abbreviations in Jonson's texts have been shown by Cyrus Hoy to be characteristic. Hoy used them as diagnostic for Jonson's contribution to the composite text of *Rollo of Normandy*. He gives the following substantial totals for *The Magnetic Lady*: '*hem* (them) 36; *i'th(e)* 44; *o'th(e)* 63; and *ha'* (have) 49. Comparable figures for *The New Inn*, written some four years earlier, are 39, 60, 67 and 44 respectively.[106]

The act and scene headings follow Jonson's usual practice in the grouping of the names of all the characters at the beginning, and in the somewhat intermittent use of *To them* as an indication of newly arriving characters. The former was derived from the first printed editions of Plautus and Terence in the fifteenth century.[107] Characteristically only one exit is marked in the text. A few centred directions are incorporated into the heading of scenes, as for 3.4.0 (p. 36 of *F*), but several—there are not many throughout—are placed in the margin in italics, as at 5.10.70. Possibly this suggests afterthoughts by Jonson, or someone else editing or annotating the copy.[108] One has an asterisk to show where it relates to the dialogue (2.2.2). Uniquely on p. 61, in a particularly busy sequence, there are ten italicised names at different points in the right margin to signify entrances. Perhaps in this case the copy Jonson was using had been marked by the stage-keeper and he decided to let the names stand in his fair copy to reduce confusion. But the overall effect, still following the fifteenth-century precedent noted above, is to make the text appear solid on the page, without interruptions for directions and without setting off new speakers on new lines unless the verse is complete. This is even the case on pp. 20–1 where it appears that the casting off left too much space on the inner forme: there is still no attempt to indent half lines for different speakers. These features suggest that the finished product was aimed primarily for reading: it is hardly a recollection of or a prescription for a performance. There are signs however that the convention broke down in places, especially at the start of 3.3, and the heading for 5.8.

Besides these features of layout, the punctuation and, to some extent, the typography are indicative that the copy was a holograph since they all follow the practice of the texts Jonson did supervise personally. His punctuation is heavy by modern standards. He uses commas very frequently to separate vocatives, to separate items such as adjectives, nouns, verbal nouns and phrases from other similar items when followed by 'and', and to separate adverbs. Semicolons are used apparently to gain rhetorical pauses. Exclamation marks are common, though these sometimes take a form similar to a modern question mark. Brackets are used for interruption of the flow of the grammar, sometimes to point up asides.[109]

The following examples illustrate from this play Jonson's normal practices in punctuation:

Fly every thing (you see) to the marke, and censure it; freely.

(Ind.125–6)

But (being away)
You'are sure to have lesse-wit-worke, gentle brother,
My humour being as stubborne, as the rest,
And as unmannageable.

(1.1.40–3)

Comforts the widow; and the fatherlesse,
In funerall Sack! Sits 'bove the Alderman!

(1.2.26–7)

It is betweene
The Lawyer, and the Courtier, which shall have her.

(1.3.33–4)

In this edition the punctuation has been lightened in accordance with modern practice, though it must be admitted that this may have obscured Jonson's intentions to some extent.

Italics were used in the original text for speakers' names (a departure from Volume Two where upper case is the norm), and for names within the text, for name-calling as in Gossip *Tittle-Tattle* (2.3.27) and *John à Noke* (2 Chor.20), for classical words such as *Logorythmes* (1.6.35) and *epitasis* (1 Chor.9), quotations, foreign expressions and the Epilogue.

An analysis of the rules and the associated headings at the top of the text indicates that certainly three skeletons were used, together with a fourth which had to be modified for some reason, probably wear and tear, after quire D, though the type in the heading is the same. The working practice appears to have been that each frame-

work was used twice in each quire. Thus in quire B the distribution
of these frameworks runs ABDCABDC. An anomaly arises in quire
G in some copies where G1v and G2v are both numbered as p. 50
because for a time during the print run the frame for the original
page number 50 (G1v) had not been cleared to make way for 52.
The distribution in quire G is DCDCABAB.

The characteristics discussed here are distributed fairly evenly
throughout the printed copies, which makes it unlikely that the text
is the work of more than one compositor. There are however a few
features which are somewhat irregular, though they do not seem
to fit together in such a way as unmistakably to confirm a second
worker. In Act 1 the characters in the lists at the beginning of the
first five scenes are separated by commas. Subsequently in all the
lists, full stops are used after each name. Another anomaly occurs
with the spellings *he/hee* and *she/shee*. As Jonson himself is inconsistent in the holographs of other work such as the *Masque of Queens*
(BL MS Royal 18A XLV), the choice may be that of the printer or
printers. On pp. 55–61 (not a complete or separate quire) the pref-
erences are in total *she:shee*::17:2 and *he:hee*::27:10. Apart from this
group of pages there are marked disproportions on only two other
individual pages: p. 14 has *she:shee*::10:1 and p. 25 has *he:hee*::14:1.
This however does not match the choice between *do* and *doe* which
is consistently in favour of *doe* throughout at 98:3. Thirdly there is
some inconsistency in the spaces inserted inside brackets, but this
does not show a discernible pattern. The unusually large spaces
noted on pp. 20–1 may suggest that the casting off was done to allow
for two compositors.[110]

One other anomaly arises with the speech prefixes. These are
always in italics and indented. Usually they consist of the first three
letters of the name: as *Lad.* for *Lady*, and *Kee.* for *Keep*. However
for *Diaphanous Silkworm* the form *Dia.* is used in 1.6, 1.7, 2.4 and
3.6; and *Silk.* or *Silke.* in 3.4, 4.8 and 5.10. In scene headings and
stage directions for these three scenes the form *Silkworm(e)* is also
used. The variation does not appear to be consistent with any com-
positorial practice: it probably originates with some anomaly in the
original copy, perhaps from Jonson's changing his mind, or incor-
porating stage keeper's notes on the manuscript.

Herford and the Simpsons judge that 'the play was not well
printed'.[111] There are errors, certainly, but few are of any great
moment, and on the whole the quantity does not seem exceptional.
The distribution of approximately seventy press variants gives some

indication of the practice of the printing house: indeed that positive attempts were made to produce accurate texts. For this edition several more beyond those identified in *H&S* have been found, but none makes any significant difference to the sense. One of the most interesting shows that there are two states of the title-page, not noticed by *H&S*. The first does not give the name of the author of the epigraph, and has no rules under the place and date. As one of the copies seen in this state was the copy possessed by the Prince of Wales (later Charles II), it may have been an early one.[112] Other quires in this copy, however, are not uniformly differentiated from those in other copies, suggesting that the print run was complete before a copy was bound and a presentation made.

Most of the variants, or corrections, are concentrated on six pages which conjugate in pairs: 3/6, 19/22 and 59/62. In some quires the correcting was done early. For some variants in quires C and F only 3 copies of the 45 seen are uncorrected; similarly in quires A and B only 6 uncorrected sheets have been seen, and for quire H the count is 8. On the other hand the corrections were much later in the print run for some sheets in quires B and G where 18 and 17 of the 45 are uncorrected. Both pages of 19/22 were corrected twice, as one variant is found in three states (*it*: 2.3.12), and two others are distributed differently among the copies from the bulk of the variants (reversed *t*, 1 Chor.27; *Daughter*, 1 Chor.22). As usual, no individual copy is found to be uniformly corrected, and quires in differing states of correction were bound together. This follows the usual practice whereby sheets already printed which were found to contain errors were not excluded from the binding process.

On pp. 31 and 49 the catchwords were altered: *Then* moved towards to the right, and the reversed *e* in *Griev'd* corrected. Those on pp. 13, 34 and 48 are inaccurate: *The* instead of *They*; *Hee* instead of *He*; and *I* instead of *It*. There are usually 50 lines per page, though p. 25 has 52.[113] On p. 32 there are only 40 lines, this being the page where the original heading for Act 3, scene 3, was apparently left out, or changed.[114] The inking is imperfect for several letters as with *P ssession* (5.3.17) in all the copies seen. On p. 40 it looks as though correcting an error at l. 123 caused the letters -lvi- in *resolving* and those in two lines above to drop, and the same thing happened with -r in *your* at l. 43 on p. 19.

As to other errors in the printing house, there are some thirteen which appear in all copies.[115] There are mistakes in lineation at 1.6.22–3, 4.1.4 and 5.2.12–13 and 29–30, and the printer wrongly assumed that 'Sirrah' required a new line at Ind.7 (see textual notes). *Palate* is missing from the heading of 4.5, and a new scene is not marked for 3.3. One textual crux remains hard to resolve: *then th'Ages* (see 4.7.45n). Four omissions have been supplied by editors.[116]

For the reprint of 1692 (usually known as *F3*), which has no independent authority, the copy was from Dawson's edition. Quires D and H are uncorrected, as is illustrated by the textual note at 2.6.23. The missing speech prefix on p. 63 (5.10.136) was supplied, presumably because it is clearly required by the dialogue.

The following list shows the forty-five copies consulted for this edition. The codes in square brackets are those for texts consulted by Herford and the Simpsons,[117] and it can thus be seen that the area of enquiry has been considerably enlarged.

London, British Library	79.l.4 [=M3?] C.39.k.9* [=M1] (*STC* reel 756) fol.1482.d.15 [=M5] C.28.m.12 [=M2]
Cambridge, Christ's College	Rouse 8.10–11
Cambridge, Gonville and Caius College	L.34.3
Cambridge, King's College	Keynes Library C.5.14 C.10.6
Cambridge, Newnham College	Young 205b
Cambridge, Trinity College	Grylls 32.140 Grylls 32.180 VI.12.11
Cambridge University Library	Keynes D.6.23 Syn 4.61.20 [Given by PS, but does not match S3] Syn.4.64.14 [PS=S1] Syn.4.64.15 [PS=S2]
Oxford, All Souls College	pp. 4.12 [=A1] pp. 4.18 [=A2]
Oxford, Bodleian Library	Douce I 303 [=B1] Don.d.66 [=B2] Vet2.d.73 Gibson 518 Gibson 520
Austin, Texas, Harry Ransom Centre	38 PFOR 560 Woodward-Ruth 1

Wh/J738 +B641
Stark 6433
Ah/J738 +B641 copy 1

Boston Public Library   G.3811.8
G.3811.8A

Cambridge, Mass., Harvard   Widener 6.10.10
   University, Houghton Library   14426.2*
14426.4F*
Smyth 5468
fAC9.H7375.Zz640j. v.2/3
STC 14754.2 [Bridgewater]

New York Public Library   Arents 211
Stuart *KC 1640
Berg Coll

New York, Pierpont Morgan Library   16255 W4D

San Marino, Huntington Library   3 RB 62103

Washington, Folger   A (STC reel 671)
   Shakespeare Library   B copy 4 m/f
C copy 6

Wellington, New Zealand,   qREng JONS Work 1640
   Alexander Turnbull Library

Cambridge University Library: Keynes D.6.23, was chosen as the basis for the present edition, as it had apparently not been used for H&S. However, the traditional idea of a copy-text is now under some doubt because the practice of binding together quires in different states of correction, as noted above, means that no one copy contains all the latest contemporary corrections. Since, in any case, Jonson did not carry out the corrections, it is hard to maintain that any individual copy is closer to his intentions than the rest.

Apart from the modification of punctuation to lighter modern conventions noted above, the following editorial procedures are adopted here. Massed lists of characters at the heads of scenes have been redistributed to places where entrances and exits occur. A few stage directions have been supplied in square brackets, but the location of scenes has been left unspecified, as in the original. Some instances of the rather irregular 'To them' direction are noted. Speech prefixes, capitals and italics have been made to conform with modern conventions. Spelling has been modernised in accordance with Revels practice, but some obsolete words have been retained in the interests of both rhythm and meaning (as with 'thorough',

5.6.17). Jonson's extensive metrical elisions have been preserved, though modern forms such as *you're* and *'em* (for Jonson's *'hem*, meaning *them*) have been introduced where they exist. Elisions such as *i' the* and *o' the* have been spaced or closed up according to the metre. The original distinctive, but occasionally eccentric, elisions are retained.

The collation notes press variants, but purely typographical changes have been largely ignored. Some readings from later seventeenth- and eighteenth-century editions have been adopted and, together with a very small number of emendations by later editors, these have been listed. A few changes in punctuation are noted, particularly with reference to the somewhat ambiguous 'question' mark.

NOTES

1 *H&S*, 6.501.
2 *JAB*, 122.
3 Jonson was born on 11 June 1572.
4 The presence of the address 'To the Reader' in the collection of poems called *Underwood* in Volume Three of *Works* suggests that Jonson had envisaged publication parallel to that of his earlier collection *The Forest* (in the First Folio of 1616). However George Parfitt, the editor of *Ben Jonson: The Complete Poems* (Harmondsworth, 1975), is in some doubt whether the order and grouping of the poems was finalised by Jonson: see pp. 19–20.
5 Riggs (p. 330) is rather doubtful about these difficulties, but this view underestimates the poems appealing for support, or appreciating it.
6 The closing of the circle has been identified as a persistent organising principle in Jonson's work: see T. M. Greene, 'Ben Jonson and the Centred Self', *SEL* 10 (1970), pp. 325–48. Donaldson suggests that Jonson used the *impresa* to symbolise the unattainability of perfection (Donaldson, p. 30).
7 The iconographical significance was well established: see the 1543 illustration by Corrozet in Riggs, p. 206, where the wording is about going beyond one's powers. Jonson considered that the perfected circle applied to John Selden, the scholar and antiquarian, whom he much admired; see *Und.*, 14.31–2, and *Conv.*, 605.
8 This idea was developed by Anne Barton, 'Harking Back to Elizabeth: Ben Jonson and Caroline Nostalgia', *English Literary History* 48 (1981), pp. 706–31: for details of contemporary plays with comparable retrospection by Nabbes and Davenant see J. L. Davis, *Sons of Ben* (Detroit, 1967), pp. 132–4, 183.
9 See M. Butler, *Theatre and Crisis, 1632–1642* (Cambridge, 1984), especially pp. 181–250.
10 For the view that Jonson trusted his audience, and was only occasion-

ally dismayed, see J. Creaser, 'Enigmatic Ben Jonson', in M. Cordner, P. Holland and J. Kerrigan (eds) *English Comedy* (Cambridge, 1994), pp. 110–16 (p. 113).

11 For the duplicity of the Jacobean Court see B. Worden, 'Ben Jonson among the Historians', in K. Sharpe and P. Lake (eds), *Culture and Politics in Early Stuart England* (Basingstoke, 1994), pp. 67–89.

12 K. Sharpe, *Criticism and Compliment: The Politics of Literature in the England of Charles I* (Cambridge, 1987), p. 211. The Queen was an active participant in plays as well as masques; see *The Shepherds' Paradise* by Walter Montague, edited by Sarah Poynting (Oxford, The Malone Society, 1998), pp. vii–xiii.

13 It was the murder in the Tower of Sir Thomas Overbury, who was opposed to the match, by the agents of Lady Frances which caused outrage and from which James had to dissociate himself: see Riggs, pp. 201–2; M. Butler 'Ben Jonson and the Limits of Courtly Panegyric', in Sharpe and Lake, *Culture and Politics*, pp. 105–6; and *DA*, 1.1.113, 1.2.1–3.

14 Leah Marcus, *The Politics of Mirth* (Chicago, 1986), p. 68; R. M. Smuts, *Court Culture and the Origins of a Royalist Tradition* (Philadelphia, 1987), p. 263.

15 D. Norbrook, *Poetry and Politics in the English Renaissance* (London, 1984), pp. 229–31.

16 Riggs, pp. 127–30.

17 *Conv.*, 315–16.

18 *Conv.*, 330–1. For a discussion of aspects of Jonson's religious changes, see Donaldson, pp. 51–6.

19 George A. E. Parfitt comments that Jonson shows 'little imaginative engagement with the great mysteries of the Christian faith' ('Ethics and Christianity in Ben Jonson', in James Hirsh (ed.) *New Perspectives on Ben Jonson* (London, 1997), pp. 77–88 (p. 79); but perhaps Jonson had learned to be circumspect about public demonstration.

20 As in 'To the Right Honourable, the Lord High Treasurer of England: An Epistle Mendicant', and 'The Humble Petition of Poor Ben to the Best of Monarchs, Masters, Men, King Charles' (*Und.*, 71 and 76).

21 The full title adds 'Celebrating the nuptials of that noble gentleman, Mr Hierome Weston, son, and heir, of the Lord Weston, Lord High Treasurer of England, with the Lady Frances Stuart, Daughter of Esmé, D[uke] of Lennox Deceased, and sister of the surviving Duke of the same name' (*Und.*, 75).

22 R. C. Evans, *Jonson and the Contexts of his Time* (Lewisburg, 1994), p. 154.

23 S. Orgel and R. Strong (eds), *Inigo Jones: The Theatre of the Stuart Court*, 2 vols (London, 1973), 1.57.

24 J. Chibnall, ' "To that secure fix'd state": The Function of the Caroline Masque Form', in D. Lindley (ed.), *The Court Masque* (Manchester, 1984), pp. 78–93.

25 C. C. Brown, 'Courtesies of Place and Arts of Diplomacy in Ben Jonson's Last Two Entertainments for Royalty', *Seventeenth Century* 9 (1994), pp. 197–212. For details of links with Cavendish see James

Fitzsimmons, 'William Cavendish and Two Entertainments by Ben Jonson', *BJJ* 5 (1998), pp. 63–80.

26 'An Expostulation with Inigo Jones' *Misc.*, 118, ll. 39–50.

27 The exception is *The Tale of a Tub*: for this Jonson, possibly disturbed by the trouble with the players over *The Magnetic Lady*, chose Queen Henrietta's Men to perform it at the Cockpit in 1633.

28 J. A. Barish, 'Jonson and the Loathèd Stage', *Celebration*, pp. 27–53 (p. 30).

29 The reference to Vitruvius is a hit at Inigo Jones, who by now had introduced complex stage settings based upon the architectural principles of Vitruvius; see Johnson, *Architecture*, p. 5n.

30 D. H. Craig, *Ben Jonson: The Critical Heritage* (London, 1990), p. 248.

31 This topic has been recently explored by Norah Yvonne Phoenix in her unpublished doctoral thesis, *Dramaturgie de l'espace-temps sur la scène Tudor: Etude de quelques formes c.1520–c.1564* (Tours, 1997).

32 The disagreement in January 1632 between Lord Thurles and Captain Essex indicates that there were boxes adjacent to the stage as well as stools on it: see Herbert Berry, 'The Stages and Boxes at the Blackfriars', *SP* 63 (1966), pp. 163–86.

33 See the poem by Alexander Gill and Jonson's riposte in Appendix I.

34 See 1 Chor.16–24, and note.

35 For a discussion of the excessive stress on moral elements in classical (New) comedy at the Renaissance, see Robert S. Miola, *Shakespeare and Classical Comedy: The Influence of Plautus and Terence* (Oxford, 1994), pp. 4–6. A precedent for 'romantic' elements in *The Magnetic Lady* may well be found in *The Case is Altered* (performed ?1597): see Robert L. Mack, 'Ben Jonson's Own "Comedy of Errors": "That Witty Play" *The Case is Altered*', *BJJ* 4 (1997), pp. 47–63.

36 There is no evidence that Brome attended Westminster. His upbringing is unknown, but see Appendix III.

37 For a discussion of the ambiguity in Jonson's protestation over too specific identification of character and plot, also found in *BF*, Ind.135–47, and *Volp.*, Epistle Dedicatory, ll. 65–70 (where the practice is called 'application'), see Donaldson, pp. 126–37.

38 I have presented some of this material in '*The Magnetic Lady*: Is the Unperformed Performable?' in Edward J. Esche (ed.), *Shakespeare and his Contemporaries in Performance* (Aldershot, forthcoming). For the interplay between reality and illusion see my '*The Alchemist* and *Le Bourgeois Gentilhomme*: Folly and Illusion', *BJJ* 4 (1997), pp. 181–6.

39 Eaves dropping has well-established precedents in classical comedy, see Miola, *Shakespeare and Classical Comedy* (Oxford, 1994) pp. 18, 83–8.

40 G. C. Thayer, *Ben Jonson: Studies in the Plays* (Norman, Ok., 1963), p. 235.

41 *The Critical and Prose Works of John Dryden*, ed. Edmund Malone (London, 1800), 1.102.

42 *H&S*, 6.501.

43 See lines 171–7 of this masque, which was performed in January 1623. Butter introduced the first newsbooks in 1622; see *Staple*, 1.4.31n (ed. Anthony Parr).

44 For more details on these actors see the note to l. 61 of Gill's poem, in Appendix I.

45 *The Control and Censorship of Caroline Drama*, ed. N. Bawcutt (Oxford, 1996), p. 184, no. 266 (from Sir Henry Herbert's lost office-book).

46 Martin Butler, 'Ecclesiastical Censorship of Early Stuart Drama: The Case of Jonson's *The Magnetic Lady*', *MP* 89 (1992), pp. 469–81 (p. 470). Pory's letter is cited at *H&S*, 9.253. Herbert's political vulnerability is discussed by Richard Dutton, ' "Discourse in the players, though no obedience": Sir Henry Herbert's Problems with the Players and Archbishop Laud', *BJJ* 5 (1998), pp. 37–61.

47 The principal 'authority' or 'allowance' for publishing had to be sought from either the Bishop of London or the Archbishop of Canterbury; see P. W. M. Blayney, 'The Publication of Playbooks', in John D. Cox and David Scott Kastan (eds) *A New History of Early English Drama* (New York, 1997), p. 396.

48 Margot Heinemann suggested that Parson Palate may have been unacceptable to Laud on the grounds that he was complaisant: see *Puritanism and Theatre: Thomas Middleton and Opposition Drama under the Stuarts* (Cambridge, 1980), p. 74.

49 In the text Palate is young, 'a venerable youth' (1.1.84), but Bateson played him as decrepit. Similarly Woodthorpe's Rut was hardly a 'young physician' (1.2.38).

50 *TLS* for 25 September 1987, p. 1049.

51 There was a comparable and equally stimulating broadcast of *The Devil is an Ass* by the same director, adapter and many of the same actors on 15 December 1987.

52 I am indebted to Brian Woolland for drawing my attention to his production and for sharing with me his thoughts on it. The account given here is dependent upon his recollections, as I did not see the performance myself.

53 See my 'Staging *The Devil is an Ass* in 1995', *BJJ* 2 (1995), pp. 239–46.

54 The *commedia dell'arte* began to show its influence in London before 1600. See K. M. Lea, *Italian Popular Comedy* (Oxford, 1934), pp. 54–73 and 350–405.

55 An extract is reprinted in Appendix II.

56 Barton, p. 302.

57 M. Butler, 'Late Jonson', in G. McMullan and Jonathan Hope (eds), *The Politics of Tragicomedy: Shakespeare and After* (London, 1992), pp. 166–88 (p. 169).

58 Barton, p. 300.

59 See *DA*, pp. 27–8.

60 'Learning great store for us to feed upon', *Jonsonus Virbius* (London, 1638), facsimile edition (Amsterdam, 1970), p. 41.

61 *H&S*, 1.86, note 5.

62 See Kay, p. 161; C. J. Simpson, 'Ben Jonson of Gresham College', *TLS*, 21 September 1951, p. 604; *H&S*, 2.417–35; Johnson, *Architecture*, p. 4.

63 Johnson, *Architecture*, pp. 5 and 159.

64 2 Chor.15–17. For further details other than the Induction and Choruses see the Notes at 1.2.47; 1.3.5; 3.6.70; 4.4.4.

65 See John Heywood, *Dial. Provs.*

66 'Speak that I may see thee', *Disc.*, 2031. Proverbs have been traced in the following: 1.3.29; 1.4.34–5; 1.4.49; 1.5.4; 1.5.34; 1.6.11; 1.7.36; 1 Chor.44 and 67; 2.1.2–3; 2.4.2 and 17; 2.5.45–6 and 48; 2.6.38; 4.4.47 (Aesop); 4.7.11 (Bible); 4.7.59; 5.1.8 (Cervantes) and 19; 5.5.44; 5.7.14, 39 and 42.; 5.10.53, 64, 83 and 136.

67 For Chaucer's influence see R. C. Evans, 'Ben Jonson's Chaucer', *English Literary Renaissance* 19 (1989), pp. 324–45. Jonson owned T. Speght's 1602 edition of Chaucer (*H&S*, 1.263).

68 For a systematic account see *H&S*, 9.391–5, where an analysis by John Jones (1571) is adumbrated.

69 See 2.3.14–17n.

70 Jonson's position in relationship to contemporary attitudes to midwives has been examined by Julie Sanders in 'Midwifery and the New Science in the Seventeenth Century: Language, Print and the Theatre', in E. Fudge, R. Gilbert and S. Wiseman (eds), *At the Borders of the Human: Beasts, Bodies, and National Philosophy in the Early Modern Period* (Basingstoke, 1998).

71 *Claudian*, ed. and trans. M. Platnauer, Loeb edition, 2 vols (London, 1963), vol. 2, pp. 234–9.

72 Gilbert's ideas may have been a fairly recent interest when Jonson wrote *The Magnetic Lady*: the copy of the treatise he owned was published in 1628. See David McPherson, 'Ben Jonson's Library and Marginalia: An Annotated Catalogue', *SP* 71 (1974), Texts and Studies, pp. 1–106, no. 66.

73 *The Navigator's Supply* (1597), b2.

74 See note 61 above.

75 I am grateful to Dr Julie Sanders for this reference. For Jane Sharp see C. F. Otten, *English Women's Voices, 1540–1700* (Miami, 1992) pp. 178–9; 197–205.

76 Barbara Smith, for example, concludes that, in spite of his male outlook, Jonson does give women 'a voice': see her *The Women of Ben Jonson's Poetry* (Aldershot, 1995) p. 117.

77 G. B. Jackson, *Vision and Judgement in Ben Jonson's Drama* (New Haven, 1968), p. 56. I gratefully acknowledge a debt to this analysis of Jonson's moral world. The delicacy of Jonson's moral and religious sentiments can be seen, for example, in these memorial lines to Lady Venetia Digby in 1633: 'To him should be her judge, true God, true man, / Jesus, the only gotten Christ! Who can / As being redeemer, repairer too / Of lapsèd nature, best know what to do, / In that great act of judgement' (*Und.*, 84.9.211–15).

78 For a general discussion of names in Jonson's plays, see Barton, pp. 170–93. Thayer points out that Jonson, by the device of naming, separates comic characters like Sir Diaphanous from symbolic ones like Compass: *Ben Jonson*, p. 160.

79 P. Hyland, *Disguise and Role-playing in Ben Jonson's Dramas* (Salzburg, 1977), p. 186.

80 Thayer draws attention to Jonson's interest in his allegorical inheritance from the morality plays, though he sees this as intimately linked to the intensely realistic elements of social satire: *Ben Jonson*, p. 15.

81 See 2.5.51, and 2.6.23.

82 *Disc.*, 2047–51.

83 J. E. Savage, *Ben Jonson's Basic Comic Characters* (Hattiesburg, 1973), p. 84.

84 R. Cave, *Ben Jonson* (London, 1991), p. 156.

85 J. A. Barish, *Ben Jonson and the Language of Prose Comedy* (Cambridge, Mass., 1960), p. 205.

86 M. McCanles, *Jonsonian Discriminations: The Humanist Poet and the Praise of True Nobility* (Toronto, 1992), p. 204. Jonson normally inscribed his own books with his motto *tamquam explorator* ('as though an explorer') from Seneca, *Epistles*, 2.5 (*H&S*, 1.261).

87 Larry S. Champion, *Ben Jonson's 'Dotages': A Reconsideration of the Late Plays* (Lexington, Ken., 1967), p. 116. In spite of this difficulty, this is undoubtedly the most sympathetic and consistent appreciation of these plays.

88 C. B. Hafer, *Themes, Techniques and Tone in Ben Jonson's Last Four Comedies* (Northern Illinois University, 1975), p. 30.

89 A. Leggatt, *Ben Jonson: His Vision and His Art* (London, 1981), pp. 148–9. For the ambiguities in these dominating manipulative characters and their appeal to a select audience, see also J. Arnold, *A Grace Peculiar: Ben Jonson's Cavalier Heroes* (University Park, Pa., 1972), p. 7.

90 The close interrelationship between wealth and love is a persistent theme and subject of imagery in *The Merchant of Venice*.

91 Cave, *Ben Jonson*, p. 155.

92 At 2.5.51, and 2.6.23. There is a press variant for the second of these; see textual note.

93 From a psychological point of view there is a concern with the fate and identity of babies—here the exchanged infants, as well as false Placentia's baby which is spirited away: Riggs (p. 333) links this with the fate of children who perish, a topic of some importance in Jonson's own life.

94 Stanley Fish, discussing Jonson's poems, suggests that Jonson developed considerable power as an author by his 'determined reticence' by which the inner self remains locked within the work and that this excludes readers, rather than including them: see his 'Authors-Readers: Jonson's Community of the Same', *Representations* 7 (1984), pp. 26–58.

95 See the letter to the Earl of Newcastle, *H&S*, 1.211.

96 For a full account of Chetwin's role in this affair see William P. Williams, 'Chetwin, Crooke, and the Jonson Folios', *SB* 30 (1977), pp. 75–95.

97 Walkley seems to have shown himself a rather dishonest character in the 1620s: he may still provide us with useful evidence, but anything depending upon his word needs corroborating: see E. A. J. Honigmann, *The Texts of 'Othello' and Shakespearean Revision* (London, 1996), pp. 22–9, and 152–8. I am grateful to Professor Honigmann for this reference.

98 *STC* 13798: see Williams, p. 88, and, for a facsimile of the title-page, *H&S*, 9.127.

99 Greg, 3.1081. In his lampoon, Alexander Gill hints that a printing of

ML was envisaged in 1633, but this may be only a jibe: see l. 24 of his verses in Appendix I.

100 See F. Marcham, 'Thomas Walkley and the Ben Jonson "Workes"', *The Library*, Fourth Series, XI (1931), pp. 225–9.

101 Greg suggests that to lead with the masques was the primary intention because they begin with quire B so as to follow a lost, or never composed, quire A which would have contained the title-page and other preparatory material (3.1080).

102 As a practical point in tracing copies, it has been found that the catalogues of some libraries assume that a composite volume with the Meighen title-page contains only the three plays listed on it.

103 Greg, 3.1082.

104 Fredson Bowers, 'Greg's "Rationale of Copy-Text" Revisited', *SB* 31 (1978), pp. 90–161 (p. 116). He discusses spellings in Jonson holographs on p. 117.

105 E. Honigmann has carried out a similar but more extensive survey in pursuit of Shakespeare's spellings surviving in the Quarto (1622) of *Othello, The Texts of 'Othello'*, Appendix C, pp. 159–61.

106 Cyrus Hoy, 'The Shares of Fletcher and his Collaborators in the Beaumont and Fletcher Canon, VI', *SB* 14 (1961), pp. 61–3. This was further developed by C. G. Petter in his study of Jonson's contribution to *Eastward Ho*: see Ben Jonson, George Chapman and John Marston, *Eastward Ho*, edited by C. G. Petter (London, 1973), pp. xx–xxi.

107 *H&S*, 9.46.

108 Another possibility arises in that p. 61 is part of the inner forme of the quire: perhaps the casting off did not allow enough space to mark individual entrances and exits on an already crowded page.

109 The general principles underlying these features of Jonson's texts have been described, and related to Jonson's discrimination exercised over much larger issues by M. McCanles, *Jonsonian Discriminations* pp. 7–42.

110 The link between casting for printing by formes and the use of more than one compositor is discussed by Charlton Hinman, *The Printing and Proof-reading of the First Folio of Shakespeare*, 2 vols (Oxford, 1963), 1.74.

111 *H&S*, 6.502.

112 Arents 211, New York Public Library. The presence of the Jonson *Works* in the Arents Collection is intriguing. Apparently the volumes were purchased, along with many other books and *objets d'art*, as materials for a social history of tobacco.

113 In Volume One (1616), and Beale's Volume Two there are 47 lines to the page (*H&S*, 9.88).

114 This is p. 32 of *F*, an outer forme where the pressure on space may have been a problem. It is the conjugate of p. 25.

115 voluptary (1.2.41); *Protesis* (1 Chor.7); Mrs. (2.2.35); Eeene (2.2.42); Timpane (2.3.33); his his (2.6.123); de defaced (3.4.16); graones (3.5.8); *Needle* omitted (5.1.7); *Iem* (5.1.11); to her, to her (5.5.43); Bak-houses (5.8.37); noofe (5.10.110).

116 These are: the (2.6.59); cried (4.2.20); *Needle* (5.1.11); *Lady* (5.10.136).

117 *H&S*, 9.107–8.

THE
MAGNETIC LADY

THE
MAGNETIC
LADY:
OR,
HUMOURS
RECONCILED.

A COMEDY composed
By
BEN: JONSON.

Iam lapides suus ardor agit ferrumque tenetur,
Illecebris.——Claud. de Magnet.

LONDON,
Printed M.DC.XL.

THE SCENE,

LONDON.

The Persons that act.

Lady LOADSTONE, the Magnetic Lady.
Mistress POLISH, her Gossip and She-parasite.   5
Mistress PLACENTIA, her Niece.
PLEASANCE, her Waiting-woman.
Mistress KEEP, the Niece's Nurse.
Mother CHAIR, the Midwife.
Master COMPASS, a Scholar mathematic.   10

Claud. de Magnet.] *not in some copies of F.*   LONDON...XL] *Under-
lined in some copies of F.*   M.DC.XL] *This ed.;* M.CD.XL. *F.*
THE SCENE, (/) LONDON.] *centred in large capitals, F.*   7. PLEAS-
ANCE,] *This ed.; Pleasance. Fu; Pleasance, Fc.*

Iam ... Magnet.] 'Rocks are stirred by a passion of their own; iron is
obedient to thy blandishments', Claudian, *Magnes*, 'The Magnet' (Loeb,
2.56–7: addressed to 'the cruel boy' (Cupid)). See Persons: Loadstone, and
Introduction, pp. 32–4.

4. *LOADSTONE*] magnetic oxide of iron, used to show the way or lode.
Claudian's poem (see epigraph on title-page) supposes the union of the
deities of Mars with an iron statue, and Venus with one of loadstone (ll.
25–6), and it shows how Venus holds Mars in check.
   5. *POLISH*] Her role is to polish Placentia (1.4.40). Perhaps there is a pun
on Pol (parrot) because of her loquacity.
   Gossip] companion (*OED* 3); cf. 1.3.37.
   She-parasite] female dependant (cf. *OED* she 10a; parasite 1a).
   6. *PLACENTIA*] suggests giving pleasure (*placere*, Lat., to give pleasure)
like Pleasance, but her name also recalls *placenta*, and it is she who is pregnant. *Placenta* (Gk), bed.
   9. *CHAIR*] suggested by French *chair* (flesh); also connected with
birth(ing) chair. Cf. birth-stool, *OED* birth 13 (1627).
   10. *COMPASS*] Compass is partly an idealisation of Jonson himself.
Jonson's personal *impresa* was a broken compass, suggesting that, although
he had a fixed and secure base for his life, he did not succeed in encom-
passing all his interests successfully; see Riggs, p. 205, and illustration on p.
206. The Boy refers to Jonson as 'near the close or shutting up of his circle',
Ind.97: see Introduction, pp. 37–8.

Captain IRONSIDE, a Soldier.
Parson PALATE, prelate of the Parish.
Dr RUT, physician to the house.
TIM ITEM, his Apothecary.
Sir DIAPHANOUS SILKWORM, a Courtier.   15
Master PRACTICE, a Lawyer.
Sir MOTH INTEREST, an Usurer or Money-bawd.
Master BIAS, a Vi-politic or Sub-secretary.
Master NEEDLE, the Lady's Steward and Tailor.

CHORUS by way of Induction.   20

[Master *Probee*, Master *Damplay*, A *Boy of the house,
Foot-boy, Varlet.*]

15. DIAPHANOUS] *This ed.; Diaph F.*   17. MOTH INTEREST,] *This ed.;
Moath F. Interest. Fu; Interest, Fc.* bawd] *This ed.; band Fu; baud Fc.*   18.
BIAS,] *This ed.; Bias Fu; Bias, Fc.*   21.] *H&S*; Servant to sir Moth, Ser-
jeants &c. *G.*

---

11. *IRONSIDE*] An irascible country parson named Ironside carried out
an inquiry into Sir Walter Raleigh's alleged atheism at Cerne Abbas in 1594:
see G. B. Harrison (ed.) *Willobie his Avisa* (London, 1922) pp. 255–71. The
name must also be associated with Mars (see l. 4n), and with the allegory
of magnetism.

12. *PALATE*] used to suggest appetite, often in a menial sense (*OED* 1b):
cf. 3.1.16–17.

15. *DIAPHANOUS*] transparent, and by implication empty: cf. 2.1.16; and
'In silk / 'Twas brought to court', 'On Court-Worm', *Ep.*, 15.1–2.

17. *MOTH INTEREST*] Interest suggests miserliness and perhaps usury.
Moth may allude to 'Lay not up for yourselves treasures upon the earth, where
moth and rust doth consume', Matthew, 6: 19 (King James Bible, 1611).

Money-bawd] a dealer in sharp financial practice; cf. *Staple*, 2.5.1.

18. *BIAS*] punned on 'ass', 1.7.50–1.

Vi-politic] One involved in political manipulation, acting as supporter or
substitute for a more eminent principal: cf. 'a sub-aiding instrument of state',
1.7.2.

21. *Probee*] derived from *probare* (Lat.) to approve.

Damplay] Dam- suggests 'damn'. The characterisation is partly aimed at
Inigo Jones, with whom he shares bad Latin according to Jonson: see
Ind.72–3n.

Boy] The Book-holder, or prompter, appears in *BF*, Ind. The Boy says he is
'the poet's servant', 1 Chor.62–3; he has some awareness of Jonson personally,
and his characterisation may reflect Jonson's earlier relationship with his
'servant', Richard Brome (?1590–1652 or 1653). However, by 1632 Brome was
an established playwright who in some respects had outstripped Jonson in
public esteem. See Ind.82–3n, 1 Chor.8–9n, and 62n, and Appendix III.

The Induction; or, Chorus

Two Gentlemen entering upon the Stage, Master PROBEE
and Master DAMPLAY. A BOY of the house *meets them.*

Boy. What do you lack, gentlemen? What is't you lack? Any
fine fancies, figures, humours, characters, ideas, defini-
tions of lords and ladies? Waiting-women, parasites,
knights, captains, courtiers, lawyers? What do you lack?
Probee. A pretty prompt boy for the poetic shop.   5
Damplay. And a bold! Where's one o'your masters, sirrah, the
poet?
Boy. Which of 'em? Sir, we have divers that drive that trade
now: poets, poet'accios, poetasters, poetitoes—
Damplay. And all haberdashers of small wit, I presume: we   10
would speak with the poet o'the day, Boy.

01.] *Centred in large capitals, F.*   Stage,] *H&S; Stage. F.*   6. sirrah] *Wha;*
Sirrah *begins new line F, perhaps mistaken as verse.*

---

   1. *What . . . lack*] Shopkeepers' cry (*H&S*) setting up the extended
metaphor of the stage as a shop; see below, l. 59. His offer of concepts (see
'idea', l. 98) for characters is thematic.
   2. *humours*] See l. 102, and cf. 'As when some one peculiar quality / Doth
so possess a man that it doth draw / All his affects, his spirits, and his powers
/ In their confluctions, all to run one way, / This may be truly said to be a
humour' (*EMO,* Ind.105–9).
   5. *prompt boy*] pun on (1) ready, active; (2) prompter. The latter implies
that this Boy was the prompter, but his actual location at the Blackfriars is
uncertain: see 125n.
   shop] Possibly an echo of 'a thinking shop' in Aristophanes, *The Clouds,* l.
94 (*H&S,* 2.210).
   9. *poet'accios*] Possibly a Jonson coinage, though *accio* (Ital.) means evil:
cf. Corbaccio in *Volp.*
   poetasters] trashy poets. Jonson's use in *CR,* 2.1 (1599) is the first citation
in *OED.* The Latin form was used by Erasmus (1521). 'The suffix *-aster*
indicates an incomplete resemblance', Tom Cain (ed.) *Poetaster* (Manchester, 1995), p. 62.
   poetitoes] paltry poets: first here in *OED.*
   10. *haberdashers*] appropriate because they dealt in small articles: associated with vanity.
   11. *o'the day*] the poet whose play is to be performed today.

Boy. Sir, he is not here. But, I have the dominion of the shop, for this time, under him, and can show you all the variety the stage will afford for the present.

Probee. Therein you will express your own good parts, Boy. 15

Damplay. And tie us two to you, for the gentle office.

Probee. We are a pair of public persons (this gentleman and myself) that are sent thus coupled unto you, upon state-business.

Boy. It concerns but the state of the stage, I hope! 20

Damplay. O, you shall know that by degrees, Boy. No man leaps into a business of state, without fording first the state of the business.

Probee. We are sent unto you, indeed, from the people.

Boy. The people! Which side of the people? 25

Damplay. The venison side, if you know it, Boy.

Boy. That's the left side. I had rather they had been the right.

Probee. So they are. Not the faeces or grounds of your people, that sit in the oblique caves and wedges of your house, your sinful sixpenny mechanics— 30

Damplay. But the better and braver sort of your people! Plush and velvet-outsides! That stick your house round like so many eminences—

---

12. *he . . . here*] Possibly Jonson's last appearance at a first performance before he became bedridden was for *Staple* in 1625–6 (*G*).

17. *public persons*] persons acting impartially on behalf of the community.

20. *but . . . hope*] a reflection of Jonson's perennial assumption that the stage always had a political dimension.

22. *fording*] crossing over.

23. *business*] pun on (1) commerce; (2) political affairs.

26. *venison*] Pun on hart/heart, i.e. (left) side of the body (*H&S*). Because the left is sinister, the Boy would prefer the more auspicious right.

28. *faeces*] sediment, *Alc.*, 2.3.63.

29. *oblique . . . house*] Derived from *caveae* (seats, Plautus, *Amphitruo*, Prologue, l. 66) and *cunei* (wedge-shaped seat-divisions, Virgil, *Aeneid*, 5.46) in Roman amphitheatres (*H&S*).

30. *sixpenny*] Damplay is accustomed to pay 'eighteen pence or two shillings': 2 Chor.61–2. For the range of admission prices see *BF*, Ind.89–91. There are many references to contemporary money values in *ML*; cf. *DA*, p. 55, n. 30.

mechanics] manual labourers, the lower orders.

31–2. *Plush . . . outsides*] Plush, a cloth with long soft nap, is priced at £3 10*s* per yard in *DA*, 1.4.40 (1616). Jonson associates plush and velvet with idleness and debauchery, *NI*, Ode, 32.

Boy. Of clothes, not understandings? They are at pawn. Well,
I take these as a part of your people though; what bring   35
you to me from these people?

Damplay. You have heard, Boy, the ancient poets had it in
their purpose still to please this people.

Probee. Ay, their chief aim was—

Damplay. Populo ut placerent: if he understands so much.   40

Boy. Quas fecissent fabulas: I understand that sin' I learned
Terence i'the third form at Westminster: go on, sir.

Probee. Now these people have employed us to you, in all their
names, to entreat an excellent play from you.

Damplay. For they have had very mean ones from this shop   45
of late, the stage as you call it.

Boy. Troth, gentlemen, I have no wares which I dare thrust
upon the people with praise. But this, such as it is, I will
venture with your people, your gay, gallant people: so as
you again will undertake for them that they shall know a   50
good play when they hear it; and will have the conscience
and ingenuity beside to confess it.

Probee. We'll pass our words for that: you shall have a brace
of us to engage ourselves.

Boy. You'll tender your names, gentlemen, to our book then?   55

Damplay. Yes, here's Master Probee: a man of most powerful
speech and parts to persuade.

---

40. if . . . much.] *G; brackets, F.*   41. *fabulas:] This ed.; fabulas.) F.*

32–3.] *That stick . . . eminences*] 'That decorate your house like so many
pinnacles or protuberances'. Damplay, perhaps out of character, expresses
Jonson's contempt for idle playgoers.

34. *pawn*] used for pledge for debt, but here with pun on peacock,
gorgeously dressed (*OED* pawn sb³).

40–1. *Populo . . . fabulas*] To see that the plays he would make should
please the people, Terence, *Andria*, prol., l. 3. See *SW*, Prol.1.1.2.

42. *Westminster*] Jonson's old school where he began his classical studies
under William Camden. In 'They make all their scholars playboys', *Staple*,
3 Intermean, 45–9, the implication is that the boys were exploited in the
theatres.

50–1. *know . . . hear it*] Possibly proverbial.

52. *ingenuity*] nobility, high-mindedness (*OED* 2); understanding.

55. *book*] perhaps a record of visitors.

Probee. And Master Damplay will make good all he
undertakes.

Boy. Good Master Probee and Master Damplay! I like your 60
securities: whence do you write yourselves?

Probee. Of London, gentlemen: but knights' brothers and
knights' friends, I assure you.

Damplay. And knights' fellows too. Every poet writes squire
now. 65

Boy. You are good names! Very good men, both of you! I
accept you.

Damplay. And what is the title of your play here? 'The
Magnetic Lady'?

Boy. Yes, sir, an attractive title the author has given it. 70

Probee. *A magnete,* I warrant you.

Damplay. O no, from *magnus, magna, magnum.*

Boy. This gentleman hath found the true magnitude—

Damplay. Of his portal or entry to the work, according to
Vitruvius. 75

---

61. securities:] *Fc;* securities, *Fu.*   72. *magnum.*] *Wha; Magnum! Fu;*
Magnum. Fc.

---

58. *will*] who will.

58–9. *make . . . undertakes*] will bring things to a firm conclusion.

61. *securities*] credentials.

whence . . . yourselves] where do you come from? (with an underlying
enquiry about social status).

62–4. *knights'. . . squire*] Poetry by Samuel Daniel (1623) and Richard
Braithwaite (1621–31) was published as by Esquires. The rank was described
as containing the 'residue of gentlemen' by Thomas Smith (1583); cf. *DA,*
4.7.30n. Jonson was exercised about titles, and in 1621 there was some
expectation he would be knighted (see Riggs, p. 271).

66. *good*] trustworthy, financially sound, *DA,* 3.1.10.

70. *attractive*] pun on (1) pleasing; (2) drawing with magnetic force.

71. *A magnete*] In italics in *F,* suggesting that it is Latin. Probee picks up
on 'attractive' (l. 70) and adds 'by a magnet' in corroboration. His remark
opens up the way to Damplay's following blunder.

72–3. *magnus . . . magnitude*] The wordplay is directed against Inigo
Jones by giving Damplay false Latin. 'Magnetic' derives from *magnes* (Lat.)
a magnet: there is no link with the declension of *magnus,* 'great' (appropriate to a schoolboy learning by rote), which Damplay offers. Cf. *T of T,*
5.7.11.

Boy. Sir, all our work is done without a portal—or Vitruvius.
　　In foro as a true comedy should be. And what is concealed
　　within is brought out and made present by report.
Damplay. We see not that always observed by your authors of
　　these times, or scarce any other.　　　　　　　　　　80
Boy. Where it is not at all known, how should it be observed?
　　The most of those your people call authors never dreamt
　　of any decorum, or what was proper in the scene, but
　　grope at it i'the dark and feel or fumble for it; I speak it
　　both with their leave and the leave o'your people.　　85
Damplay. But why 'Humours Reconciled'? I would fain know.
Boy. I can satisfy you there too, if you will. But perhaps you
　　desire not to be satisfied.
Damplay. No? Why should you conceive so, Boy?
Boy. My conceit is not ripe yet: I'll tell you that anon.　　90
　　The author, beginning his studies of this kind with
　　'Every Man in his Humour', and after 'Every Man out
　　of his Humour', and since continuing in all his plays,
　　especially those of the comic thread, whereof 'The New
　　Inn' was the last, some recent humours still or manners　　95
　　of men that went along with the times, finding himself

---

77. *In*] *H&S;* In *F.*

76. *Vitruvius*] Roman architect whose work inspired Inigo Jones, the
architect and designer with whom Jonson collaborated over Court masques
for many years. Jones used complex scenery, hence Jonson's scorn for 'portal'
as distinct from the plainer sets of classical comedy. See Introduction, pp.
10–11, and *H&S*, 3.3, 10.689–92 and 709–10.

77. In foro] In open court, see *NI*, 2.6.184; but the remark continues the
attack upon the staging of Inigo Jones.

78. *present by report*] as in classical drama where the narrative of
offstage events is a marked characteristic: cf. 'Many things may be told
which cannot be showed', Sidney, *Apology*, p. 135.

82–3. *authors... decorum*] In 'To my Old Faithful Servant: and (by his
continued virtue) my Loving Friend', his dedicatory poem to Richard
Brome's *Northern Lass* (1632), Jonson remarks 'Both learned and unlearned
all write plays', *H&S*, 8.409–10, l. 12.

85. *their... people*] with the permission of popular authors and the people
who would approve them (ironic).

86. *Humours Reconciled*] the subtitle of the play, justified by 5.10.126.

90. *My conceit... yet*] the Boy suspects prejudice, but does not allege it.

92–5. *Every Man... Inn*] *EMI* performed 1598 and printed 1601, revised
1616; *EMO* performed 1599 and printed 1600; *NI* performed 1629 and
printed 1631.

now near the close or shutting up of his circle, hath
fancied to himself in idea this magnetic mistress. A lady,
a brave, bountiful housekeeper and a virtuous widow,
who, having a young niece ripe for a man and marriage-   100
able, he makes that his centre attractive to draw thither
a diversity of guests, all persons of different humours to
make up his perimeter. And this he hath called 'Humours
Reconciled'.

Probee. A bold undertaking! And far greater than the recon-   105
ciliation of both churches, the quarrel between humours
having been much the ancienter and, in my poor opinion,
the root of all schism and faction both in church
and commonwealth.

Boy. Such is the opinion of many wise men that meet at this   110
shop still; but how he will speed in it, we cannot tell, and
he himself, it seems, less cares. For he will not be
entreated by us to give it a prologue. He has lost too
much that way already, he says. He will not woo the
gentile ignorance so much. But careless of all vulgar   115
censure, as not depending on common approbation, he
is confident it shall superplease judicious spectators, and
to them he leaves it to work with the rest by example or
otherwise.

---

97. *circle*] The motto of Jonson's emblem was 'Deest quod duceret
orbem': that is lacking which should complete the circle, *Conv.*, 578–9. See
Introduction, pp. 37–8, and p. 53 note 6.

98. *in idea*] in conception or imagination, as opposed to reality; cited in
OED 8d.

99. *housekeeper*] one who keeps a bountiful house, (*OED* 2).

101. *centre attractive*] centre (*OED*, 6b); attractive (*OED*, B.2): 'that which
draws like a magnet'. Possibly the concept is derived from the 'handsome
hostess' in Earle's *Microcosmographie*: 'she is the loadstone that attracts men
or iron, gallants and roarers' (Peck); see Introduction, p. 32.

103. *perimeter*] circumference, continuing the compass-circle imagery.

106. *of both churches*] that is of the Protestant and Catholic Churches.

113. *lost*] Terence claims in the Prologue to *Andria* that he has to spend
time answering slanderous attacks in his prologues: a priority not un-
familiar to Jonson.

115. *gentile*] Probably the ignorance 'of the tribe' from *gentilis* (Lat.);
perhaps heathen or pagan. Cf. *CR*, Ind.116n.

117. *superplease*] please exceedingly: a Jonson coinage? Not in *OED*.
judicious spectators] For Jonson's concern with discriminating spectators
see Introduction, p. 10.

Damplay. He may be deceived in that, Boy: few follow   120
examples now, especially if they be good.

Boy. The play is ready to begin, gentlemen; I tell you lest you
might defraud the expectation of the people for whom
you are delegates. Please you take a couple of seats, and
plant yourselves here, as near my standing as you can. Fly   125
everything you see to the mark and censure it—freely. So
you interrupt not the series or thread of the argument to
break or pucker it with unnecessary questions. For, I
must tell you, not out of mine own dictamen but the
author's, a good play is like a skein of silk: which, if you   130
take by the right end, you may wind off at pleasure on
the bottom or card of your discourse in a tale or so, how
you will: but if you light on the wrong end, you will pull
all into a knot, or elf-lock, which nothing but the shears
or a candle will undo or separate.   135

Damplay. Stay! Who be these, I pray you.

126. it—freely] *This ed.;* it; freely *F.*

125. *standing*] The prompter's location during the performance is not
known but, for the convenience of Damplay and Probee, it must have
commanded a good view of the action. 'Take' and 'plant' suggests that the
seats were movable, and would most probably be on the stage itself.

125–6. *Fly . . . mark*] used in falconry for the hawk's marking the location
of prey; see *BF*, 2.4.42.

127. *series*] connected sequence of discourse (*OED* 4).

128. *pucker*] distort into wrinkles or folds.

unnecessary questions] contrasts with the role of the onlookers Mitis and
Cordatus in *EMO* who are to 'Speak your opinions upon every scene',
Ind.155.

129. *dictamen*] authoritative statement; cf. *NI*, 3.1.52, and the title of
Und., 2.9, 'Her man described by her own dictamen'.

130. *skein of silk*] This is the beginning of a series of metaphors related
to embroidery, as in 4 Chor.20, 5.10.81, and 115–16: see Helen Ostovich,
'The Appropriation of Pleasure in *The Magnetick Lady*', *SEL* 34 (1994),
pp. 434–6.

131. *the right end*] Cf. 5.10.81.

132. *bottom*] a nucleus on which to wind thread (*OED* 15): hence Bottom,
the weaver, in *MND*. Cf. 'to bottom it', *Gent.*, 3.2.53.

card] instrument with iron teeth used to comb fibres (*OED* 1.2).

134. *elf-lock*] tangle, created by elves.

136. *these*] the first characters appear on the stage.

Boy. Because it is your first question and these be the prime
persons, it would in civility require an answer: but I
have heard the poet affirm that to be the most unlucky
scene in a play which needs an interpreter, especially   140
when the auditory are awake: and such are you, he pre-
sumes. *Ergo* . . .

137–8. these . . . persons,] *G;* (these . . . persons) *F.*

137. *prime*] first to appear, or first in rank.
139. *poet affirm*] For Jonson's attitude to plot see Introduction, pp. 39–40.
142. Ergo] Therefore.

Act I

[Enter] COMPASS *[and]* IRONSIDE.

Compass. Welcome, good Captain Ironside, and brother;
You shall along with me. I'm lodged hard by,
Here at a noble lady's house i'th' street,
The Lady Loadstone's—one will bid us welcome
Where there are gentlewomen, and male guests   5
Of several humours, carriage, constitution,
Profession too: but so diametral
One to another, and so much opposed
As if I can but hold them all together,
And draw'em to a sufferance of themselves   10
But till the dissolution of the dinner,
I shall have just occasion to believe

Heading centred in large capitals: THE (/) MAGNETICK (/) LADY: (/)
OR, (/) HUMORS (/) RECONCIL'D. *F.*

0.1] The whole of Act I takes place in the street in front of Lady
Loadstone's house. Compass and Ironside enter the house at 1.2.48, and
reappear at the beginning of 1.5. See 1.2.47n.
   1. *brother*] Compass and Ironside are apparently not blood brothers
('adopted', 2.6.145). The word 'brother' appears many times in the rest of
this scene.
   4. *Loadstone*] See Persons.
   will] who will.
   6. *several*] different.
   humours] see above Ind.2n.
   carriage] habitual conduct (*OED* 15).
   7. *Profession*] belief or occupation.
   diametral] directly opposed (*OED* 3; and cf. diametrical 2b).
   10. *draw'em*] a single syllable (draw'm).
   sufferance] toleration.
   11. *dissolution*] termination, but spoken with a somewhat sinister
irony.

My wit is magisterial; and ourselves
Take infinite delight i'the success.

Ironside. Troth, brother Compass, you shall pardon me: 15
    I love not so to multiply acquaintance
    At a meal's cost—'twill take off o' my freedom
    So much—or bind me to the least observance.

Compass. Why, Ironside, you know I am a scholar
    And part a soldier. I have been employed   20
    By some the greatest statesmen o' the kingdom
    These many years, and in my time conversed
    With sundry humours, suiting so myself
    To company, as honest men and knaves,
    Good-fellows, hypocrites, all sorts of people,   25
    Though never so divided in themselves,
    Have studied to agree still in the usage,
    And handling of me, which hath been fair too.

Ironside. Sir, I confess you to be one well read
    In men and manners; and that usually   30
    The most ungoverned persons, you being present,
    Rather subject themselves unto your censure
    Than give you least occasion of distaste,
    By making you the subject of their mirth:
    But, to deal plainly with you, as a brother,   35
    Whenever I distrust i' my own valour,
    I'll never bear me on another's wit,

---

13. *magisterial*] This has an alchemical meaning deriving from *magisterium*, the philosopher's stone: see G. C. Thayer, *Ben Jonson: Studies in the Plays* (Norman, Ok., 1963), p. 241. This sentence establishes Compass's managing role.

14. *success*] result.

16–17. *I love . . . cost*] I don't like having to meet so many people just in order to have a meal.

18. *bind . . . observance*] force me to comply in trivial ways.

25. *Good-fellows*] revellers; thieves (*OED*).

26–8. *Though . . . too*] 'Though all these different types of people have nevertheless managed to treat me in the same way, usually to good effect.' The sentiment implies a threat.

27. *usage*] being used.

28. *handling*] treatment.

32. *subject . . . censure*] accept your judgement.

33. *distaste*] displeasure; quarrel, *DA*, 3.3.77.

37. *bear me*] rely upon.

Or offer to bring off or save myself
On the opinion of your judgement, gravity,
Discretion, or what else. But, being away,   40
You're sure to have less wit-work, gentle brother,
My humour being as stubborn as the rest,
And as unmanageable.

Compass.   You do mistake
My caract of your friendship all this while!
Or at what rate I reckon your assistance,   45
Knowing by long experience to such animals,
Half-hearted creatures, as these are, your fox, there,
Unkennelled with a choleric, ghastly aspect,
Or two or three comminatory terms,
Would run their fears to any hole of shelter,   50
Worth a day's laughter! I am for the sport:
For nothing else.

Ironside.   But brother, I ha' seen
A coward, meeting with a man as valiant
As our St George (not knowing him to be such,
Or having least opinion that he was so)   55
Set to him roundly, ay, and swinge him soundly:
And i' the virtue of that error, having
Once overcome, resolved for ever after
To err; and think no person nor no creature

---

41. less] *Wha;* lesse- *F.*

41. *wit-work*] need to be ingenious.
44. *caract*] valuation, (*OED* carat 4); see *EMI*, 3.3.22.
47. *fox*] Ironside's sword; cf. *BF*, 2.6.56.
48. *Unkennelled*] unsheathed, referring to the sword: foxhunting term for dislodging a fox (*H&S*).
49. *comminatory*] threatening.
50. *run . . . shelter*] would force them to run away to any refuge they could find.
53. *coward*] This anticipates the 'duel' between Diaphanous and Ironside in 2.6.
56. *Set to*] set upon.
   swinge] thrash.
57. *virtue*] strength.

More valiant than himself.

Compass.   I think that too.   60
But, brother, could I over-entreat you,
I have some little plot upon the rest,
If you would be contented to endure
A sliding reprehension at my hands,
To hear yourself, or your profession glanced at   65
In a few slighting terms: it would beget
Me such a main authority, o' the by:
And do yourself no disrepute at all!

Ironside. Compass, I know that universal causes
In nature produce nothing; but as meeting   70
Particular causes, to determine those,
And specify their acts. This is a piece
Of Oxford science stays with me e'er since
I left that place; and I have often found
The truth thereof in my private passions.   75
For I do never feel myself perturbed
With any general words 'gainst my profession
Unless by some smart stroke upon myself
They do awake and stir me: else to wise
And well-experienced men, words do but signify;   80

---

61. over-entreat] *Wi.;* over intreat *F.*   66. terms] *Wha;* terme *Fu;* termes
Fc.   75. my] *Fc;* ym *Fu.*

---

61. *over-entreat*] ask beyond your predetermined wishes: a Jonson
coinage?

64. *sliding*] passing, temporary.
reprehension] finding of faults.

65. *glanced at*] criticised obliquely.

67. *main*] strong.
o'the by] as well; cf. 1.7.69; *Cat.,* 3.77.

69–72. *universal causes . . . acts*] Aristotle's doctrine of universals notes
that there are common, universal characteristics which may be perceived
as real, but they only exist in relation to individual instances, and not in
a separate ideal world like Plato's. Ironside's subsequent example shows
that particular insults stir him, while general condemnation does not (ll.
76–9).

80. *but signify*] only carry meaning. As he explains in the next line, words
have no real power. The idea has proverbial analogues in 'Foul words break
no bones' (Tilley, W801); and 'Words are but wind' (Tilley, W833).

They have no power; save with dull grammarians,
Whose souls are nought but a syntaxis of them.
Compass. Here comes our parson, Parson Palate, here,
A venerable youth! I must salute him,
And a great clerk! He's going to the lady's,   85
And though you see him thus, without his cope,
I dare assure you he's our parish pope!

[*Enter* PALATE.]

God save my reverend clergy, Parson Palate.

ACT I   SCENE 2

Palate. The witty Master Compass! How is't with you?
Compass. My lady stays for you, and for your counsel,
Touching her niece, Mistress Placentia Steele!
Who strikes the fire of full fourteen today,
Ripe for a husband.
Palate.   Ay, she chimes, she chimes.   5

87.1] *G.*

1.2] *Palate, Compasse, Ironside. F.*   5. chimes.] *Wha; chimes, F.*

___

82. *syntaxis*] arrangement (jocular).
85. *clerk*] cleric.
86. *cope*] ecclesiastical outer garment, often ceremonial. Along with
'prelate' (1.2.15), this may suggest the influence of Laud.
87. *pope*] Alluding to 'a pope in every parish'. Cf. 1.2.15.
88. *clergy*] clergyman, one in priestly orders.

2. *stays*] waits.
4. *strikes the fire*] play on Steele.
fourteen] This is a distinctly early age for marriage: see Graph 3 showing
the median age (c.1650) for first marriage of females in the squirearchy
and above as over twenty, in Lawrence Stone, *The Family, Sex and Marriage
in England, 1500–1800* (Harmondsworth, 1979), p. 43. He shows that the
illegitimacy rate in rural areas declined from 4 per cent in 1590 to 1.5
per cent in 1650 (p. 105). John R. Gillis, *For Better, For Worse: British
Marriages 1600 to the Present* (Oxford, 1985), has similar figures for the
illegitimacy ratio, and slightly older ages for marriage; see fig. 11 (p. 111).
He notes that some Puritans advocated raising the age of majority to twenty-
four (p. 86).
5. *Ripe . . . husband*] Virgil, *Aeneid*, 7.53 (*H&S*).
chimes] indicates her age like a bell chiming.

Saw you the Doctor Rut, the house physician?
He's sent for too.
Palate.   To counsel? 'Time you'were there.
Make haste, and give it a round quick dispatch:
That we may go to dinner betimes, parson:
And drink a health or two more to the business.   10

> [*Exit* PALATE.]

Ironside. This is a strange put-off! A reverend youth,
You use him most surreverently methinks!
What call you him? Palate Please? or Parson Palate?
Compass. All's one, but shorter! I can gi' you his character.
He is the prelate of the parish, here;   15
And governs all the dames; appoints the cheer;
Writes down the bills of fare; pricks all the guests;
Makes all the matches and the marriage feasts
Within the ward; draws all the parish wills;
Designs the legacies; and strokes the gills   20
Of the chief mourners; and, whoever lacks
Of all the kindred, he hath first his blacks.
Thus holds he weddings up, and burials,

---

10. health] *Fc;* health, *Fu.*   10.1] *G.*   13. What] *Fc;* What? *Fu.*   21.
whoever lacks] *G; in parenthesis F.*

---

7. '*Time*] Elliptical for 'It's time'.
8. *round*] thorough.
dispatch] speedy completion.
9. *betimes*] soon.
11. *put-off*] snub.
12. *surreverently*] not reverently, perhaps derived from the saying 'saving your reverence'; a Jonson coinage? Sole citation in *OED*: 'without reverence,' *T of T,* 1.6.25. This may also allude to sirreverence as excrement (*OED* 2).
14. *character*] description.
15–32] The 'character' of Palate is in couplets; see l.36 below.
15. *prelate*] religious dignitary (ironic, perhaps a hint at Laud).
16. *cheer*] food, or entertainment.
17. *pricks*] records (v).
19. *ward*] administrative local district; cf. 5.6.17.
20. *Designs*] Arranges; with a hint that Palate may be a beneficiary of the legacies.
strokes the gills] Tickling trout in this way leads to catching them.
22. *blacks*] black hangings at funerals (*OED* 4b), *Ep.,* 44.3: there would be income from these. Possibly the reference is to mourning clothes, often bequeathed to relatives.

As his main tithing; with the gossips' stalls,
Their pews. He's top still at the public mess;   25
Comforts the widow, and the fatherless,
In funeral sack! Sits 'bove the alderman!
For of the wardmote quest he better can
The mystery than the Levitic law:
That piece of clerkship doth his vestry awe.   30
He is as he conceives himself, a fine
Well-furnished and apparellèd divine.
Ironside. Who made this epigram, you?
Compass.   No, a great clerk
As any'is of his bulk: Ben Jonson made it.
Ironside. But what's the other character, Doctor Rut?   35
Compass. The same man made 'em both: but his is shorter,
And not in rhyme but blanks. I'll tell you that, too.
Rut is a young physician to the family:
That, letting God alone, ascribes to nature
More than her share; licentious in discourse,   40

---

30. clerkship] *Wha; Clark-ship F.*   34. bulk:] *This ed.; bulke. F.*

24. *tithing*] income from taxes, originally tenths.
24–5. *with . . . pews*] income from the hire of stalls and pews (elliptic).
gossips'] godparents'.
25. *top . . . mess*] always sits at the head of the table at public feasts.
27. *sack*] white wine.
28–9. *For . . . law*] For he knows more about the intricacies of secular inquiries than about religious laws.
28. *wardmote quest*] judicial inquiry made by citizens of a town ward.
29. *Levitic*] from Levites, Israelite priests (*OED*, first here).
30. *clerkship . . . awe*] his knowledge of secular matters overawes his parish council.
clerkship] scholarship.
33. *epigram*] short poem which leads to a witty conclusion.
34. *bulk*] pun on (1) Jonson's scholarship; (2) his physique. By his own admission he was just short of 20 stone (*Und.*, 54.12).
37. *blanks*] in blank verse (i.e. unrhymed), contrasting with the couplets, ll. 15–32.
39–40. *That . . . share*] Rut leaves God out of his calculations, relying instead upon Nature excessively; perhaps an echo of Chaucer's comment on the Physician's study which 'was but litel on the Bible', *Gen. Prol.*, l. 438.
40. *licentious in discourse*] saying more than he should, perhaps lewdly. Burton has 'who have no skill but prating ignorance', *Anatomy*, 1.2.3.15.

And in his life a professed voluptuary;
The slave of money, a buffoon in manners;
Obscene in language; which he vents for wit;
Is saucy in his logics and, disputing,
Is anything but civil, or a man.   45
See here they are! And walking with my lady,
In consultation, afore the door;
We will slip in, as if we saw 'em not.   [*Exeunt.*]

ACT I   SCENE 3

[*Enter*] LADY [LOADSTONE], PALATE, [*and*] RUT.

Lady. Ay, 'tis his fault she's not bestowed,
       My brother Interest's.
Palate.   Who, old Sir Moth?
Lady. He keeps off all her suitors, keeps the portion
       Still in his hands: and will not part withal,
       On any terms.

41. voluptuary] *Wha;* Voluptary *F.*   48.1] *This ed.; Iron. and Com. go into
the house. G.*

1. 'tis] *Wha;* tis *F.*   4. withal] *Wha;* with all *F.*

___

41. *voluptuary*] lewd sensualist (*OED*, first 1610); cf. *CR*, 5.4.331. See
textual note.
42. *slave of money*] Cf. Chaucer's Physician: 'For gold in phisik is a
cordial, / Therefore he lovede gold in special', *Gen. Prol.*, ll. 443–4; and
Burton, *Anatomy*, 1.2.3.15.
   buffoon] a low jester; cf. *EMI*, 2.5.8. (Jonson spells 'buffon'.)
43. *Obscene*] indecorous; but Jonson would have known the Latin,
inauspicious: see *OED* 3, Cowley, 1635–6, first here.
   vents] releases, discharges.
47. *afore the door*] Terentian comedy tended to take place in the street
with doors opening from houses.

1. *bestowed*] given in marriage.
3. *portion*] This practice of keeping the portion, or dowry, and forbidding
marriage reflects the close link between marriage and property. Jonson was
concerned by the predicament of women; cf. *DA*, 4.7.67–9.

Palate.   *Hinc illae lacrimae;*   5
    Thence flows the cause o' the main grievance.
Rut.   That,
    It is a main one! How much is the portion?
Lady. No petty sum.
Palate.   But sixteen thousand pound.
Rut. He should be forced, madam, to lay it down.
    When is it payable?
Lady.   When she is married.   10
Palate. Marry her, marry her, madam.
Rut.   Get her married.
    Lose not a day, an hour—
Palate.   Not a minute.
    Pursue your project real. Master Compass
    Advised you, too. He is the perfect instrument
    Your ladyship should sail by.
Rut.   Now Master Compass   15
    Is a fine witty man: I saw him go in, now.
Lady. Is he gone in?
Palate.   Yes, and a feather with him,
    He seems a soldier.
Rut.   Some new suitor, madam.
Lady. I am beholden to him: he brings ever
    Variety of good persons to my table,   20
    And I must thank him, though my brother Interest
    Dislike of it a little.
Palate.   He likes nothing
    That runs your way.

---

5. lacrimae] *This ed.; lachrymae F.*   6. That,] *H&S; That F; That!—G.*

---

5. Hinc . . . lacrimae] 'Hence come these tears', Terence, *Andria*, 126;
paraphrased in the next line. This is also found in Horace, *Epodes*, 1.19.41,
and is quoted by Burton, *Anatomy*, 1.3.2.4.
   9. *lay it down*] release it.
   13. *real*] actual, genuine: but used for property (*OED* a^2.II.6c, 1641).
   17. *feather*] man of dashing or decorative appearance. Not in *OED*.
Ironside later wears a feather on his beaver, 3.4.61–2: cf. *NI*, 2.5.40.
   22. *Dislike*] disapproves.
   22–3. *likes . . . way*] [Sir Moth] does not approve anything favourable to
you.

Rut.   Troth, and the other cares not.
  He'll go his own way, if he think it right.
Lady. He's a true friend! And there's Master Practice,   25
  The fine young man of law, comes to the house:
  My brother brooks him not, because he thinks
  He is by me assignèd for my niece:
  He will not hear of it.
Rut.   Not of that ear:
  But yet your ladyship doth wisely in it—   30
Palate. 'Twill make him to lay down the portion sooner,
  If he but dream you'll match her with a lawyer.
Lady. So Master Compass says. It is between
  The lawyer and the courtier, which shall have her.
Palate. Who, Sir Diaphanous Silkworm?
Rut.   A fine gentleman,   35
  Old Master Silkworm's heir?
Palate.   And a neat courtier,
  Of a most elegant thread.
Lady.   And so my gossip
  Polish assures me. Here she comes!

          [*Enter* MISTRESS POLISH.]

                Good Polish
  Welcome in troth! How dost thou, gentle Polish?
Rut. Who's this?
Palate.   Dame Polish, her she-parasite,   40
  Her talking, soothing, sometime governing gossip.

---

25. there's] *Wi;* ther's *F.*   35. *Palate*] *This ed.; Pal. F3; Bal. F, not indented.*
37. thread.] *Wha;* thred *F.*   38. S.D.] *G.*   40. this?] *G adds: Aside to*
Palate.

---

  27. *brooks*] tolerates.
  29. *Not . . . ear*] proverbial (Dent E11: 'He cannot hear on that ear'). A
convenient deafness like Falstaff's, *2H4*, 1.2.66–77.
  35. *Diaphanous*] See Persons.
  36. *neat*] elegant.
  37. *thread*] making.
  gossip] companion; cf. Persons, l. 5.
  40. *she-parasite*] female dependant: a Jonson coinage?

ACT I   SCENE 4

Palate. Your ladyship is still the Lady Loadstone
That draws, and draws unto you guests of all sorts:
The courtiers, and the soldiers, and the scholars,
The travellers, physicians, and divines,
As Doctor Ridley writ, and Doctor Barlow;   5
They both have wrote of you, and Master Compass.
Lady. We mean they shall write more, ere it be long.
Polish. Alas, they are both dead, and't please you; but
Your ladyship means well, and shall mean well
So long as I live. How does your fine niece,   10
My charge, Mistress Placentia Steele?
Lady. She is not well.
Polish.   Not well?
Lady.   Her doctor says so.
Rut. Not very well; she cannot shoot at butts,
Or manage a great horse, but she can cranch
A sack of small coal! Eat you lime, and hair,   15
Soap-ashes, loam, and has a dainty spice

1.4] ACT. *F.*   1. *Palate*] *Pal. F; Pol. Wha.*   5. Barlow;] *H&S; Barlow? F.*
10. niece,] *Wha;* Neice? *F.*   13. butts,] *G;* Buts. *F.*

5. *Ridley . . . Barlow*] Mark Ridley (1560–1624) published *The Navigators
Supply* (1597), and William Barlow (d. 1625) *Magneticall Advertisements . . .
experiments concerning the nature and properties of the Load-stone* (1616):
both discussed compasses, and engaged in controversy. They owed much to
the monumental *De magnete* (1600) by Dr William Gilbert (1540–1603; see
Introduction, pp. 32–4).
7. *mean*] intend that.
10. *I*] i.e. You: the first of many word muddles.
13. *shoot at butts*] shoot arrows in target practice.
14. *great horse*] war horse, charger (*OED* horse 22).
cranch] crush with the teeth: earlier form of *crunch* (*OED* 1814+).
15. *Eat you*] ethical dative, implying only an indirect interest (*OED*
ethical 3).
lime] earth, mud.
15–16. *lime . . . hair . . . loam*] used in the making of walls.
16. *Soap-ashes*] wood ash used in making soap.
dainty] rare (Peck): cf. l. 63n.
spice] trace of an illness (*OED* sb.5).

　　　　O'the green sickness!
Polish.　　　　　　　　'Od shield!
Rut.　　　　　　　　　　　　Or the dropsy!
　　　A toy, a thing of nothing. But my lady here,
　　　Her noble aunt—
Polish.　　　　　　　She is a noble aunt!
　　　And a right worshipful lady, and a virtuous;　　　　20
　　　I know it well.
Rut.　　　　　　Well, if you know it, peace.
Palate. Good sister Polish, hear your betters speak.
Polish. Sir, I will speak, with my good lady's leave,
　　　And speak, and speak again. I did bring up
　　　My lady's niece, Mistress Placentia Steele,　　　　25
　　　With my own daughter, who's Placentia too,
　　　And waits upon my lady, is her woman.
　　　Her ladyship well knows Mistress Placentia
　　　Steele, as I said, her curious niece, was left
　　　A legacy to me, by father and mother,　　　　30
　　　With the nurse, Keep, that tended her: her mother,
　　　She died in child-bed of her, and her father
　　　Lived not long after: for he loved her mother!
　　　They were a godly couple. Yet both died,
　　　As we must all. No creature is immortal,　　　　35
　　　I have heard our pastor say: no, not the faithful.
　　　And they did die, as I said, both in one month.

24. again.] *This ed.;* againe; *F.*　　30. mother,] *Wha;* Mother *F.*　　35.
immortal,] *Wha;* immortal; *F.*

---

17. *green sickness*] chlorosis, a disease affecting young women at puberty.
H&S point out that a 'depraved appetite' is a sign of the green sickness; it
may also accompany pregnancy, as Rut ought to know.
　　'*Od shield*] bland form of 'God shield us!'. On putative blasphemy in *ML*
see Introduction, p. 25.
　　dropsy] insatiable craving (*OED* 2).
　　20. *worshipful*] worthy of respect.
　　26. *Placentia too*] perhaps a proleptic clue.
　　29. *curious*] fastidious, discriminating.
　　34–5. *died . . . all*] proverbial commonplace probably deriving from 'What
man is he that liveth and shall not see death?' Psalm 89: 48; also *2H4*,
3.2.36–7.

Rut. Sure she is not long lived, if she spend breath thus.

Polish. And did bequeath her to my care and hand,
    To polish and bring up. I moulded her,   40
    And fashioned her, and formed her; she had the sweat
    Both of my brows and brains, my lady knows it,
    Since she could write a quarter old.

Lady.   I know not
    That she could write so early, my good gossip.
    But I do know she was so long your care,   45
    Till she was twelve year old; that I called for her,
    And took her home, for which I thank you, Polish,
    And am beholden to you.

Rut.   I sure thought
    She had a lease of talking, for nine lives—

Palate. It may be she has.

Polish.   Sir, sixteen thousand pound   50
    Was then her portion! For she was, indeed,
    Their only child! And this was to be paid
    Upon her marriage, so she married still
    With my good lady's liking here, her aunt:
    I heard the will read. Master Steele, her father,   55
    The world condemned him to be very rich,
    And very hard, and he did stand condemned

---

42. brains, my . . . it,] *G;* braines. My . . . it *F.*

38. *long lived*] likely to live long.

41–2. *sweat . . . brains*] Possibly proverbial; cf. Genesis, 3: 19.

43. *a quarter old*] three months old: mischievously, in order to tease Polish, Lady Loadstone at l. 45 interprets this common impersonal phrase 'write herself' (meaning 'was', as in 'Though I now write fifty years' *Und.,* 2.9.3) as 'able to write'.

49. *lease*] legal arrangement which lasted for life, or for a very long period: sometimes these were granted for a specified number of lives (Honigmann).

nine lives] proverbial of cats: 'Good king of cats, nothing but one of your nine lives', *RJ,* 3.1.75; *ODEP,* p. 108: but compare 'Tost: To speak thick or fast or (as we say) nine words at once', Cotgrave.

53. *so*] provided that.

still] consistent.

56. *condemned*] ironic: for Jonson's exploitation of Polish's bizarre use of words see Introduction, pp. 19, 40.

57. *very hard*] exceptionally so (i.e. rich).

With that vain world, till, as 'twas proved after,
He left almost as much more to good uses
In Sir Moth Interest's hands, my lady's brother,   60
Whose sister he had married: he holds all
In his close grip. But Master Steele was liberal,
And a fine man; and she a dainty dame,
And a religious, and a bountiful—

ACT I   SCENE 5

[*Enter*] COMPASS [*and*] IRONSIDE *to them.*

[*Polish.*] You knew her, Master Compass?
Compass.   Spare the torture,
   I do confess without it.
Polish.   And her husband?
   What a fine couple they were! And how they lived?
Compass.   Yes.
Polish. And loved together, like a pair of turtles?
Compass.   Yes.
Polish. And feasted all the neighbours?
Compass.   Take her off,   5
   Somebody that hath mercy.
Rut.   O, he knows her
   It seems!
Compass.   Or any measure of compassion:
   Doctors, if you be Christians, undertake
   One for the soul, the other for the body!

62. grip] *This ed.; *gripe *F.*

1.5] *In right margin:* To them. *Centred:* ACT I. SCENE V. *Compasse, Ironside.*
F. Enter Compass and Ironside from the house. *G.*   2–3. husband? . . . were!]
This ed.; husband, . . . were? *F.*

   63. *dainty*] This word has a wide range of meanings: Jonson would
probably know the Latin origin, *dignus,* worthy.

   4. *turtles*] turtle doves, proverbially loving (Dent T624: 'As true as a turtle
to her mate').
   8. *Doctors*] Palate and Rut: see l. 9.
   undertake] take responsibility for (*OED* 5).

Polish. She would dispute with the Doctors of Divinity   10
     At her own table! And the Spital preachers!
     And find out the Armenians.
Rut.   The Arminians?
Polish. I say the Armenians.
Compass.   Nay, I say so too!
Polish. So Master Polish called 'em, the Armenians!
Compass. And Medes, and Persians, did he not?
Polish.   Yes, he knew 'em,   15
     And so did Mistress Steele! She was his pupil!
     The Armenians, he would say, were worse than papists!
     And then the Persians, were our puritans,
     Had the fine piercing wits!
Compass.   And who, the Medes?
Polish. The middle men, the lukewarm Protestants!   20
Rut. Out, out.
Polish.   Sir, she would find them by their branching:

---

12. Arminians] *Fc;* Armenians *Fu.*   20. Protestants!] *H&S;* Protestants?
F.

---

11. *Spital preachers*] Sermons, attended by the Lord Mayor, were preached at St Mary Spittle (i.e. hospital) of Bishopsgate Without, Spital-fields; cf. *Und.,* 42.71.

12. *Armenians . . . Arminians*] The followers of James Arminius (1560–1609) modified Calvin's concept of absolute predetermination, and were therefore seen as imperfect Protestants by some, and sympathetic to the quasi-Catholic Laudian position. Polish's malapropisms continue with Medes, and Persians. See Introduction, pp. 25–6, and Martin Butler, 'Ecclesiastical Censorship of Early Stuart Drama: The Case of Jonson's *The Magnetic Lady*', *MP* 89 (1992), pp. 469–81.

15. *Medes, Persians*] Compass mischievously follows the erroneous national name Armenians (l. 13) with these two additions; but Polish interprets Medes (mede (adj.) middle) as those in the middle way of religious observance, and understands Precisians, those with radical Puritan views, as Persians. She praises the Puritan view in l. 19.

18–19. *Persians . . . piercing*] homophonic, both being pronounced like 'pursing'.

20. *lukewarm*] 'Forsake . . . thy lukewarmenes . . . hange not any longer in the midst between the reformed Churches and that that is Antichristian', Thomas Brightman (1615), cited by Butler, p. 476.

21. *Out, out*] Rut objects to the middle way.

          Their branching sleeves, branched cassocks, and
               branched doctrine,
          Beside their texts.
Rut.   Stint, carline, I'll not hear:
          Confute her, parson.
Polish.   I respect no persons,
          Chaplains, or doctors; I will speak.
Lady.   Yes, so't be reason,   25
          Let her.
Rut.   'Death, she cannot speak reason.
Compass. Nor sense, if we be masters of our senses!
Ironside. What mad woman ha' they got, here, to bait?
Polish. Sir, I am mad, in truth, and to the purpose;
          And cannot but be mad; to hear my lady's   30
          Dead sister slighted, witty Mistress Steele!
Ironside. If she had a wit, death has gone near to spoil it,
          Assure yourself.
Polish.   She was both witty, and zealous,
          And lighted all the tinder o' the truth,
          As one said, of religion, in our parish:
          She was too learnèd to live long with us!   35
          She could the Bible in the holy tongue:
          And read it without pricks: had all her Masoreth;

---

23. hear:] *H&S;* heare, *F.*   24. her,] *Wha;* her *F.*   36. learned] *Wha;*
learn'd *F.*

---

   22. *branching*] embroidery; cf. *NI*, 5.1.17, where the priest described is 'a
good crammed divine': but Polish's ostensible meaning unwittingly suggests
'diverging'. Her claim is that Mistress Steele would detect near papists by
their vestments: another anti-Laudian point.
   23. *Stint*] Stop!
   carline] old witch, *OED* carline[1] b.
   24. *persons*] This *F* spelling suggests a pun on persons/parsons, especially
as the former could also mean 'parson'. When spoken the sound would be
a clue to interpretation(s).
   26. *'Death*] a blasphemy (by God's death) here rendered inoffensive.
   28. *bait*] torment.
   34. *tinder . . . truth*] possibly proverbial.
   37. *could*] knew.
   holy tongue] Hebrew, which has pricks, or points for vowels and other
linguistic functions.
   38. *Masoreth*] traditional and learned edition of the Talmud.

Knew Burton, and his bull; and scribe Prynne, gent.
Presto begone: and all the Pharisees.

Lady.　　　　　　　　　　　　　　Dear gossip,　　　40
Be you gone, at this time, too, and vouchsafe
To see your charge, my niece.

Polish.　　　　　　I shall obey
If your wise ladyship think fit: I know
To yield to my superiors.　　　　[*Exit* POLISH.]

Lady.　　　　　　A good woman!
But when she is impertinent, grows earnest,　　　45
A little troublesome, and out of season:
Her love and zeal transport her.

Compass.　　　　　　I am glad
That anything could port her hence. We now
Have hope of dinner, after her long grace.
I have brought your ladyship a hungry guest here,　　　50
A soldier, and my brother, Captain Ironside:
Who being by custom grown a sanguinary,
The solemn and adopted son of slaughter,
Is more delighted i' the chase of an enemy,
An execution of three days and nights,　　　55

---

39. Prynne, gent.] *This ed.; Prin*-Gent! *F;* Prin, gent. *Wha.*　　44. S.D.] *G.*

39. *Burton*] Henry Burton (1578–1648) published *The Baiting of the Popes Bull* (1627).

Prynne] William Prynne (1600–69), prolific author of *Histriomastix* (1633), attacking the stage. He was pilloried and mutilated in 1634 for alleged attacks upon the King and Queen, and again with Burton in 1637; both were pursued by Archbishop Laud.

gent.] short for gentleman, though it is not clear why Polish should use an abbreviation.

40. *Presto begone*] Quibble on John Preston (1527–1628), Protestant divine (*Wha.*): and a conjuring term (*H&S*).

Pharisees] Hebrew sect which valued the written law.

41. *vouchsafe*] condescend.

45. *impertinent*] off the point. See *Disc.*, 250.

48. *port*] carry; playing on *transport*, l. 47.

49. *long grace*] A Puritan characteristic satirised in *BF*, 1.3.88: 'as long as thy tablecloth'.

52. *a sanguinary*] one given to bloodshed.

55. *execution . . . nights*] an action requiring three days and nights to complete; but there is a quibble on putting to death.

Than all the hope of numerous succession,
Or happiness of issue could bring to him.
Rut. He is no suitor then?
Palate.   So't should seem.
Compass. And, if he can get pardon at heaven's hand
    For all his murders, is in as good case   60
    As a new christened infant (his employments
    Continued to him, without interruption
    And not allowing him or time or place
    To commit any other sin, but those).
    Please you to make him welcome for a meal, madam.   65
Lady. The nobleness of his profession makes
    His welcome perfect: though your coarse description
    Would seem to sully it.
Ironside.   Never, where a beam
    Of so much favour doth illustrate it,
    Right knowing lady.
Palate.   She hath cured all well.   70
Rut. And he hath fitted well the compliment.

ACT I   SCENE 6

[*Enter*] SIR DIAPHANOUS [SILKWORM *and*] PRACTICE
to them.

Compass. No; here they come. The prime magnetic guests
    Our Lady Loadstone so respects; the Arctic!

67. coarse] *Wha;* course *F.*   71. compliment] *Wha;* Complement *F.*

1.6] *In right margin:* To them. *F. Centred:* Sir *Diaphanous. Practise. In this and
all subsequent scene headings the characters are separated by full stops in F.*

56–7. succession . . . issue] He preferred slaughter to the hope of begetting
descendants.
   59–61.] Compass outrageously suggests that Ironside had been so busy
committing murders that he had no time for other sins: to forgive his
murders would reduce him to the innocence of an infant.
   69. *illustrate*] illuminate.
   71. *compliment*] Ironside has matched Loadstone's compliment; but
the *F* spelling is 'complement' which also suggests that Ironside completes
Loadstone, Claudian's theme, see Persons 4. The spellings were alternatives.

   1. *prime magnetic*] The courtier, Sir Diaphanous, and the lawyer, Practice, are most likely to attract others: they are seen as Arctic and Antarctic,
the poles of the earth's magnet (ll. 2–3).

And th'Antarctic! Sir Diaphanous Silkworm!
A courtier extraordinary; who by diet
Of meats and drinks, his temperate exercise,   5
Choice music, frequent baths, his horary shifts
Of shirts and waistcoats, means to immortalise
Mortality itself; and makes the essence
Of his whole happiness the trim of Court.

Diaphanous. I thank you, Master Compass, for your short   10
Encomiastic.

Rut.   It is much in little, sir.

Palate. Concise and quick: the true style of an orator.

Compass. But Master Practice here, my lady's lawyer,
Or man of law (for that's the true writing)
A man so dedicate to his profession,   15
And the preferments go along with it,
As scarce the thund'ring bruit of an invasion,
Another eighty-eight, threat'ning his country
With ruin, would no more work upon him
Than Syracusa's sack on Archimede: 20
So much he loves that night-cap! The bench-gown!
With the broad guard o'th' back! These show a man
Betrothed unto the study of our laws.

---

18. threat'ning] *This ed.;* threatning *F.*   22. o'th'] *Wha;* o'th *F.*   22–3.
show a man / Betrothed] *G;* shew / A man betroth'd *F.*

---

6. *horary*] hourly (*OED* 2, first here).
shifts] changes of clothing (*OED* 9).
7–8. *immortalise / Mortality*] to make change unchangeable.
9. *trim*] fashionable dress.
11. *Encomiastic*] commendation (*OED* B, first here, but as adj. *CR,*
1.4.89).
much in little] proverbial (Dent M1284).
12. *quick*] lively.
14. *man of law*] Chaucer's name for a lawyer, *Canterbury Tales,* Fragment
II.
17. *bruit*] uproar, rumour, report.
18. *eighty-eight*] 1588, the year of the Spanish Armada.
19. *work upon*] affect, discompose.
20. *Archimede*] Archimedes, the mathematician, was too engrossed in a
problem to defend himself from a Roman soldier at the siege of Syracuse
(212 B.C.).
21. *night-cap*] a reference to the lawyer's cap, or biggen, as at *Volp.,* 5.9.5.
bench-gown] lawyer's formal gown.
22. *guard*] ornamental trimming; but perhaps a pun on looking behind
him.

Practice. Which you but think the crafty impositions
 Of subtle clerks, feats of fine understanding,   25
 To abuse clots and clowns with, Master Compass,
 Having no ground in nature to sustain it,
 Or light from those clear causes: to the inquiry
 And search of which, your mathematical head
 Hath so devowed itself.
Compass.   Tut, all men are   30
 Philosophers to their inches. There's within
 Sir Interest, as able a philosopher
 In buying and selling, has reduced his thrift
 To certain principles, and i' that method,
 As he will tell you instantly, by logarithms,   35
 The utmost profit of a stock employed:
 Be the commodity what it will, the place,
 Or time, but causing very, very little,
 Or, I may say, no parallax at all,
 In his pecuniary observations!   40
 He has brought your niece's portion with him, madam,
 At least the man that must receive it. Here
 They come negotiating the affair;
 You may perceive the contract in their faces;
 And read th'indenture, if you'd sign 'em—so.   45

---

27. it,] *Wha;* it *F.* 34. method,] *Wha;* method! *F.* 35. logarithms]
Wha; Logorythmes F.

---

 26. *clots*] dull fellows (*OED* 4, first here).
 27. *nature*] Practice suggests that the law is based upon nature, which
Compass studies through mathematics.
 30. *devowed*] dedicated (Lat. *devovere*).
 31. *to their inches*] clever or scientific to the best of their abilities.
 35. *logarithms*] mathematical function invented by John Napier, c.1614:
abstruse calculation.
 36. *stock*] investment.
 37. *commodity*] what is being traded.
 39. *parallax*] alteration (in astronomy).
 45. *indenture*] a metaphor based upon the interlocking of the two parts of
an indenture (*dent* Fr. tooth), or written agreement, which was divided
between the participants by being torn apart.

ACT I   SCENE 7

[Enter SIR MOTH] INTEREST *[and]* BIAS *to them.*

Palate. What is he, Master Compass?
Compass.   A vi-politic,
  Or a sub-aiding instrument of state.
  A kind of a laborious secretary
  To a great man. And likely to come on.
  Full of attendance. And of such a stride   5
  In business politic or economic,
  As well his lord may stoop t'advise with him
  And be prescribèd by him in affairs
  Of highest consequence, when he is dulled
  Or wearied with the less.
Diaphanous.   'Tis Master Bias,   10
  Lord Whach'um's politic.
Compass.   You know the man?
Diaphanous. I ha' seen him wait at Court, there, with his
     maniples
  Of papers and petitions.
Practice.   He is one
  That overrules though by his authority
  Of living there; and cares for no man else: 15
  Neglects the sacred letter of the law;
  And holds it all to be but a dead heap
  Of civil institutions; the rest only

1.7] *In right margin:* To them. *Centred:* Interest. Bias. *F.*   them] em *slipped*
downwards in some copies of F.   14. though] *G;* tho' *F.*

1. *vi-politic*] See Persons.
2. *sub-aiding*] giving secret aid to; cf. *OED* subaid (1597).
3. *laborious*] one who does all the work.
4. *come on*] be promoted.
5. *attendance*] assiduous service (*OED* 3).
6. *politic*] i.e. political.
7. *advise . . . him*] be advised by him.
8. *prescribèd*] directed.
12. *maniples*] bundles (*OED*, first here); cf. 'my politic bundles', 2.6.14.
13-15. *one . . . there*] has overbearing power by virtue of living at
Court.
18. *rest*] resort.

Of common men, and their causes, a farrago,
Or a made dish in Court; a thing of nothing.   20
Compass. And that's your quarrel at him? A just plea.
Interest. I tell you, sister Loadstone—
Compass.   Hang your ears
This way, and hear his praises, now Moth opens.
Interest. I ha' brought you here the very man. The jewel
Of all the Court. Close Master Bias. Sister,   25
Apply him to your side. Or you may wear him
Here o' your breast. Or hang him in your ear:
He's a fit pendant for a lady's tip.
A chrysolite, a gem: the very agate
Of state and polity: cut from the quar   30
Of Machiavel, a true cornelian,
As Tacitus himself. And to be made
The brooch to any true state-cap in Europe.
Lady. You praise him, brother, as you had hope to sell him.
Compass. No, madam, as he had hope to sell your niece   35
Unto him.
Lady.   'Ware your true jests, Master Compass;
They will not relish.
Interest.   I will tell you, sister,

---

20. nothing.] *Wha;* nothing: *F.*   23–4. Hang . . . opens.] *G,*   *marked*
[*Aside.;* (Hang . . . opens) *F.*   25. Sister,] *Fc;* Sister! *Fu.*

---

19. *farrago*] hotchpotch.
20. *made dish*] something concocted.
25. *Close*] secret, reticent (*OED* 7).
27. *hang . . . ear*] Besides the literal sense, this suggests conspiracy.
28. *tip*] ear lobe.
29. *chrysolite*] green gem.
   agate] variegated precious stone.
30–1. *quar / Of Machiavel*] quarry of Machiavelli, by reputation the craftiest of political manipulators: 'a great doctor of state', *Disc.*, 1430.
31–2. *cornelian . . . Tacitus*] a jewel; punning on Cornelius Tacitus, the Roman historian.
33. *brooch . . . state-cap*] he would embellish any political authority; cf. 'Honour's a good brooch to wear in a man's hat', *Poet.*, 1.2.161–2.
34. *hope to sell*] Perhaps proverbial.
36. *true jests*] proverbial (Tilley W772: 'There is many a true word spoken in jest').

I cannot cry his caract up enough:
He is unvaluable: all the lords
Have him in that esteem, for his relations,   40
Courants, advices, correspondences
With this ambassador, and that agent. He
Will screw you out a secret from a statist—
Compass. So easy, as some cobbler worms a dog.
Interest. And lock it in the cabinet of his memory—   45
Compass. Till't turn a politic insect, or a fly
      Thus long.
Interest.   You may be merry Master Compass,
      But though you have the reversion of an office,
      You are not in't, sir.
Bias.   Remember that.
Compass. Why should that fright me, Master *Bi-*, from telling   50
      Whose *-as* you are?
Interest.   Sir, he's one, can do
      His turns there: and deliver too his letters
      As punctually, and in as good a fashion,
      As e'er a secretary can in Court.
Ironside. Why, is it any matter in what fashion   55
      A man deliver his letters, so he not open 'em?
Bias. Yes, we have certain precedents in Court
      From which we never swerve once in an age:

---

50. Why] *Wha;* Why, *F.*   51. *-as*] *H&S;* as *F;* ass *F3.*

38. *caract*] pun on (1) character; (2) carat, weight of gold.
39. *unvaluable*] invaluable, but also worthless: cf. *OED* 1 and 2.
40. *relations*] accounts, narratives.
41. *Courants*] express messengers: 'the weekly corrants', *Und.,* 43.81.
advices] information (advises in *F*).
43. *statist*] skilled politician.
44. *worms . . . dog*] to extract a ligament from a dog's tongue as a preventative for rabies (*OED* II.3).
45. *cabinet*] treasure-chamber, storehouse (*OED* 6); the first *OED* citation for a political cabinet is 1644, and it may be an overtone here.
48. *reversion*] right of succession to an office: see l. 74 below.
50–1. Bi- . . . as] In the radio performance the actors constantly made this name disyllabic: see Introduction, p. 26.
51–2. *do . . . turns*] knows the tricks of the trade.
56. *so*] provided that.

And whatso'er he thinks, I know the arts
And sciences do not directlier make   60
A graduate in our universities,
Than an habitual gravity prefers
A man in Court.
Compass.   Which by the truer style,
Some call a formal, flat servility.
Bias. Sir, you may call it what you please. But we,   65
That tread the path of public businesses,
Know what a tacit shrug is, or a shrink;
The wearing the calotte; the politic hood:
And twenty other *parerga*, o' the by,
You seculars understand not. I shall trick him,   70
If his reversion come i' my lord's way.
Diaphanous. What is that, Master Practice? You sure know?
Mas'Compass's reversion?
Practice.   A fine place,
Surveyor of the projects general;
I would I had it.
Palate.   What is't worth?
Practice.   O, sir,   75
A *nemo scit.*
Lady.   We'll think on't afore dinner.   [*Exeunt.*]

---

71. come] *F3;* came *F.*

---

62. *habitual ... prefers*] having the right kind of aplomb ensures promo-
tion at Court.
    64. *formal*] outward, external (*OED* A.1.c).
    67. *shrink*] body language suggesting withdrawal or fear.
    68. *calotte*] the coif, or white cap of a Sergeant-at-law (*OED* calotte 1; and
coif 3).
    politic hood] in apposition to calotte, a link between politics and the law
frequently made by Jonson.
    69. parerga] secondary features (*parergon*, Gk).
    o' the by] on the side.
    70. *seculars*] laymen, those not 'in the know': cf. *NI*, 5.2.9n, 'unlearned'.
    74. *Surveyor ... general*] Projects are associated with monopolies in *DA*,
1.7.5. The office, held by Thinwit (4.6.16–17 below), is a hit at an untraced
Court corruption, but Inigo Jones was Surveyor General of the Works from
1615 (*DNB*).
    76. nemo scit] Something no one knows, but may be guessed at; cf.
Staple, 1.5.105.

[I] CHORUS

[BOY, PROBEE *and* DAMPLAY.]

Boy. Now, gentlemen, what censure you of our *protasis*, or first
  Act?

Probee. Well, Boy, it is a fair presentment of your actors. And
  a handsome promise of somewhat to come hereafter.

Damplay. But, there is nothing done in it, or concluded: there-   5
  fore I say, no Act.

Boy. A fine piece of logic! Do you look, Master Damplay, for
  conclusions in a *protasis*? I thought the law of comedy had
  reserved 'em to the *catastrophe*: and that the *epitasis*, as
  we are taught, and the *catastasis* had been intervening   10
  parts to have been expected. But you would have all come
  together, it seems: the clock should strike five, at once,
  with the Acts.

Damplay. Why, if it could do so, it were well, Boy.

Boy. Yes, if the nature of a clock were to speak, not strike. So,   15
  if a child could be born, in a play, and grow up to a man
  i'the first scene, before he went off the stage: and then
  after to come forth a squire, and be made a knight: and

---

1 CHORUS] *This ed.; Chorus. F.*   6. no Act] *F; noAct in some copies.*   8.
protasis] Wha; Protesis F.   8–9. comedy . . . reserved] *Fc; Comedy, . . .*
reserv'd, *Fu.*   9. 'em] *Wi; not in F;* [them] *G.*

---

1. *censure you*] is your opinion.

protasis] See note at ll. 8–9, and Introduction, pp. 13–14.

3. *presentment*] performance, so used by Rowley (1605) and Dryden
(1668); but the word also has ecclesiastical and legal resonances (*OED* 5,
and cf. with 1 and 2).

8–9. protasis . . . epitasis] For the classical terminology see Introduction,
pp. 13–14, and T. W. Baldwin, *Shakespere's Five-act Structure* (Urbana, Ill.,
1947), p. 320. The Boy's expertise here may relate to the poem to Brome (see
Ind.82–3n) which compliments the latter's stage practice—'By observation
of those comic laws / Which I, your master, first did teach the age', ll.
7–8.

12. *the clock . . . five*] The play would be over all at once, and all the appropriate parts concluded.

16–24. *child . . . miracles*] like a similar passage in *EMI*, Prol. 7–12,
perhaps modelled upon Sir Philip Sidney's mockery of playwrights ignoring
the Unity of Time: 'for ordinary it is that two young princes fall in love. After
many traverses, she is got with child, delivered of a fair boy, he is lost, groweth
a man, falls in love, and is ready to get another child, and all this is two
hours' space', *Apology*, p. 134.

that knight to travel between the Acts, and do wonders
i'the Holy Land, or elsewhere; kill paynims, wild boars, 20
dun cows, and other monsters; beget him a reputation,
and marry an emperor's daughter for his mistress;
convert her father's country; and at last come home,
lame, and all-to-beladen with miracles.

Damplay. These miracles would please, I assure you: and take 25
the people. For there be of the people that will expect
miracles, and more than miracles from this pen.

Boy. Do they think this pen can juggle? I would we had
Hocus Pocus for 'em then, your people; or Travitanto
Tudesko. 30

Damplay. Who's that, Boy?

Boy. Another juggler with a long name. Or that your expec-
tors would be gone hence, now, at the first Act; or expect
no more hereafter than they understand.

Damplay. Why so, my peremptory jack? 35

Boy. My name is John, indeed—Because who expect what is
impossible or beyond nature defraud themselves.

---

20. Land, . . . paynims] *This ed.;* land, . . . Pannims *Fu;* land . . . Paynims
Fc.   21. monsters;] *Fc;* Monsters: *Fu.*   22. daughter] *Fc;* Daughter: *Fu.*
22–3. mistress; convert] *Wi;* Mrs.Convert *F.*   24. lame, . . . miracles.]
Wha; lame, . . . miracles: *changed to* lame . . . miracles. *in some copies of F.*
27. than] *Wha.;* then *Fu, with* t *inverted;* then *Fc.*   29. then, . . . people;]
Wha; then, . . . People; *changed to* then; . . . People, *in some copies of F.*   30.
Tudesko] *Wha;* Tudeske *Fu;* Tudesko *Fc.*

---

20. *paynims*] pagans, frequently killed in romances.

20–1. *boars . . . cows . . . monsters*] Peck notes how Guy killed a boar and
a dragon (chap. 11) and a dun cow (chap. 6) in *The History of Guy, Earl of
Warwick.*

24. *all-to-beladen*] entirely laden; cf. all-to-bemarried, 5.2.2.

25. *take*] captivate (*OED* 10).

29. *Hocus Pocus*] Name of juggler at the time of James I who used this
phrase for conjuring and was so called (*OED* 1655): *Staple* 2 Intermean 15,
Augurs, 268.

29–30. *Travitanto Tudesko*] Untraced: in Italian *tedesco* means German. Cf.
travisare (Ital.) change; *traviare* mislead.

33–4. *expect . . . understand*] one of the items in the contract with the
audience in *BF*, Ind.113–15.

35. *peremptory*] too confident, dogmatic.

jack] common person (condescending).

36. *who*] those who.

37. *defraud*] cheat.

Probee. Nay, there the Boy said well: they do defraud themselves indeed.

Boy. And therefore, Master Damplay, unless, like a solemn   40
justice of wit, you will damn our play unheard or unex-
amined, I shall entreat your Mistress, Madam Expectation, if she be among these ladies, to have patience but a
pissing while: give our springs leave to open a little, by
degrees! A source of ridiculous matter may break forth   45
anon that shall steep their temples and bathe their brains
in laughter, to the fomenting of stupidity itself, and the
awaking any velvet lethargy in the house.

Probee. Why do you maintain your poet's quarrel so with
velvet and good clothes, Boy? We have seen him in indif-   50
ferent good clothes, ere now.

Boy. And may do in better, if it please the King, his master,
to say Amen to it, and allow it, to whom he acknowled-
geth all. But his clothes shall never be the best thing about
him, though; he will have somewhat beside, either of   55
humane letters or severe honesty, shall speak him a man
though he went naked.

Probee. He is beholden to you, if you can make this good,
Boy.

Boy. Himself hath done that, already, against envy.   60

Damplay. What's your name, sir? Or your country?

---

38. well:] *Fc;* well. *Fu.*   42. your] r *dropped in most copies.*   45. degrees!]
Fc; degrees: *Fu.*

40–1. *like . . . wit*] paradoxical: a serious judge with powers of condemnation over witty matters.

44. *pissing while*] a very short time (*OED* pissing b). Proverbial (Dent
P355: 'To stay a pissing-while'); cf. *Gent.*, 4.4.18. This leads to a series of
watery images: *springs, source* (stream), *steep* (soak), *bathe* (ll. 44–6).

47. *fomenting*] bathing with warm liquid.

48. *velvet lethargy*] idle sleepiness; cf. Ind.31–2n.

50–1. *indifferent*] fairly, quite.

52. *King*] a reference to Jonson's continuing dependence upon patronage.

53. *say Amen to*] agree to.

56. *humane letters*] study of classical learning, 'literae humaniores':
earliest citation in *OED* humane, 1691.

58.] The author will owe much to you if the play supports your claim.

60. *envy*] refers to the baffling of Envy in the Induction to *Poet.*

Boy. John Trygust my name: a Cornish youth, and the poet's
  servant.
Damplay. West-country breed, I thought, you were so
  bold.   65
Boy. Or rather saucy: to find out your palate, Master
  Damplay. Faith, we do call a spade a spade, in Cornwall.
  If you dare damn our play i'the wrong place we shall take
  heart to tell you so.
Probee. Good, Boy.   70

---

67. Damplay.] *Wha; Damplay, F.*

---

62. *Trygust*] One who tests matters of taste: cf. 'to find out your palate'
l. 66. Virtually nothing is known of Richard Brome's origins, though this
Cornish identity may be a clue: see Appendix III.
  63. *servant*] See Boy in Persons.
  67. *spade*] proverbial (Dent S699: 'To call a spade a spade').

Act 2

[*Enter*] KEEP, PLACENTIA, [*and*] PLEASANCE.

Keep. Sweet mistress, pray you be merry: you are sure
    To have a husband now.
Placentia.   Ay, if the store
    Hurt not the choice.
Pleasance.   Store is no sore, young mistress,
    My mother is wont to say.
Keep.   And she'll say wisely
    As any mouth i'the parish. Fix on one,   5
    Fix upon one, good mistress.
Placentia.   At this call, too,
    Here's Master Practice, who is called to the bench
    Of purpose.
Keep.   Yes, and by my lady's means—
Pleasance. 'Tis thought to be the man.
Keep.   A lawyer's wife—
Pleasance. And a fine lawyer's wife!
Keep.   Is a brave calling.   10
Pleasance. Sweet Mistress Practice!
Keep.   Gentle Mistress Practice!
Pleasance. Fair, open Mistress Practice!
Keep.   Ay, and close

---

9. wife—] *This ed.;* wife. F.

   2–3. *store . . . sore*] If the abundance of suitable husbands does not make
the choice difficult: but abundance does no harm. Proverbial (Dent S903:
'store is no sore'). Perhaps Placentia questions whether there is abundance.
   4. *wisely*] as wisely.
   6. *call*] opportunity, with pun on Practice's professional calling—'called', 1.7.
   7. *bench*] to be a judge.
   8. *Of purpose*] because of the plan to marry: Lady Loadstone has used her
influence.
   10. *brave*] fine (a general epithet of admiration or praise: *OED*).
   12. *open*] frank; unreserved; free, liberal.
   close] secretive.

And cunning Mistress Practice!
Placentia.   I not like that;
   The courtier's is the neater calling.
Pleasance.   Yes,
   My Lady Silkworm.
Keep.   And to shine in plush.   15
Pleasance. Like a young night-crow, a diaphanous silkworm.
Keep. Lady Diaphanous sounds most delicate!
Pleasance. Which would you choose, now, mistress?
Placentia.   Cannot tell.
   The copy does confound one.
Pleasance.   Here's my mother.

ACT 2   SCENE 2

[*Enter*] POLISH.

Polish. How now, my dainty charge, and diligent nurse,
   What were you chanting on?

18. now,] *Wha;* now *F.*

---

   13. *cunning*] wise; crafty (*OED* 1,5).
   14. *neater*] more elegant.
   15. *plush*] expensive cloth with long soft nap: associated by Jonson with debauched aristocrats; see *DA*, 1.4.40.
   16. *night-crow*] A glossy black bird supposed to croak or cry at night and be of evil omen; possibly for the Greeks the night heron, but more likely an owl or nightjar in England; applied abusively to persons (*OED*). See also *SW*, 3.5.17.
   diaphanous] Cf. Persons.
   17. *Lady Diaphanous*] Keep is apparently wrong about this title: Placentia would be Lady Silkworm.
   delicate] delightful; exquisitely fine.
   18. *Cannot tell*] I cannot say: cf. *BF*, 1.3.10.
   19. *copy*] abundance (Lat. *copia*), *EMO*, 2.3.70.
   confound] defeat; confuse.

   1. *dainty*] delicate in health (*OED* 7).
   charge] a person entrusted to the care of another.
   2–3. *chanting . . . enchanting*] Playing on (1) gossiping and (2) casting a spell.
   2. *on*] about.

To her daughter kneeling.
God bless you, maiden.

Keep. We were enchanting all; wishing a husband
    For my young mistress here. A man to please her.
Polish. She shall have a man, good nurse, and must have a
      man: 5
    A man and a half, if we can choose him out:
    We are all in council within, and sit about it:
    The doctors and the scholars, and my lady,
    Who's wiser than all us. Where's Master Needle?
    Her ladyship so lacks him to prick out   10
    The man.   [*Exit* PLEASANCE.]
          How does my sweet young mistress?
    You look not well, methinks. How do you, dear charge?
    You must have a husband, and you shall have a husband;
    There's two put out to making for you: a third
    Your uncle promises: but you must still   15
    Be ruled by your aunt: according to the will
    Of your dead father and mother, who are in heaven.
    Your lady-aunt has choice i'the house for you.
    We do not trust your uncle; he would keep you
    A bachelor still, by keeping of your portion: 20
    And keep you not alone without a husband,
    But in a sickness: ay, and the green sickness,

---

2. S.D.] *In right margin opposite ll. 2–3, with (*) before* God.   2. God . . .
maiden] *in parenthesis, F.*   11. S.D.] *G.*   20. bachelor] *Wi;* Batchler *F.*

    2.1 kneeling] i.e. kneeling for her mother's blessing.
    6. *and a half*] an exceptional man worth one and a half ordinary ones.
Peck suggests half as a compliment on the analogy of one's better half.
    7. *sit about it*] sit in session like a formal court.
    10. *prick out*] choose (*OED* 15), with play on his name: another is at 4.1.1.
See also *CR*, 5.2.79.
    14. *to making*] to be made.
    third] Bias.
    18. *i'the house*] from within the family.
    20. *bachelor*] unmarried woman (*OED* 5, first here).
    portion] marriage portion, dowry; i.e. he wants to hang on to her dowry,
which he would have to surrender if she married.
    21. *alone*] only.
    22. *green sickness*] See 1.4.17n. According to Polish, Sir Moth wants to
keep Placentia unmarried.

The maiden's malady, which is a sickness,
A kind of a disease, I can assure you,
And like the fish our mariners call remora—   25
Keep. Aremora, mistress!
Polish.   How now, goody nurse?
Dame Keep of Katerne's? What, have you an oar
I'the cockboat, 'cause you are a sailor's wife?
And come from Shadwell?

                    [*Enter* NEEDLE.]

                    I say a remora;

For it will stay a ship that's under sail.   30
And stays are long and tedious things to maids.
And maidens are young ships that would be sailing,
When they be rigged: wherefore is all their trim else?
Needle. True; and for them to be stayed—
Polish.   The stay is dangerous:
You know it, Master Needle.

---

25. remora] *Wi;* '*remora F.*   26. Aremora] *This ed.; Aremora F; A remora
H&S: see Notes.*   29. S.D.] *G.*   35. Master] *G;* Mr. *F3;* Mrs. *F.*

---

25. *remora*] 'the sucking-fish believed by the ancients to have the power
of staying the course of any ship to which it attached itself' (*OED*); also in
Poet., 3.2.4. H&S cite Pliny, *Natural History*, 9.25; but see the reference to
Ridley, Introduction, p. 33.
26. *Aremora*] The *F* reading suggests that Keep, making a mistake of her
own, tries to correct Polish, but is scornfully ignored: cf. l. 29.
  goody] (married) woman, usually a respectful term, though it could sometimes be condescending towards social inferiors.
27. *Dame* . . . *Katerne's*] A mock title. St Katharine's old hospital, east of
London, on the north bank of the River Thames was a place of ill-repute;
see *Alc.*, 5.3.54–6.
27–8. *oar* . . . *cockboat*] Proverbial (Tilley O4: 'He will have an oar in every
man's boat'). The variant for cockboat (small boat, often towed behind larger
ship) suggests impertinence.
29. *Shadwell*] Dock area on north bank of Thames; but known for its
whores (Chalfant).
31. *stays*] Play on (1) rope support for sails (l. 30); (2) delays; (3)
stiffening support for corset. The play between (2) and (3) may have been
proverbial: cf. 'Stay (a thing few women can do . . . therefore they had need
wear satin stays)', Middleton, *Trick* (1608), 1.1.50 (*OED* sb2.3).
33. *rigged*] Pun on (1) dressed up; (2) *rig* a wanton girl (*OED* sb⁴).
  trim] used for a ship prepared to sail, but also for dress (*OED* 1 and 3).

Needle.   I know somewhat,   35
And can assure you from the doctor's mouth
She has a dropsy; and must change the air
Before she can recover.
Polish.   Say you so, sir?
Needle. The doctor says so.
Polish.   Says his worship so?
I warrant 'em he says true then: they sometimes   40
Are soothsayers and always cunning men.
Which doctor was it?
Needle.   E'en my lady's doctor:
The neat house-doctor: but a true stone-doctor.
Polish. Why? Hear you, nurse? How comes this gear to pass?
This is your fault in truth—it shall be your fault,   45
And must be your fault—why is your mistress sick?
She had her health the while she was with me.
Keep. Alas, good Mistress Polish, I am no saint,
Much less, my lady, to be urged give health
Or sickness at my will: but to await   50
The stars' good pleasure, and to do my duty.
Polish. You must do more than your duty, foolish nurse:
You must do all you can, and more than you can,

---

42. E'en] *Wha;* Eeene *F.*

35. *I know somewhat*] 'Well, there is something I know [but it is not what you think].'
37. *dropsy*] Pun on (1) illness involving excessive fluid; (2) an insatiable craving (*OED* 2): cf. 2.3.34n.
   change the air] have a change of air.
39. *worship*] general title showing respect.
41. *soothsayers*] literally 'speakers of the truth', but ironic; cf. 2.3.1.
   cunning men] 'wise' men, wizards; also at 5.9.17.
43. *neat*] skilful (*OED* 9b).
   stone-doctor] Obscure. *Stone puritan* (*BF*, 3.2.118) suggests full, or complete, perhaps even 'not castrated': possibly this might go with 'rut' to suggest lechery. Stone was also used for loadstone (*OED* 8b).
44. *gear*] goings on (*OED* 11b).
45–6. *is . . . shall . . . must*] Possibly proverbial.
48–50. *I am . . . will*] 'I am not a saint, and I am certainly not my lady [who is even more powerful and gracious] and so I cannot be petitioned like a saint to decide whether to grant sickness or health'.
50. *but . . . await*] 'instead it is my role to wait'.

More than is possible, when folks are sick,
Especially a mistress, a young mistress.   55
Keep. Here's Master Doctor himself cannot do that.
Polish. Doctor Do-all can do it. Thence he's called so.

ACT 2   SCENE 3

[*Enter*] RUT [*and*] LADY [LOADSTONE].

Rut. Whence? What's he called?
Polish.   Doctor, do all you can,
    I pray you, and beseech you, for my charge, here.
Lady. She's my tendering gossip, loves my niece.
Polish. I know you can do all things, what you please, sir,
    For a young damsel, my good lady's niece, here.   5
    You can do what you list.
Rut.   Peace, tiffany.
Polish. Especially in this new case o' the dropsy.
    The gentlewoman, I do fear, is leavened.
Rut. Leavened? What's that?

56. that.] *Wha; that F.*

2.3] Needle *not in F heading.*   7. Especially in] *Fc;* Especially'in *Fu (Cf.
other corrections on its conjugate sheet, and Introduction, p. 50.)*

---

57. *Do-all . . . so*] Rut is capable of doing everything, and so is called
Do-all (ironic in view of his failure to recognise a pregnancy in the following scene). Earliest citation in *OED* is 1633: also 'Do-all at Court' Fuller
1655. Do-all may be suggested by Know-all.

1. *do all*] the word play continues from the previous scene, suggesting
that Polish was deliberately sarcastic.
3. *tendering*] showing affection; not in *OED* in this sense where the
earliest citation is 1640, affecting.
gossip] friend (*OED* 2).
6. *list*] please.
tiffany] flimsy or transparent fabric; trivial person here, but not in this
figurative sense in *OED*. Peck links this with sophistry.
7. *dropsy*] Cf. l. 34.
8. *leavened*] The primary sense is 'fermented', hence 'swollen' (like dough
that rises); figuratively 'transformed' (*OED*). Rut's rebuke (ll. 10–11) points
to a malapropism by Polish.

Polish.   Puffed, blown, and't please your worship.
Rut. What! Dark, by darker? What is blown? puffed? Speak
    English—   10
Polish. Tainted, and't please you, some do call it.
    She swells and swells so with it—
Rut.   Give her vent,
    If she do swell. A gimlet must be had:
    It is a *tympanites* she is troubled with.
    There are three kinds: the first is *anasarca*   15
    Under the flesh, a tumour: that's not hers.
    The second is *ascites*, or *aquosus*,
    A watery humour: that's not hers neither.
    But *tympanites*, which we call the drum.
    A wind bomb's in her belly, must be unbraced,   20
    And with a faucet, or a peg let out,
    And she'll do well: get her a husband.
Polish.   Yes,
    I say so Master Doctor, and betimes too.
Lady.   As

---

10. darker? What] *Fc;* darker: what *Fu.*   English—] *Fu;* English—. *Fc.*
12. it—] *Wha;* it. *Fu;* it—. *Fc(1);* it.—*Fc(2).*   her vent] *Fc;* heaven *Fu.*
14. with.] *G;* with *Fu;* with; *Fc.*   18. hers] *Fc;* hers, *Fu.*   19. drum.]
Wi; Drum) *F.*   20. bomb's] *Wi;* bombes *F.*

<hr/>

   10. *Dark by darker*] An obscure point is not illuminated by ignorance, or
by one that is more obscure: perhaps a variant of 'All colours will agree in
the dark', Heywood, *Dial. Provs*, 1.5. Peck offers a Latinism: *obscurum per
obscuras.*
   11. *Tainted*] contaminated, but Polish is being circumspect.
   12. *vent*] outlet.
   13. *gimlet*] tool for piercing holes: see *faucet,* l. 21n.
   14–17. *tympanites . . . anasarca . . . ascites*] Jonson may have found these
types of dropsy (*aquosus:* water-filled, l. 17) in John Halle's translation of *Lanfranke of Mylayne his brief* (1565), p. 53 (*H&S*): *tympanites* sounded like a
drum; *anasarca* spread through all the flesh; *ascites* stretched the arteries (like
a wine-skin). Lanfrank rejected the theory that there were four kinds in
favour of the Arabs' three. See also *Lanfrank's 'Science of Chirurgie'*, EETS
o.s. 102, 1894, pp. 281–5.
   20. *unbraced*] loosened, relaxed: 'an unbraced drum', *Staple*, Ind.68.
   21. *faucet*] a tap, as a means of release. *Gimlet* (l. 13) and *faucet* may
suggest the grotesque equipment of the comic doctor in the folk plays.
   23. *betimes*] quickly.

Soon as we can: let her bear up today,
Laugh, and keep company, at gleek or crimp.   25
Polish. Your ladyship says right: crimp, sure, will cure her.
Rut. Yes, and gleek, too; peace, Gossip Tittle-Tattle.
  She must, tomorrow, down into the country
  Some twenty mile—a coach and six brave horses—
  Take the fresh air a month there, or five weeks;   30
  And then return a bride up to the town,
  For any husband i' the hemisphere
  To chuck at, when she has dropped her tympany.
Polish. Must she then drop it?
Rut.   Thence 'tis called a dropsy.
  The *tympanites* is one spice of it;   35
  A toy, a thing of nothing, a mere vapour:
  I'll blow't away.
Lady.   Needle, get you the coach
  Ready, against tomorrow morning.
Needle.   Yes, madam.
                              [*Exit* NEEDLE.]
Lady. I'll down with her myself, and thank the doctor.
Polish. We all shall thank him. But, dear madam, think,   40
  Resolve upon a man this day.
Lady.   I ha' done't.
  To tell you true, sweet gossip—here is none

---

26. right:] *This ed.;* right, *F.*   27. Tattle.] *H&S; Tattle, F.*   30. weeks;]
Wha; weekes! *Fu;* weeks: *Fc.*   33. tympany] *F3; Timpane F.*   38.1] *G.*
42. To] *Fc; (To Fu.*

---

24. *bear up*] keep up her spirits.
  25. *gleek*] a card game for three persons; cf. *DA*, 5.2.31.
  crimp] card game. Here both words are punning: *gleek* as a trick (*OED*
sb2) and *crimp* as a means of entrapping (cf. *OED* v2).
  32. *hemisphere*] visible world above the horizon (*OED* 2).
  33. *chuck at*] chuckle at, as in *NI*, 1.3.133; but the sense of a gentle,
affectionate blow under the chin would also be appropriate as in *OED*
v².1.
  34. *drop*] Pun on (1) get rid of; and (2) let fall in birth (*OED* 14). Rut's
etymology for *dropsy* is bogus. *OED* gives *ydropsy* from ME: see also *Hydropsy*
(Gk).
  35. *spice*] a touch of, *OED* 5b.
  36. *toy*] something of little importance (*OED* 5).
  38. *against*] in readiness for.

But Master Doctor, he shall be o'the council—
The man I have designed her to, indeed,
Is Master Practice. He's a neat young man,   45
Forward, and growing up, in a profession.
Like to be somebody, if the Hall stand,
And pleading hold. A prime young lawyer's wife,
Is a right happy fortune.
Rut.   And she bringing
So plentiful a portion, they may live   50
Like king and queen, at common law together.
Sway judges; guide the courts; command the clerks
And fright the evidence; rule at their pleasures,
Like petty sovereigns in all cases.
Polish.   O that
Will be a work of time; she may be old   55
Before her husband rise to a chief judge;
And all her flower be gone. No, no, a lady
O' the first head I'd have her; and in Court
The Lady Silkworm, a diaphanous lady:
And be a viscountess to carry all   60
Before her, as we say: her gentleman usher,

44. to] *Fc;* too *Fu.*   45. Practice.] *This ed.;* Practise! *Fu;* Practise: *Fc.*
man,] *Fc;* man! *Fu.*   47–8. stand, . . . hold.] *This ed.;* stand! . . . hold! *F.*
61. say: . . . usher,] *Wi;* say:) . . . usher, *H&S;* say) . . . usher: *F.*

---

45. *neat*] skilful; cf. 2.2.43.
46. *Forward*] precocious, with a suggestion of presumption (*OED* A.7, 8).
47. *the Hall*] Westminster Hall, haunt of lawyers, as in *DA*, 1.1.73.
48. *pleading hold*] arguing legal cases continues.
prime] youthful (*OED* 1), sexually excited, ruttish (*OED* 5).
51. *at common law*] play on (1) being involved in law, and (2) being together in marriage.
53. *fright the evidence*] suggests illegal influencing of witnesses.
55. *work of time*] something which takes a long time to achieve.
58. *O' the first head*] said of a deer with its first antlers, hence a person newly ennobled (*OED* 6b: in this sense first in 1509); cf. *EMO*, 3.3.48.
59. *diaphanous*] See Persons 15.
60. *viscountess*] With bawdy puns in 'vice' and 'cunt'; cf. 2.5.77–8. No doubt the pronunciation of 'visc-' could be adjusted to signal the pun.
61. *gentleman usher*] originally an attendant upon a monarch, but later used for anyone of importance.

And cast-off pages, bare, to bid her aunt
Welcome unto her honour, at her lodgings.
Rut. You say well, lady's gossip; if my lady
    Could admit that, to have her niece precede her.   65
Lady. For that, I must consult mine own ambition,
    My zealous gossip.
Polish.   O, you shall precede her:
You shall be a countess. Sir Diaphanous
Shall get you made a countess. Here he comes,
Has my voice certain. O fine courtier!   70
O blessed man! The bravery pricked out,
To make my dainty charge a viscountess!
And my good lady, her aunt, countess at large!

ACT 2   SCENE 4

[*Enter*] DIAPHANOUS [*and*] PALATE *to them.*

Diaphanous. I tell thee, parson, if I get her, reckon
    Thou hast a friend in Court; and shalt command
    A thousand pound to go on any errand,
    For any church preferment thou hast a mind to.

---

69. comes,] *H&S;* comes; *F.*   70. certain.] *Enter behind Sir Diaphanous
Silkworm and Palate, in discourse. G.*   73. large!] *Fc;* large *Fu.*

2.4] *In right margin: To them. Centred: Diaphanous. Palate. F.*

---

62. *cast-off*] slipped, like hounds: moving freely.
bare] bare-headed: to have outdoor servants so was a sign of conspicuous
extravagance. Cf. *DA*, 2.3.36–7.
65. *admit*] accept that as a viscountess Pleasance would take precedence
over a Lady Loadstone, a mere knight's wife (2.4.11).
66. *I . . . ambition*] I must consider whether I still have ambitions.
70. *Has . . . certain*] who certainly has my support.
71. *bravery*] finery.
pricked out] dressed up (*OED* 20c), with bawdy undertone.
72. *dainty*] fine, pleasing.
73. *at large*] Pun on (1) in full size, not belittled (*OED* C.II.5d); (2)
recognised as such everywhere, perhaps with erotic implication.

2. *friend in court*] proverbial (Dent F687: 'Better is a friend in court than
a penny in purse').
3–4. *errand . . . preferment*] as expenses to promote his advancement.
4. *thou hast*] Possibly should be slurred as 'thou'st'.

Palate. I thank your worship. I will so work for you,   5
    As you shall study all the ways to thank me:
    I'll work my lady, and my lady's friends,
    Her gossip, and this doctor, and Squire Needle,
    And Master Compass, who is all in all,
    The very fly she moves by. He is one   10
    That went to sea with her husband, Sir John Loadstone,
    And brought home the rich prizes—all that wealth
    Is left her; for which service she respects him—
    A dainty scholar in the mathematics,
    And one she wholly employs. Now Dominus Practice   15
    Is yet the man appointed by her ladyship,
    But there's a trick to set his cap awry,
    If I know anything: he hath confessed
    To me in private that he loves another,
    My lady's woman, Mistress Pleasance: therefore   20
    Secure you of rivalship.
Diaphanous.   I thank thee,
    My noble parson: there's five hundred pound
    Waits on thee more for that.
Palate.   Accost the niece:
    Yonder she walks alone: I'll move the aunt.
    But here's the gossip: she expects a morsel.   25
    Ha'you ne'er a ring, or toy to throw away?

---

16. appointed . . . ladyship] *brackets, F.*   17. awry,] *Wha; awry: F.*

7. *work*] work on.
9. *all in all*] all-powerful: a reminder of the power of Compass to encompass all.
10. *fly*] compass card fly, a device for pointing the way (*OED* sb2.5a); and demon (sb1.5a). See Introduction, p. 33.
12. *prizes*] vessels captured (during a war).
14. *dainty*] excellent (*OED* 1).
15. *Dominus*] Lord; academic title, perhaps ironic here.
16. *yet*] already.
17. *a trick . . . awry*] a device to upset him: perhaps proverbial. Cf. Tilley N219: 'to put his nose out of joint'.
21. *Secure . . . rivalship*] Do not worry about rivalry.
23. *Waits . . . more*] You shall receive.
Accost] '"Accost" is front her, board her, woo her, assail her', *TwN*, 1.3.55–6.
24. *move*] persuade, suggest to (*OED* v. 14).
25. *gossip*] associate.
morsel] portion, a little something.

Diaphanous. Yes, here's a diamond of some threescore pound,
   I pray you, give her that.
Palate.   If she will take it.
Diaphanous. And there's an emerald, for the doctor too:
   Thou, parson, thou shalt coin me: I am thine.   30
Palate. Here Master Compass comes.

              [*Enter* COMPASS.]

                     Do you see my lady?
And all the rest? How they do flutter about him.
He is the oracle of the house and family!
Now, is your time: go nick it with the niece:
I will walk by, and hearken how the chimes go.   35
      [*Exit* SIR DIAPHANOUS. PALATE *walks aside.*]

            ACT 2   SCENE 5

Compass. Nay, parson, stand not off; you may approach.
   This is no such hid point of state we handle
   But you may hear it: for we are all of counsel.
   The gentle Master Practice hath dealt clearly
   And nobly with you, madam.
Lady.   Ha' you talked with him?   5
   And made the overture?
Compass.   Yes, first I moved
   The business trusted to me by your ladyship,

---

31. S.D.] *G.*   33. family!] *Fc;* family? *Fu.*   35.1] *Following G.*

2.5] *In right margin:* To them. *Centred:* Compasse. *F: Compass has entered at 2.4.31.*

---

27. *diamond . . . pound*] The ring given as a present at *DA*, 2.8.52, is worth
'forty or fifty pound'.
   30. *coin*] make money out of (*OED* v[1].2c).
   32. *about*] Possibly shortened to 'bout.
   34. *nick it*] take advantage of the opportunity (*OED* v[2].7b, first in 1634).
   35. *how . . . go*] pass the time; or perhaps see whether the others
harmonise (Peck).

   2. *point of state*] Matter of national importance (and therefore requiring
secrecy).
   3. *of counsel*] in the know.

I' your own words, almost your very syllabes,
Save where my memory trespassed 'gainst their elegance,
For which I hope your pardon. Then I enlarged,   10
In my own homely style, the special goodness
And greatness of your bounty, in your choice,
And free conferring of a benefit
So without ends, conditions, any tie
But his mere virtue, and the value of it,   15
To call him to your kindred, to your veins,
Insert him in your family, and to make him
A nephew, by the offer of a niece,
With such a portion; which when he had heard
And most maturely acknowledged (as his calling   20
Tends all unto maturity) he returned
A thanks as ample as the courtesy,
In my opinion; said it was a grace
Too great to be rejected or accepted
By him. But as the terms stood with his fortune   25
He was not to prevaricate with your ladyship
But rather to require ingenious leave
He might with the same love that it was offered
Refuse it, since he could not with his honesty,
Being he was engaged before, receive it.   30

---

8. syllabes] *This ed.;* Sillabes *F;* Syllables *F3.*   16. veins,] *Wha;* veines *Fu;*
veines, *Fc.*

---

8. *syllabes*] syllables: *F*'s spelling, *sillabes*, is an example of Jonson's classical vocabulary; cf. *OED* and *Und.,* 70.63, and see Introduction, p. 46.
9. *Save . . . elegance*] 'Except where I could not speak as elegantly as you'.
10. *enlarged*] spoke fully about. Lines 10–25 are all one sentence.
13. *free*] voluntary.
14. *without ends*] without concealed purposes.
15. *mere*] pure.
20–1. *calling . . . maturity*] as his profession (law) is disposed to be mature (ironic).
maturity] due deliberation (*OED* 1).
25. *stood with*] made common cause with (*OED* stand with, 79b).
26. *prevaricate*] be evasive.
27. *ingenious*] noble (*OED* 4, frequently used for *ingenuous*).
28. *that*] with which.
30. *Being*] because.

Palate. The same he said to me.
Compass.   And named the party?
Palate. He did, and he did not.
Compass.   Come, leave your schemes
    And fine amphibolies, parson.
Palate.   You'll hear more.
Polish. Why now your ladyship is free to choose
    The courtier, Sir Diaphanous—he shall do it;   35
    I'll move it to him myself.
Lady.   What will you move to him?
Polish. The making you a countess.
Lady.   Stint, fond woman.
    (*To Compass*) Know you the party Master Practice means?
Compass. No, but your parson says he knows, madam.
Lady. I fear he fables; parson, do you know   40
    Where Master Practice is engaged?
Palate.   I'll tell you.
    But under seal, her mother must not know:
    'Tis with your ladyship's woman, Mistress Pleasance.
Compass. How?
Lady.   He is not mad.
Palate.   O, hide the hideous secret
    From her, she'll trouble all else. You do hold   45
    A cricket by the wing.
Compass.   Did he name Pleasance?
    Are you sure, parson?
Lady.   O, 'tis true, your mistress.

---

31. named] *G;* name *F.*   37.1] *in right margin, F.*   44. mad.] *F;* mad?
Wha.

---

33. *amphibolies*] contrary senses, deliberately ambiguous.
36. *to him*] Possibly scanned as 'to'm' (twice).
37. *Stint*] stop.
 fond] foolish, over-affectionate.
42. *under seal*] in confidence.
45–6. *hold . . . wing*] to have to submit to unendurable noise: proverbial (Dent G425: 'To hold a grasshopper by the wing'): 'fill every ear with noise', *Poet.,* Apol. Dial.112–13. This ancient proverb is found in Archilocus and Erasmus, and is roughly equivalent to 'to hold a tiger by the tail'.

I find where your shoe wrings you, Master Compass:
But you'll look to him there.

[*Enter* INTEREST, PRACTICE *and* BIAS.]

Compass.   Yes, here's Sir Moth,
Your brother, with his Bias, and the party   50
Deep in discourse: 'twill be a bargain and sale;
I see by their close working of their heads,
And running them together so in council.
Lady. Will Master Practice be of council against us?
Compass. He is a lawyer, and must speak for his fee,   55
Against his father and mother, all his kindred;
His brothers or his sisters; no exception
Lies at the common law. He must not alter
Nature for form, but go on in his path—
It may be he will be for us. Do not you   60
Offer to meddle, let them take their course:
Dispatch, and marry her off to any husband;
Be not you scrupulous; let who can, have her,
So he lay down the portion, though he geld it.
It will maintain the suit against him: somewhat,   65
Something in hand is better than no birds;
He shall at last account for the utmost farthing

---

49. S.D.] *Wi; G adds this entry after l. 53.*   64. geld] *Wha;* gueld *F.*
65. him: somewhat,] *F;* him, somewhat: *G.*

---

48. *where . . . wrings*] Where your sensitive spot is: proverbial (Heywood,
Dial. Provs, 2.5, ultimately from Plutarch *Lives*, Aemilius Paulus 5.2, and
found in Chaucer, *Merchant's Tale*, l. 309). Cf. Tilley M129: 'Every man
knows best where the shoe wrings'.
49. *look to him*] put him right.
51. *bargain*] negotiation, discussion.
54. *of council*] i.e. be retained for his professional services.
55. *must . . . fee*] must argue in favour whatever he is paid for.
for his] Possibly 'for's'.
58–9. *He . . . form*] He must not put natural affections in place of what is
required by formal legal procedures (see *OED* form sb.11).
63. *scrupulous*] too particular.
64. *So . . . geld*] Provided that he pays the marriage portion, even though
it be incomplete; cf. 2.6.21–2.
66. *something . . . birds*] proverbial (Dent B363: 'a bird in the hand is
better than two in the bush').
67. *utmost farthing*] possibly proverbial.

If you can keep your hand from a discharge.

                                                    [*Exit* LADY.]

Polish. Sir, do but make her worshipful aunt a countess
And she is yours: her aunt has worlds to leave you!   70
The wealth of six East Indian fleets at least!
Her husband, Sir John Loadstone, was the governor
O'the company, seven years.

Diaphanous.   And came there home
Six fleets in seven years?

Polish.   I cannot tell;
I must attend my gossip, her good ladyship.   [*Exit.*]   75

Placentia. And will you make me a viscountess too? For
How do they make a countess? In a chair?
Or 'pon a bed?

Diaphanous.   Both ways, sweet bird, I'll show you.

                        [*Exeunt* DIAPHANOUS *and* PLACENTIA.]

                        ACT 2   SCENE 6

            [INTEREST, PRACTICE *and* BIAS *come forward.*]

Interest. The truth is, Master Practice, now we are sure
That you are off, we dare come on the bolder:

68.1] *G.*   75.1] *G.*   78.1] *G.*

2.6] *Centred: Interest. Practise. Bias. Compasse. Palate. Rut. (*/*) Ironside. In right
margin:* To them. *F.*   Rut] *Fc; Rnt Fu.*   0.1] *G.*

──

68. *If . . . discharge*] if you can refrain from signing any form of release.
69. *Sir*] Diaphanous.
70. *she*] Placentia.
71. *East Indian*] Merchant vessels belonging to the East India Company,
founded in 1600. The earliest ventures are said to have produced 100 per
cent profits.
    fleets] groups of several ships.
77–8. *chair . . . bed*] sexual innuendoes: cf. the name Mother Chair in
Persons (flesh), and 2.3.60n.
78. *'pon a bed*] i.e. by sexual activity, with pun on *Placentia/Placenta*
meaning bed: cf. Persons 6n.
    bird] Young maiden: used in a similarly patronising way by Fitzdottrel in
DA, 2.7.28.

2. *off*] not a suitor, with play on 'on'.

The portion left was sixteen thousand pound,
I do confess it, as a just man should.
And call here Master Compass, with these gentlemen,   5
To the relation: I will still be just.
Now for the profits every way arising:
It was the donor's wisdom those should pay
Me for my watch and breaking of my sleeps.
It is no petty charge, you know, that sum,   10
To keep a man awake for fourteen year.
Practice. But, as you knew to use it i' that time,
It would reward your waking.
Interest.   That's my industry;
As it might be your reading, study and counsel;
And now your pleading; who denies it you?   15
I have my calling too. Well, sir, the contract
Is with this gentleman, ten thousand pound—
An ample portion for a younger brother,
With a soft, tender, delicate rib of man's flesh
That he may work like wax, and print upon.   20
He expects no more than that sum to be tendered,
And he receive it: those are the conditions.
Practice. A direct bargain and sale in open market.
Interest. And what I have furnished him withal o'the by,
To appear, or so: a matter of four hundred,   25
To be deduced upo' the payment—

---

21. more] *Fc;* more, *Fu.*   23. sale in open] *Fc;* in open sale, *Fu, and F3.*

---

6. *To the relation*] to the report, probably as witnesses.
8. *those*] the profits, l. 7.
9. *watch*] wakefulness.
10. *charge*] responsibility.
13. *industry*] diligence.
15. *pleading*] argument, but with a legal flavour referring ironically to Practice's profession.
17. *ten thousand pound*] Sir Moth, by this agreement will keep back £6,000 of the total marriage portion of £60,000: see l. 30n.
19. *rib . . . flesh*] woman, like Eve, Genesis, 2: 21.
20. *work like wax*] Cf. 'the clay is soft—you will mould it to what you will' (*argilla quidvis imitaberis uda*), Horace, *Epistles*, 2.2.8.
print upon] use to produce his own likeness: cf. 'print off', Partridge.
24. *o'the by*] on the side.
26. *deduced*] deducted, *OED* 7: the £400 for Practice to draw up the agreement.

Bias.   Right.
    You deal like a just man still.
Interest.   Draw up this,
    Good Master Practice, for us, and be speedy.
Practice. But here's a mighty gain, sir, you have made
    Of this one stock. The principal first doubled   30
    In the first seven year; and that redoubled
    I'the next seven! Beside six thousand pound,
    There's threescore thousand got in fourteen year,
    After the usual rate of ten i'the hundred,
    And the ten thousand paid.
Interest.   I think it be!   35
Practice. How will you 'scape the clamour and the envy?
Interest. Let 'em exclaim and envy: what care I?
    Their murmurs raise no blisters i' my flesh.
    My moneys are my blood, my parents, kindred:
    And he that loves not those, he is unnatural: 40
    I am persuaded that the love of money
    Is not a virtue only in a subject,
    But might befit a prince. And, were there need,
    I find me able to make good the assertion
    To any reasonable man's understanding   45

---

36. 'scape] *This ed.;* scape *F.*   44. assertion] *Wi;* Assertion. *F.*   45.
understanding] *This ed.;* understanding. *F.*

---

30. *stock*] dowry, *OED* 48c.

principal] The principal of £16,000 would double twice at 10 per cent in
fourteen years to approximately £64,000. If Sir Moth then pays out only
£10,000 as the marriage portion (l. 17), keeping back £6,000, he is left with
£54,000 + £6,000 = £60,000—'threescore thousand got in fourteen year' (l.
33).

34. *ten i'the hundred*] Ten per cent, the old maximum rate; noted as
reduced in 1624 by two per cent at *Staple*, 2.1.4. Sir Moth's interest in the
amount began before the reduction.

36. *clamour*] outcry.

38. *murmurs . . . flesh*] Possibly proverbial but not traced: perhaps a
variation of 'Sticks and stones may break my bones, but words will never
hurt me'.

murmurs] complaints.

41. *love of money*] scripture reversed: 'The love of money is the root of all
evils', 1 Timothy, 6: 10.

43. *prince*] It is even a virtue in a prince (irony).

And make him to confess it.

Compass.   Gentlemen,
Doctors, and scholars, you'll hear this, and look for
As much true secular wit and deep lay-sense
As can be shown on such a commonplace.
Interest. First, we all know the soul of man is infinite   50
I' what it covets. Who desireth knowledge
Desires it infinitely. Who covets honour
Covets it infinitely. It will be then
No hard thing for a coveting man to prove,
Or to confess, he aims at infinite wealth.   55
Compass. His soul lying that way.
Interest.   Next, every man
Is i' the hope or possibility
Of a whole world: this present world being nothing
But the dispersèd issue of the first one:
And therefore I not see but a just man   60
May with just reason, and in office ought
Propound unto himself—
Compass.   An infinite wealth!
I'll bear the burden: go you on, Sir Moth.

---

51. I' what] *H&S;* I wh at *F.*   53. infinitely.] *Wha;* infinitely, *F.*   59.
²the] *H&S; not in F;* th' *Wha.*

---

46. *confess it*] believe it.
48. *secular*] worldly, but Jonson also uses this to mean 'common' or
'vulgar': *NI,* 5.2.9 (*OED* 2b).
49. *commonplace*] a statement of a general truth upon which disputation
might be based: here ll. 41–2 above upon which Sir Moth dilates until l. 101.
56. *lying*] Pun on (1) being that way inclined; (2) telling lies.
58. *whole*] complete, perfect.
59. *issue*] result.
first one] first world, before the flood (*Wha.*). But perhaps the contrast is
between the perfect world before the Fall of Man and the world contaminated afterwards.
60–2. *therefore . . . himself*] 'therefore I cannot think otherwise but that a
just man may legally put forward this proposition for his own advantage, and
indeed it is an obligation that he should'.
61. *in office*] acting according to his responsibility.
62. *Propound*] put forward legally.
63. *bear the burden*] Pun on (1) provide the chorus or refrain to Moth's
speech (also at l. 70); (2) put up with being wealthy.

Interest. Thirdly, if we consider man a member
   But of the body politic, we know   65
   By just experience that the prince hath need
   More of one wealthy than ten fighting men.
Compass. There you went out o' the road a little from us.
Interest. And therefore if the prince's aims be infinite,
   It must be in that which makes all.
Compass.   Infinite wealth.   70
Interest. Fourthly, 'tis natural to all good subjects
   To set a price on money; more than fools
   Ought on their mistress' picture; every piece
   Fro'the penny to the twelvepence being the hieroglyphic,
   And sacred sculpture of the sovereign.   75
Compass. A manifest conclusion, and a safe one.
Interest. Fifthly, wealth gives a man the leading voice
   At all conventions; and displaceth worth,
   With general allowance to all parties.
   It makes a trade to take the wall of virtue,   80
   And the mere issue of a shop right honourable.
   Sixthly, it doth enable him that hath it
   To the performance of all real actions,
   Referring him to himself still; and not binding

73. mistress' picture] *Wha;* Mrs. Picture *F.*   77. Fifthly] *F3;* Fiftly *F.*
82. Sixthly] *F3;* Sixtly *F.*

---

68. *There . . . us*] This does not quite fit us [perhaps because Compass is not too wealthy].

70. *It . . . all*] It must be so in the case of that which facilitates everything [i.e. money].

71. *natural*] Pun on (1) appropriate; (2) foolish.

72. *set . . . money*] to fix a value for money, but also in a more literal sense to mark coin with a value.

74. *hieroglyphic*] sacred symbol (*hieros* sacred, Gk): see also the stage business about the hieroglyphic (a paper emblem) in *Poet.*, 5.3.31–151.

75. *sculpture*] engraving.

76. *manifest*] clearly revealed.

78. *conventions*] public meetings.

78–9. *and displaceth . . . parties*] and is generally allowed to outweigh all values.

80. *take the wall*] to take the inner and safer position (*OED* wall 16 a and b). Trade is thus privileged over virtue; cf. *RJ*, 1.1.12.

81. *And . . . honourable*] and a mere shopkeeper's son can become a lord.

83–4. *To . . . still*] To carry out all actions in reality, referring constantly to his own interests throughout.

His will to any circumstance without him.   85
It gives him precise knowledge of himself:
For, be he rich, he straight with evidence knows
Whether he have any compassion
Or inclination unto virtue, or no;
Where the poor knave erroneously believes   90
If he were rich, he would build churches, or
Do such mad things. Seventhly, your wise poor men
Have ever been contented to observe
Rich fools, and so to serve their turns upon them:
Subjecting all their wit to the others' wealth,   95
And become gentlemen parasites, squire bawds,
To feed their patron's honourable humours.
Eighthly, 'tis certain that a man may leave
His wealth or to his children or his friends:
His wit he cannot so dispose, by legacy,   I00
As they shall be a harrington the better for't.
Compass. He may entail a jest upon his house, though:

Enter IRONSIDE.

Or leave a tale to his posterity,
To be told after him.

---

95. others'] *Wi;* others *F.*   100. legacy,] *Wha;* Legacie? *Fu;* Legacie, *Fc.*
102.1] *in left margin, F.*

---

85. *without him*] away from him.
87. *be . . . rich*] supposing he be rich.
87–9. *he . . . no*] he immediately finds plenty of evidence to show whether
he should give pity or favour to virtue.
90. *Where*] whereas.
92–4. *Seventhly . . . them*] Recalls Iago's self-description, *Oth.*, 1.1.49–55.
94. *serve their turns*] take their advantage.
99. *or . . . or*] either . . . or.
100. *His . . . legacy*] Jonson notes this as a Spanish saying: 'arts cannot be
shared among heirs', *Disc.*, 251–2.
101. *As*] So that.
harrington] a brass farthing: Lord Harrington was patented to coin them
in 1613, and they became proverbial as at 4.8.74–5 below.
102–3. *He . . . tale*] He may entail his properties [placing certain obsta-
cles to the inheritance] as a jest [against his heirs], or leave behind a story
or tale, possibly scandalous.
103. *tale*] Pun on (1) entail; (2) tale.

Ironside.   As you have done here?
    To'invite your friend and brother to a feast,   105
    Where all the guests are so mere heterogene
    And strangers, no man knows another, or cares
    If they be Christians or Mohammedans
    That here are met.
Compass.   Is't any thing to you, brother,
    To know religions more than those you fight for?   110
Ironside. Yes, and with whom I eat. I may dispute;
    And how shall I hold argument with such
    I neither know their humours, nor their heresies,
    Which are religions now, and so received?
    Here's no man among these that keeps a servant   115
    To'inquire his master of: yet i' the house,
    I hear it buzzed there are a brace of doctors,
    A fool, and a physician: with a courtier
    That feeds on mulberry leaves, like a true silkworm:
    A lawyer, and a mighty money-bawd,   120
    Sir Moth, has brought his politic Bias with him—
    A man of a most animadverting humour,
    Who, to endear himself unto his lord,
    Will tell him, you and I, or any of us
    That here are met, are all pernicious spirits,   125
    And men of pestilent purpose, meanly affected

---

105. To'invite] *This ed.;* T'invite *F.*   117. doctors,] *Wha;* Doctors; *F.*
121. Moth,] *G; Moath! F.*   123. his] *Wha;* his his *F.*

---

106. *mere heterogene*] completely different in character; also at *Alc.,* 2.5.11.

109–10. *Is't . . . for*] 'Do you need to know, brother, what religion you are fighting against? Your own is sufficient for you.'

111. *Yes . . . eat*] Cf. *MerVen.,* 1.3.32–3, where eating with someone similarly raises the question of religious allegiance.

113–14. *heresies . . . religions*] a change characteristic of the Reformation settlements.

115–16. *Here's . . . of*] no one here is sufficiently important to have a servant from whom one might enquire about his master.

117. *buzzed*] rumoured (*OED* 5).

brace] Pair consisting of Rut, the 'physician', and Palate, the 'fool' in l. 118.

122. *animadverting*] critical, censorious (*OED* 4: first in 1665).

126–7. *affected / Unto*] disposed towards.

Unto the state we live in: and beget
Himself a thanks with the great men o' the time,
By breeding jealousies in them of us,
Shall cross our fortunes, frustrate our endeavours   130
Twice seven years after: and this trick be called
Cutting of throats with a whispering, or a penknife.
I must cut his throat now: I'm bound in honour,
And by the law of arms, to see it done.
I dare to do it; and I dare profess   135
The doing of it, being to such a rascal,
Who is the common offence grown of mankind,
And worthy to be torn up from society.
Compass. You shall not do it here, sir.
Ironside.   Why? will you
Entreat yourself into a beating for him,   140
My courteous brother? If you will, have at you,
No man deserves it better, now I think on't,
Than you: that will keep consort with such fiddlers,
Pragmatic flies, fools, publicans, and moths:
And leave your honest and adopted brother.   145
Interest. 'Best raise the house upon him to secure us;

---

133. I'm] *This ed.;* I'am *F.*

127. *state*] nation, country.
129. *jealousies*] suspicions (*OED* 5).
130. *cross*] thwart.
132. *Cutting . . . whispering*] causing murder by evil report, as in *Sej.*,
1.30–1: ultimately from Juvenal, *Satires*, 4.110, 'Whose gentle whisper would
cut men's throats' (*tenui iugulos aperire susurro*).
135. *profess*] confirm openly.
136–7. *being . . . mankind*] as I am speaking of such a rogue who has
become the common disgrace to mankind: for *offence* see *OED* 5d.
136. *rascal*] rogue.
140. *Entreat*] negotiate (ironic).
143. *consort*] Pun on (1) concert (n); and (2) consort [with].
fiddlers] triflers (*OED*).
144. *Pragmatic*] busy, interfering, *DA*, 1.6.56.
flies] Cf. 2.4.10.
publicans] tax gatherers.
145. *adopted*] 'called so twenty year', 3.4.50.
146. *'Best*] The apostrophe suggests the anxious omission of 'It were . . .'
secure us] make us safe.

He'll kill us all!
Palate.   I love no blades in belts.
Rut. Nor I.
Bias.   Would I were at my shop again,
     In Court, safe stowed up with my politic bundles.
Compass. How they are scattered!
Ironside.   Run away like *cimici*   150
     Into the crannies of a rotten bedstead.
Compass. I told you such a passage would disperse 'em,
     Although the house were their fee-simple in law,
     And they possessed of all the blessings in it.
Ironside. Pray heaven they be not frighted from their
          stomachs   155
     That so my lady's table be disfurnished
     Of the provisions!
Compass.   No, the parson's calling
     By this time all the covey again together.
     Here comes good tidings.

[*Enter* PLEASANCE.]

Dinner's o' the board.
[*Exit all except* COMPASS *and* PLEASANCE.]

ACT 2   SCENE 7

Compass. Stay, Mistress Pleasance, I must ask you a question:
     Ha' you any suits in law?
Pleasance.   I, Master Compass?
Compass. Answer me briefly, it is dinner time.

---

159. S.D.] *G.*   159.1] *This ed.*

147. *blades . . . belts*] knife and sword blades stuck into belts without proper sheaths.
148. *shop*] place of business.
150. *they*] the humours characters.
cimici] bed-bugs (Ital.).
152. *passage*] course of events.
153. *fee-simple*] possession without complications in law.
156. *disfurnished*] deprived: he wants the feast to go on, not be brought to a premature end.
158. *covey*] party, usually of game-birds.

They say you have retained brisk Master Practice
Here, of your counsel; and are to be joined   5
A patentee with him.
Pleasance.   In what? Who says so?
You are disposed to jest.
Compass.   No, I am in earnest.
It is given out i' the house so, I assure you;
But keep your right to yourself, and not acquaint
A common lawyer with your case. If he   10
Once find the gap a thousand will leap after.
I'll tell you more anon.   *[Exit* COMPASS.]
Pleasance.   This riddle shows
A little like a love-trick o' one face
If I could understand it: I will study it.   *[Exit.]*

[2] CHORUS

[DAMPLAY, BOY *and* PROBEE.]

Damplay. But whom doth your poet mean now by this—
Master Bias? What lord's secretary doth he purpose to
personate or perstringe?
Boy. You might as well ask me what alderman or alderman's
mate he meant by Sir Moth Interest? Or what eminent   5

---

12. S.D.] *G.*   14.1] *G.*

2 CHORUS] *This ed.; Chorus. F.*   0.1] *This ed.*

---

4. *retained*] employed as legal representative.
5–6. *joined . . . patentee*] made joint beneficiary of a document of agreement: legal joke for marriage settlement.
9. *keep . . . yourself*] remain in full control [of your heart]: expressed in
legal word play.
not] do not.
10. *case*] Pun on (1) legal case; and (2) vagina; cf. Partridge, citing *MWW*,
4.1.49–54.
11. *gap . . . after*] proverbial? Not in Dent.
13. *love-trick*] courtship: she spots Compass's amorous interest.

3. *personate*] represent.
perstringe] censure (*perstringere*, Lat.).
4–12.] A similar idea is elaborated in the Articles of Agreement read by
the Scrivener in *BF*, Ind.135–45: see Introduction, p. 14.

lawyer by the ridiculous Master Practice? Who hath
rather his name invented for laughter than any offence or
injury it can stick on the reverend professors of the law:
and so the wise ones will think.

Probee. It is an insidious question, Brother Damplay. Iniquity   10
itself would not have urged it. It is picking the lock of
the scene; not opening it the fair way with a key. A play,
though it apparel and present vices in general, flies from
all particularities in persons. Would you ask of Plautus
and Terence, if they both lived now, who were Davus or   15
Pseudolus in the scene? Who Pyrgopolinices or Thraso?
Who Euclio or Menedemus?

Boy. Yes, he would: and inquire of Martial, or any other
epigrammatist whom he meant by Titius or Seius (the
common John à Noke, or John à Stile) under whom they   20
note all vices and errors taxable to the times. As if there
could not be a name for a folly fitted to the stage but
there must be a person in nature found out to own it.

---

20. Stile] *Wha;* Style *F.*

6–7. *Who . . . laughter*] Whose name was invented for a joke.

8. *professors of*] those professionally involved in.

10. *insidious*] crafty, underhand.

Iniquity] The evil-minded; traditional name for the Vice in the
interludes, and used by Shakespeare and Jonson. See *DA*, 1.1.41–3n (Revels
edition).

11. *picking . . . lock*] Cf. 'any state-decipherer, or politic picklock of the
scene', *BF*, Ind.138–9.

13–14. *vices . . . persons*] 'modest rhymes / That spare men's persons, and
but tax their crimes', *Poet.*, 3.5.134–5: a recurrent theme in Jonson's critical
theory.

15. *Davus*] a slave in Terence's *Andria.*

16. *Pseudolus*] Eponymous hero, 'the Liar', in Plautus' play.

Pyrgopolonices] a braggart in Plautus' *Miles gloriosus.*

Thraso] in Terence's *Eunuchus.*

17. *Euclio*] in Plautus' *Aulularia.*

Menedemus] in Terence's *Heautontimorumenos.*

18–20. *Martial . . . Stile*] fictitious names used in law cases. Juvenal has
Seius and Titius in *Satires*, 4.13; Martial has Gaius and Lucius in *Epigrams*,
5.14.5. The English equivalents used here are John from the Oak, and John
from the Stile.

21. *taxable to*] which can be blamed upon.

Damplay. Why, I can fancy a person to myself, Boy: who shall
    hinder me?   25

Boy. And in not publishing him you do no man an injury. But
    if you will utter your own ill meaning on that person,
    under the author's words, you make a libel of his comedy.

Damplay. O, he told us that in a prologue long since.

Boy. If you do the same reprehensible ill things, still the   30
    same reprehension will serve you, though you heard it
    afore. They are his own words. I can invent no better,
    nor he.

Probee. It is the solemn vice of interpretation that deforms the
    figure of many a fair scene by drawing it awry: and indeed   35
    is the civil murder of most good plays. If I see a thing
    vively presented on the stage that the glass of custom,
    which is comedy, is so held up to me, by the poet, as I
    can therein view the daily examples of men's lives and
    images of truth in their manners so drawn for my delight   40
    or profit as I may either way use them: and will I, rather
    than make that true use, hunt out the persons to defame,
    by my malice of misapplying? And imperil the innocence

---

24. *fancy*] invent, imagine.

27. *utter*] give currency to; assign.

28. *you . . . comedy*] you use the comedy as a vehicle for your own
libel.

29. *prologue*] 'They make a libel which he made a play', *SW*, Second
Prologue, 14.

31. *reprehension*] rebuke.

34. *vice of interpretation*] *Staple*, Int.2.21–8.

35. *drawing it awry*] Pun on (1) making an inaccurate drawing; (2) pulling
it out of shape.

36–43. *If . . . misapplying*] If I see something presented on stage in so
lively a manner that the mirror of fashion, which is comedy, is so held
up for me by the poet that I can see in it daily examples of men's lives and
pictures of truth for my use as either pleasure or profit, shall I then try to
find people to defame by means of my own malicious distortion rather than
benefiting?

37. *vively*] clearly (*OED* 2 cites this).

37–8. *glass . . . comedy*] *speculum consuetudinis*, Cicero, quoted at *EMO*,
3.6.204–7.

40–1. *for . . . profit*] Derived from Horace, *Ars poetica*, 343–4 which Jonson
translated: 'As doctrine and delight together go'. This became fundamental
to Jonson's critical principles, as at *EMO*, Ind.202.

and candour of the author by his calumny? It is an unjust
way of hearing and beholding plays, this, and most   45
unbecoming a gentleman to appear malignantly witty in
another's work.

Boy. They are no other but narrow and shrunk natures,
shrivelled up, poor things, that cannot think well of
themselves, who dare to detract others. That signature   50
is upon them and it will last. A half-witted barbarism,
which no barber's art, or his balls, will ever expunge or
take out.

Damplay. Why, Boy? This were a strange empire, or rather a
tyranny, you would entitle your poet to, over gentle-   55
men, that they should come to hear and see plays and say
nothing for their money.

Boy. O, yes; say what you will, so it be to purpose, and in
place.

Damplay. Can anything be out of purpose at a play? I see no   60
reason if I come here and give my eighteen pence or two
shillings for my seat but I should take it out in censure
on the stage.

Boy. Your two shilling worth is allowed you: but you will
take your ten shilling worth, your twenty shilling worth,   65

---

44. his calumny] *F;* this calumny *Wha: see Notes.*   65. ten] *Fc;* ten, *Fu.*

44. *by his calumny*] By calumniating the author (*H&S*). Whalley's
emendation makes the phrase parallel with the previous one: the author
would thus not be threatened by the calumny of others.

44–7.] 'But the sinister application / Of the malicious ignorant and base /
Interpreter, who will distort and strain / The general scope and purpose of
an author, / To his particular and private spleen', *Poet.*, 5.3.135–9, deriving
from Martial, *Epigrams*, 1, Prol.9–10.

50. *detract others*] damage the reputation of others.

signature] distinctive mark (*OED* 4).

52. *no barber's art*] Cinnamus, the barber, was credited with removing
stains and brands, *Volp.*, Ded.141–2, from Martial, *Epigrams*, 6.64.24–6.

balls] spherical soap (*OED* sb[1].10b).

54. *empire*] absolute rule: Jonson associates this word with tyranny, *DA*,
3.3.45.

55. *entitle*] give a legal right.

60. *out of purpose*] Damplay's view is heretical to Jonson who promoted
the integrity of poems and plays.

61. *eighteen pence*] See Ind.33n. The same theme of being able to critise
the play because of paying the fee occurs in *BF*, Ind.88–97.

and more: and teach others about you to do the like that
follow your leading face; as if you were to cry up or down
every scene by confederacy, be it right or wrong.

Damplay. Who should teach us the right or wrong at a play?

Boy. If your own science can not do it, or the love of modesty   70
and truth, all other entreaties or attempts are vain. You
are fitter spectators for the bears than us, or the puppets. This is a popular ignorance indeed, somewhat
better apparelled in you than the people: but a hard-
handed and stiff ignorance, worthy a trowel or a hammer-   75
man; and not only fit to be scorned but to be triumphed
o'er.

Damplay. By whom, Boy?

Boy. No particular, but the general neglect and silence. Good
Master Damplay, be yourself still, without a second.   80
Few here are of your opinion today, I hope; tomorrow I am sure there will be none, when they have rumi-
nated this.

Probee. Let us mind what you come for, the play, which will
draw on to the *epitasis* now.   85

---

71. attempts] *Wha;* attempts—*F.*   78. *Damplay . . . Boy?*] *after ore (i.e.*
o'er) *Fu; separate line, Fc.*

---

68. *by confederacy*] by unlawful conspiracy (*OED* 1b).

70. *science*] knowledge: emphasises that Jonson was interested in spectators prepared to think about moral issues.

72–3. *bears . . . puppets*] Bear baiting was practised on Bankside, often in
the same theatre as the plays. Puppets aroused Jonson's contempt at *Alc.*,
5.1.14n, but he used them in *BF*, 5.4.

73. *popular*] of the common people.

73–4. *somewhat . . . apparelled*] rather better dressed.

75. *trowel*] perhaps a recollection of Jonson's past as a bricklayer.

79. *No . . . silence*] Not by any particular person, but by the neglect and
silence shown by all.

80. *second*] supporter.

81. *here are*] here are men.

85. *epitasis*] In accordance with Terentian structure this begins with Act
3: cf. 1 Chor.8–9n.

Act 3

[*Enter*] ITEM, NEEDLE, [*and*] KEEP.

Item. Where's Master Doctor?
Needle.   O, Master Tim Item,
　　His learned pothecary! You are welcome:
　　He is within at dinner.
Item.   Dinner! Death!
　　That he will eat now, having such a business
　　That so concerns him!
Needle.   Why, can any business   5
　　Concern a man like his meat?
Item.   O, twenty millions
　　To a physician that's in practice: I
　　Do bring him news from all the points o' the compass,
　　(That's all the parts of the sublunary globe)
　　Of times and double times.

3.1. SCENE I.] *stop lowered in some copies of F.*   1. *Item*] *Fc; Iem Fu.*

---

2. *pothecary*] apothecary, who makes and sells medicines.
3. *within*] off stage, as at 3.1.33.1. The action onstage depends upon what is imagined offstage in another room of Loadstone's house: see Introduction, p. 11.
Death] sanitised oath: by God's death. There was a strong Puritan reaction against swearing: cf. Stubbes, *Abuses* (1583), pp. 129–36. The players in 1632 were found responsible for introducing unacceptable material, but this may not have been oaths; see Introduction, p. 25.
4. *That*] To think that.
5–6. *business . . . meat*] Possibly proverbial, but not identified.
6–7. *twenty . . . practice*] the doctor in practice has twenty million things more important than his food.
8. *points*] part of the sustained imagery about Compass: here points are the directions the compass may indicate.
9. *sublunary*] terrestrial, under the moon: cited in *OED* 2.
10. *double*] suggests either time twice filled up with business or times

Needle.   In, in, sweet Item,
And furnish forth the table with your news.
Deserve your dinner; sow out your whole bag full;
The guests will hear it.
Item.   I heard they were out.
Needle. But they are pieced and put together again.
You may go in; you'll find them at high eating.   15
The parson has an edifying stomach
And a persuading palate, like his name.
He hath begun three draughts of sack in doctrines,
And four in uses.
Item.   And they follow him.
Needle. No, Sir Diaphanous is a recusant   20
In sack. He only takes it in French wine,
With an allay of water. In, in, Item,
And leave your peeping.   [*Exit* ITEM.]
Keep.   I have a month's mind

---

17. name.] *This ed.;* name: *Fu;* name:) *Fc.*   18–19. in . . . uses] *italics, F.*
19. him.] *F;* him? *Wha.*   23. S.D.] *G.*

involving deception.
   11. *furnish forth*] provide (*OED* 8): cf. 'did coldly furnish forth the marriage tables', *Ham.*, 1.2.181.
   12. *Deserve*] earn.
   sow out] throw around as though seeding.
   13. *out*] fallen out.
   14. *pieced*] mended: cf. *DA*, 4.1.37.
   15. *high eating*] eating luxuriously; cf. *OED* high 8: luxurious (of food and drink: *obsolete*).
   16. *edifying*] pun on (1) building in a physical sense (as a result of eating) (2) morally benefiting.
   18. *sack*] white wine, usually Spanish.
   18–19. *doctrines . . . uses*] Puritan expressions for discourse (*H&S*).
   20. *recusant*] one who rejects, usually a religion (such as a Catholic rejecting Protestantism): here Diaphanous rejects sack in favour of French wine. Jonson himself was accused of recusancy in 1605, after the Gunpowder Plot.
   22. *an allay of water*] mixture of water, dilution. Cf. *OED* 4, 5, and 'hot wine with not a drop of allaying Tiber in't', *Cor.*, 2.1.49.
   23. *peeping*] Perhaps a concealed stage direction.
   month's mind] intention, from commemorative mass one month after death, but used playfully: see *OED* sb⁵.2, and cf. *Gent.*, 2.1.134.

To peep a little too. Sweet Mas' Needle,
    How are they set?
Needle.   At the board's end my lady—   25
Keep. And my young mistress by her?
Needle.   Yes, the parson
    On the right hand (as he'll not lose his place
    For thrusting) and 'gainst him, Mistress Polish:
    Next, Sir Diaphanous against Sir Moth;
    Knights, one again another: then the soldier,   30
    The man of war, and man of peace, the lawyer:
    Then the pert doctor, and the politic Bias,
    And Master Compass circumscribeth all.
                                    A noise within.

                        [*Enter* PLEASANCE.]

Pleasance. Nurse Keep! Nurse Keep!
Needle.   What noise is that within?
Pleasance. Come to my mistress, all their weapons are out.   35
Needle. Mischief of men! What day, what hour is this?
Keep. Run for the cellar of strong waters, quickly.   [*Exeunt.*]

---

24. Sweet] *F;* O sweet *H&S.*   32. Then] *cw p. 31 moved further to right in
some copies.*   33.1] *In left margin, F.*   *Enter* PLEASANCE] *This ed.*   34,
35. Pleasance] *F; within (S.D.s) G.*   37.1] *G.*

---

25. *set*] seated.
At . . . lady] Lady Loadstone is at the head of the table.
28. *For thrusting*] in spite of pushing by anyone else.
30. *again*] against, next to.
32. *pert*] ostensibly skilled (ironic here), but it can also mean 'unbecom-
ingly ready to express an opinion' (*OED* 3 and 4).
33. *circumscribeth*] completes the circle: he must be on Lady Loadstone's
left hand: but there is also the sense of containing them all as the circumference of a circle.
36. *Mischief of men!*] How wicked men are! Possibly read 'on' for 'of': 'A
curse on men!'
37. *cellar*] case of bottles (*OED*, first here).
strong waters] stimulants, usually containing alcohol.
37.1] The stage is empty at this point, presumably with interesting noises
off.

ACT 3 SCENE 2

To them after.

[*Enter*] COMPASS [*and*] IRONSIDE.

Compass. Were you a mad man to do this at table?
    And trouble all the guests, to affright the ladies
    And gentlewomen?

Masculinity

Ironside.   Pox upo' your women,
    And your half man there, Court-Sir Ambergris:
    A perfumed braggart, he must drink his wine   5
    With three parts water, and have amber in that too.

Compass. And you must therefore break his face with a glass,
    And wash his nose in wine?

Ironside.   Cannot he drink
    In orthodox, but he must have his gums
    And paynim drugs?

Compass.   You should have used the glass   10
    Rather as balance than the sword of justice:
    But you have cut his face with it, he bleeds.
    Come, you shall take your sanctuary with me;
    The whole house will be up in arms 'gainst you else
    Within this half hour; this way to my lodging.   15

                           [*Exeunt.*]

3.2] *In right margin:* To them after. *Centred:* Compasse. Ironside. *F.*   10.
paynim] *G;* Panym *F.*   15.1] *G.*

   0.1] *To them after* is usually Jonson's way of adding new characters to a scene; the addition of *after* suggests that this entry is to be timed to follow the rapid *exeunt* at 3.1.37.

   4. *Court-Sir*] ironically deferential title for courtier.

   Ambergris] grey amber, waxy substance from the whale used as perfume: cf. *Nept. Tr.*, 494.

   5. *braggart*] boaster.

   6. *amber*] used to flavour wine (*H&S*).

   9. *orthodox*] in a proper manner: normally of religious opinions at this time. See Introduction, pp. 25–6.

   gums] resins used as medicine: exotic, in accordance with *paynim* in next line.

   10. *paynim*] heathen.

   11. *balance*] something which produces equilibrium (*OED* 12): contrasting here evaluation with retribution, with pun on 'glass' as means of seeing. The traditional figure of Justice carries scales and a sword.

   13. *sanctuary*] place of refuge where a sentence might be avoided.

ACT 3   SCENE 3

[*Enter*] RUT, LADY [LOADSTONE], POLISH, [*and*] KEEP
carrying PLACENTIA *over the Stage,* [*followed by*]
PLEASANCE [*and*] ITEM.

Rut. A most rude action! Carry her to her bed;
And use the fricace to her, with those oils.
    Keep your news, Item, now, and tend this business.
Lady. Good gossip, look to her.
Polish.   How do you, sweet charge?
Keep. She's in a sweat.
Polish.   Ay, and a faint sweat, marry.   5
Rut. Let her alone to Tim: he has directions.
    I'll hear your news, Tim Item, when you ha' done.

                        [*Exeunt* ITEM, POLISH, KEEP *and*
                        PLEASANCE, *with* PLACENTIA.]

Lady. Was ever such a guest brought to my table?
Rut. These boisterous soldiers ha' no better breeding.

                [*Enter* COMPASS.]

    Here Master Compass comes. Where's your captain,   10
    Rudhudibras de Ironside?
Compass.   Gone out of doors.
Lady. Would he had ne'er come in them, I may wish.
    He has discredited my house and board
    With his rude, swaggering manners, and endangered

3.3.0.1.] *G and H&S; Rut. Lady. Polish. Keepe, carrying Placentia (l) over the
Stage. (l) Pleasance. Item. Centred in F, without new scene: see Introduction,
p. 47.*   4. How] H *damaged in many copies.*   7.1] *G.*   9.1] *G.*

3.3] No new scene in F.
2. *fricace*] rubbing, massage; cf. *Volp.*, 2.2.106.
3. *Keep*] hold back.
tend] attend to.
4. *gossip*] friend.
charge] responsibility, person for whom one has a duty (*OED* 14).
6. *to Tim*] for Tim to deal with.
9. *boisterous*] roughly behaved.
11. *Rudhudibras*] Sir Rud Hudibras, legendary son of King Leil of Britain,
supposed founder of Carlisle, Canterbury and Winchester: see Geoffrey
of Monmouth, *Historia*, 2.9: cf. 4.8.77, 5.1.20 and *NI*, 2.5.75. This part of
the name does not appear in Persons, and may be seen as a sarcastic
attribution.

My niece's health, by drawing of his weapon,   15
God knows how far; for Master Doctor does not.
Compass. The doctor is an ass then, if he say so,
    And cannot with his conjuring names, Hippocrates,
    Galen or Rasis, Avicen, Averroes,
    Cure a poor wench's falling in a swoon: 20
    Which a poor farthing changed in *rosa solis*
    Or cinnamon water would.

                    [*Enter* KEEP *and* POLISH.]

Lady.   How now? How does she?
Keep. She's somewhat better. Master Item has brought her
    A little about.
Polish.   But there's Sir Moth, your brother,
    Is fallen into a fit o'the happyplex.   25
    It were a happy place for him and us

---

22. S.D.] *This ed. following G.*

---

15. *weapon*] obscene pun: cf. Partridge 215, and *OED* 3. The crude joke, together with the following phrase about the ignorance of the Doctor anticipates ironically Placentia's pregnancy. In 3 Chor. 6–9 below, the Boy draws attention to the deliberate anticipation for the benefit of the audience.

18. *conjuring*] calling upon by magic.

Hippocrates] Greek physician, born c.460 B.C., developed theory of humours, influential in medieval times; cf. *Volp.*, 2.2.121.

19. *Galen*] Greek physician, A.D. c.130–c.200. Strong supporter and disseminator of the theory of humours.

Rasis] ninth-century Arab physician.

Avicen] Ibn-Sina or Avicenna, from Bokhara (980–1037).

Averroes] Ibn-Roshd (1126–98) born at Cordoba, translated Aristotle. A Latin translation of his work was printed at Venice in 1552 (*H&S*). This group of physicians is mentioned in Chaucer, *Gen. Prol.*, 431–3.

20. *swoon*] faint.

21. *farthing*] small quantity of something: cf. small piece (*OED* 2).

changed] infused with: but this is unsupported by other usages. *Wi* reads 'charged'.

rosa solis] cure for swooning made from spirits and flavoured, sometimes with orange; cf. *EMO*, 4.8.123.

22. *cinnamon water*] aromatic drink from cinnamon (*OED*, first in 1834, but also found in Lyly, *Pappe with a Hatchet*, 1589 (*H&S*)).

23–4. *brought . . . about*] recovered her a little.

25. *happyplex*] apoplexy; punned as 'happy place', l. 26.

26. *happy place*] Polish wishes him in heaven for his own benefit, and dead and gone for the benefit of herself and Placentia.

If he could steal to heaven thus. All the house
Are calling 'Master Doctor! Master Doctor!'
                                        [*Exit* RUT.]
The parson, he has gi'n him gone, this half hour;
He's pale in the mouth already, for the fear   30
O'the fierce captain.
Lady.   Help me to my chamber,
Nurse Keep. Would I could see the day no more,
But night hung over me, like some dark cloud;
That, buried with this loss of my good name,
I and my house might perish, thus forgotten—   35
        [*Exeunt* LADY LOADSTONE, KEEP *and* POLISH.]
Compass. Her taking it to heart thus more afflicts me
Than all these accidents, for they'll blow over.

ACT 3 SCENE 4

[*Enter*] PRACTICE [*and* SIR DIAPHANOUS] SILKWORM.

Practice. It was a barbarous injury, I confess:
But if you will be counselled, sir, by me,
The reverend law lies open to repair
Your reputation. That will gi' you damages;
Five thousand pound for a finger, I have known   5
Given in court. And let me pack your jury.
Diaphanous. There's nothing vexes me but that he has stained
My new, white satin doublet; and bespattered
My spick and span silk stockings, o' the day
They were drawn on. And here's a spot i'my hose too.   10

28.1] *G.*   35.1] *G.*

3.4] *H&S;* ACT III. SCENE III. *F.*   3.4.0.1] *Silkworme (not Diaphanous) F.*
7. *Diaphanous*] *Wi; Silk. F, and for remaining speech prefixes of 3.4.*

29. *gi'n . . . gone*] considered him dead.
37. *blow over*] pass away.

3. *reverend*] worthy of respect.
6. *pack . . . jury*] arrange a jury which is not impartial, (*OED* v^2.4).
9. *spick and span*] quite new and not worn: *OED* first in 1665, though the
form 'spick and span new' occurs earlier, as in *BF*, 3.5.38.
10. *drawn on*] put on.
hose] stockings.

Compass. Shrewd maims! Your clothes are wounded
   desperately,
   And that, I think, troubles a courtier more,
   An exact courtier, than a gash in his flesh.
Diaphanous. My flesh? I swear had he giv'n me twice so much,
   I never should ha' reckoned it. But my clothes   15
   To be defaced and stigmatised so foully!
   I take it as a contumely done me
   Above the wisdom of our laws to right.
Compass. Why then, you'll challenge him?
Diaphanous.   I will advise,
   Though Master Practice, here, doth urge the law;   20
   And reputation it will make me of credit
   Beside great damages (let him pack my jury).
Compass. He speaks like Master Practice, one that is
   The child of a profession he's vowed to,
   And servant to the study he hath taken   25
   A pure apprentice at law! But you must have
   The counsel o' the sword; and square your action
   Unto their canons, and that brotherhood,
   If you do right.
Practice.   I tell you, Master Compass,
   You speak not like a friend unto the laws   30

---

16. defaced] *Wha;* de defac'd *F.*   21. reputation] *F;* reparation *Wha.*

11. *Shrewd maims*] grievous injuries (ironic).
13. *exact*] refined (*OED* 2).
15. *reckoned*] noticed.
16. *stigmatised*] branded, disgraced (*OED* 2).
17. *contumely*] contemptuous insult.
18. *to right*] able to be put right.
19. *advise*] consider (*OED* 6 intransitive).
21. *And . . . credit*] And it will improve my reputation.
22. *let . . . jury*] Refers to Practice, as at l. 6.
24. *vowed to*] devoted to (*OED* 1b).
26. *pure*] uncorrupted, but perhaps ironical.
apprentice at law] barrister-at-law of less than sixteen years' standing (*OED* 2).
27. *counsel . . . sword*] Advice from those who settle matters by duelling, with a word play on legal terms as in 'counsel', and 'canons'.
27-8. *square . . . canons*] make your behaviour conform with their laws.

Nor scarce a subject, to persuade him thus
Unto the breach o'the peace. Sir, you forget
There is a court above, o' the Star Chamber
To punish routs and riots.
Compass.   No, young master,
Although your name be Practice there in term time,   35
I do remember it. But you'll not hear
What I was bound to say; but like a wild
Young haggard justice, fly at breach o'the peace,
Before you know whether the amorous knight
Dares break the peace of conscience in a duel.   40
Diaphanous. Troth Master Compass, I take you my friend;
You shall appoint of me in any matter
That's reasonable, so we may meet fair,
On even terms.
Compass.   I shall persuade no other;
And take your learned counsel to advise you—   45
I'll run along with him. You say you'll meet him,
On even terms. I do not see indeed
How that can be, 'twixt Ironside and you,

---

45. And . . . you] *in parenthesis, F.*

---

31. *Nor scarce*] nor even.

33. *above*] Perhaps the action requires a pause to suggest 'heaven' above.
Star Chamber] Room in Westminster Palace where royal Council tried
cases; also at 3.6.140.

34. *routs*] disturbances (*OED* 8).

35. *term time*] during legal terms: the implication is that Practice appears
a skilful lawyer in his professional context.

37. *bound*] on my way.

38. *haggard*] untrained falcon who might 'fly at' something unauthorised
prematurely: cf. *TwN*, 3.1.62–3.
fly at] attack (*OED* 8b).

39. *amorous knight*] Sir Diaphanous is a suitor, but the phrase suggests
the hero of the romances.

41. *take . . . friend*] accept you as my second.

42. *appoint of me*] settle on my behalf.

43. *so . . . fair*] so that we might meet fairly.

44. *even terms*] a technical condition in duelling in which there were no
odds taking account of the greater skill of one participant, as in the odds laid
in favour of Laertes by Claudius (*Ham.*, 5.2.144–75). The point recurs below
at ll. 87–91.

46. *run*] go.

Now I consider it. He is my brother,
I do confess; we ha' called so twenty year: 50
But you are, sir, a knight in Court, allied there,
And so befriended you may easily answer
The worst success: he a known, noted, bold
Boy o'the sword, hath all men's eyes upon him;
And there's no London jury but are led   55
In evidence as far by common fame
As they are by present deposition.
Then you have many brethren, and near kinsmen.
If he kill you, it will be a lasting quarrel
'Twixt them, and him. Whereas Rud. Ironside,   60
Although he ha' got his head into a beaver,
With a huge feather, 's but a currier's son,
And has not two old Cordovan skins to leave
In leather caps to mourn him in, if he die.
Again, you are generally beloved; he hated   65
So much that all the hearts and votes of men
Go with you, in the wishing all prosperity
Unto your purpose. He's a fat, corpulent,

49. brother,] *Wha;* brother. *F.*   50. confess; we] *This ed.;* confesse (wee
F.   called] a *faint in some copies.*   60. 'Twixt] *Wha;* T'wixt *F.*   63.
Cordovan] *Wha;* Cordov'an *F.*

---

50. *called so*] They are not born brothers, but behave as though they were.
51. *allied there*] with allies there.
52-3. *answer... success*] respond to the worst eventuality.
54. *Boy... sword*] one who settles quarrels by duelling. Though Jonson
himself fought when younger, he mocks duelling, as in the satire on
Dependancies in *DA*, 3.3.62-147. Official concern produced an *Edict...
against Private Combats and Duels* in 1614: see *DA*, 3.3.64-6n.
55-7. *there's... deposition*] 'All London juries are convinced by the
evidence of popular assumptions rather than by any proper and immediate
testimony'. The unreliability of juries outraged Jonson for years: cf. *EMI*,
1.2.89 and *DA*, 1.1.21.
60. *Rud.*] The shortened form may be an allusion to Sir Benjamin
Rudyard, Jonson's friend: see *DNB*.
61. *beaver*] visor, standing for helmet here.
62. *currier*] one who colours leather after tanning.
63. *Cordovan skins*] Spanish leather from Cordoba in Spain: appropriate
for currier in l. 62.
66. *votes*] prayers: *OED* 2 cites *Fort. Isles* (1626) (*H&S*, 7.723, l. 476).
68. *fat*] There is no other evidence for Ironside's being so: the attribution
is part of the rhetorical distortion practised by Compass throughout this
speech. Perhaps his corpulence recalls Jonson's own; cf. next.

Unwieldy fellow: you, a dieted spark,
Fit for the combat. He has killed so many   70
As it is ten to one his turn is next;
You never fought with any; less, slew any:
And therefore have the hopes before you.
I hope these things thus specified unto you
Are fair advantages: you cannot encounter   75
Him upon equal terms. Beside, Sir Silkworm,
He hath done you wrong in a most high degree:
And sense of such an injury received
Should so exacuate and whet your choler
As you should count yourself an host of men   80
Compared to him. And therefore you, brave sir,
Have no more reason to provoke or challenge
Him, than the huge, great porter has to try
His strength upon an infant.
Diaphanous.   Master Compass,
You rather spur me on than any way   85
Abate my courage to the enterprise.
Compass. All counsel's as it's taken. If you stand
On point of honour not t'have any odds,
I have rather then dissuaded you than otherwise:

---

73. hopes] *F;* better hopes *conj. Wha.*   76.] *cw (p. 34) Hee does not match*
He (p. 35).

69. *dieted spark*] a dashing young warrior with a slim figure: ironic. This could be made a visual joke.

76. *Sir Silkworm*] As at 1.6.32, this unconventional form may be significant, and possibly contemptuous here. However, it may be part of the textual anomaly concerning the uses of this name: see Introduction, p. 49.

79. *exacuate*] sharpen (*OED* 1, first here).

83. *great porter*] William Evans (d. 1636), porter to Charles I, reputedly over seven feet tall: noted in T. Fuller, *History of the Worthies* (1662) by *H&S.*

86. *Abate*] reduce.

87. *All's . . . taken*] All advice is what you make of it. Perhaps proverbial: cf. Tilley A154: 'If the counsel be good, no matter who gave it'.

87–91. *If . . . you*] If you base your intention to fight on even terms without odds in your favour [as in l. 44 above], on grounds of honour I have in effect given you advice not to risk your reputation: if fighting on even terms comes from your fiery temperament and desire for revenge what I have said will give you courage.

If upon terms of humour and revenge,   90
I have encouraged you. So that I think
I have done the part of a friend on either side:
In furnishing your fear with matter first,
If you have any: or, if you dare fight,
To heighten and confirm your resolution.   95
Practice. I now do crave your pardon, Master Compass:
I did not apprehend your way before
The true perimeter of it: you have circles,
And such fine draughts about!
Diaphanous.   Sir, I do thank you,
I thank you, Master Compass, heartily.   100
I must confess I never fought before,
And I'll be glad to do things orderly,
In the right place: I pray you instruct me.
Is't best I fight ambitiously, or maliciously?
Compass. Sir, if you never fought before, be wary   105
Trust not yourself too much.
Diaphanous.   Why? I assure you,
I'm very angry.
Compass.   Do not suffer, though,
The flatuous, windy choler of your heart
To move the clapper of your understanding,
Which is the guiding faculty, your reason: 110
You know not, if you'll fight, or no, being brought
Upo' the place.
Diaphanous.   O yes, I have imagined
Him treble armed, provoked too, and as furious

---

98. perimeter] *H&S;* Perimiter *F.*   103. instruct] *F;* to instruct *H&S.*
107. I'm] *Wha;* I'am *F.*

---

 93. *matter*] a basis.
 98. *perimeter*] scope.
 99. *draughts about*] lines drawn around the circle, suggesting clever
draughtsmanship. Practice accepts that he was wrong at ll. 29–34.
 106. *Trust . . . much*] Don't be over-confident.
 108. *flatuous*] flatulent.
 choler] one of the four humours supposed to cause anger.
 109. *clapper*] something which makes a noise, as in a bell: tongue here.

As Homer makes Achilles; and I find
Myself not frighted with his fame one jot.   115
Compass. Well, yet take heed. These fights imaginary
Are less than skirmishes; the fight of shadows.
For shadows have their figure, motion,
And their umbratile action from the real
Posture and motion of the body's act: 120
Whereas, imaginarily, many times,
Those men may fight, dare scarce eye one another,
And much less meet. But if there be no help,
Faith I would wish you send him a fair challenge.
Diaphanous. I will go pen it presently.
Compass.   But word it   125
In the most generous terms.
Diaphanous.   Let me alone.
Practice. And silken phrase: the courtliest kind of quarrel.
Compass. He'll make it a petition for his peace.
Practice. O, yes, of right, and he may do it by law. [*Exeunt.*]

120. body's] *Wha;* bodies *F.*   128-9] *speech headings in roman type; speeches in italics in F.*   129.1] *G.*

---

114. *Homer*] *H&S* point out that Homer's Achilles is less furious than indignant, and suggest that Jonson followed Horace's *iracundus* (angry) in *Ars poetica*, l. 121.

115. *jot*] tiniest amount.

116-23. *These . . . meet*] Compass is being deliberately confusing, but his meaning, which derives from the uncertainty in ll. 111-12, appears to be 'These fights, like that of Hercules, which are made up in fiction, are not proper fights, but only fights of shadows: shadows can have the appearance of the reality which they copy or imitate without being the real thing. On the other hand there are men who do come to real fighting even though they might be afraid to look one another in the eye, and could not have been expected to bring themselves to meet.'

117. *skirmishes*] not proper conflicts.

119. *umbratile*] shadowy (*OED* 2, first here).

120. *Posture*] physical attitude.

122. *eye*] look at threateningly.

125. *presently*] at once.

126. *generous*] noble, high-minded.

Let . . . alone] leave it to me.

128. *a . . . peace*] Refers to a legal bond for maintaining peace between two or more parties (*OED* surety 5c): cf. Lesley Hotson, *Shakespeare versus Shallow* (London, 1931), p. 9.

129. *of right . . . law*] justifiably, providing he does it according to the law. Whalley suggests this refers to the Petition of Right (1628).

ACT 3 SCENE 5

[*Enter*] RUT, PALATE [*and*] BIAS *bringing out*
INTEREST *in a chair*; ITEM [*and*] POLISH *following.*

Rut. Come, bring him out into the air a little:
    There set him down. Bow him—yet bow him more—
    Dash that same glass of water in his face:
    Now tweak him by the nose. Hard, harder yet:
    If it but call the blood up from the heart,   5
    I ask no more. See, what a fear can do!
    Pinch him in the nape of the neck now: nip him, nip him.
Item. He feels, there's life in him.
Palate.   He groans and stirs.
Rut. Tell him the captain's gone.
Interest.   Ha!
Palate.   He's gone, sir.
Rut. Gi' him a box, hard, hard, on his left ear.   10
Interest. O!
Rut.   How do you feel yourself?
Interest.   Sore, sore.
Rut.   But where?
Interest. I' my neck.
Rut.   I nipped him there.
Interest.   And i' my head.
Rut. I boxed him twice, or thrice, to move those sinews.
Bias. I swear you did.
Polish.   What a brave man's a doctor,
    To beat one into health! I thought his blows   15
    Would e'en ha' killed him: he did feel no more
    Than a great horse.

3.5] *H&S;* ACT III. SCENE IV. *F.*   8. groans] *Wha;* graones *F.*   11. But
where?] *H&S; separate line in F.*

    2. *Bow*] bend (*OED* v¹ 9): cf. 'cut her lace, and bow her forward', Richard
Brome, *The Sparagus Garden* (1640), 5.12, sig. L2v (*H&S*).
    6. *fear*] shock.
    7. *Pinch . . . nip*] The cause of Moth's indisposition seems to be his
fear of Ironside (cf. ll. 16–17), but Rut's crude treatment revives him. In the
rest of the scene, Rut's learned theories make little impact upon Moth's
avaricious humour, and both men are ridiculed: cf. 4.3.50.
    14. *brave*] excellent: ironic here.

Interest.   Is the wild captain gone?
     That man of murder?
Bias.   All is calm and quiet.
Interest. Say you so, cousin Bias? Then all's well.
Palate. How quickly a man is lost!
Bias.   And soon recovered!   20
Polish. Where there are means and doctors, learned men,
     And their apothecaries, who are not now,
     As Chaucer says, their friendship to begin.
     Well, could they teach each other how to win
     I'their swath-bands—
Rut.   Leave your poetry, good gossip,   25
     Your Chaucer's clouts, and wash your dishes with 'em;
     We must rub up the roots of his disease,
     And crave your peace a while, or else your absence.
Polish. Nay, I know when to hold my peace.
Rut.   Then do it.
     Gi' me your hand, Sir Moth. Let's feel your pulse.   30
     It is a pursiness, a kind of stoppage,
     Or tumour o'the purse, for want of exercise,
     That you are troubled with: some ligatures
     I'th' neck of your *vesica* or *marsupium*

---

22. now] *F; see Notes l. 23.*   25. bands—] *Wha;* bands-. *F.*   gossip,]
Wha; Gossip. *F.*   34. I'th'] *Wha;* I'th *F.*

---

19. *all's well*] Proverbial (Tilley A154: 'All's well that ends well').

23. *Chaucer*] *Gen. Prol.*, 425–8. *F*'s 'now' makes sense but it may be
Jonson's error for Chaucer's 'newe', l. 428, as at *BF*, 2.4.46.

25. *swath-bands*] swaddling bands (*OED* 1a cites this).

26. *clouts*] play on (1) shreds (*OED* 1); (2) swaddling-clothes (*OED* 5).
The comment refers to 'swath-bands' which are added by Polish to her
Chaucer reference.

27. *rub up*] remove, uproot (not in *OED*; nearest 6a).

28. *crave*] request, usually with respect.

31. *pursiness*] shortness of breath, Cotgrave: possibly flatulence.

32. *tumour o'the purse*] Anatomically a purse is a bag, such as the scrotum,
or possibly the lungs: this might be a swelling or impediment there, but Rut's
use of these terms appears pretentious. The play on a purse for money (l.
46) may be the main intent: the interweaving of medical and monetary
imagery runs from here to 'anatomical', l. 71.

33. *ligatures*] ligaments (medical), and purse-strings.

34. vesica] bladder (*OED* first in 1693).
marsupium] pouch (*OED* first in 1698); perhaps it suggests stomach here.

Are so close knit that you cannot evaporate;   35
And therefore you must use relaxatives.
Beside, they say, you are so restive grown,
You cannot but with trouble put your hand
Into your pocket, to discharge a reckoning.
And this we sons of physic do call *chiragra*,   40
A kind of cramp or hand-gout. You shall purge for't.

Item. Indeed, your worship should do well to'advise him
To cleanse his body, all the three high ways;
That is by sweat, purge and phlebotomy.

Rut. You say well, learned Tim; I'll first prescribe him   45
To give his purse a purge once, twice a week
At dice or cards: and when the weather is open,
Sweat at a bowling alley; or be let blood
I'the lending vein, and bleed a matter of fifty,
Or threescore ounces at a time. Then put   50
Your thumbs under your girdle, and have somebody
Else pull out your purse for you, till with more ease
And a good habit, you can do it yourself.
And then be sure always to keep good diet;
And ha' your table furnished from one end   55

---

55. ha'] *Wha; h' F.*

35. *knit*] tied.
evaporate] pass off as vapour, presumably equivalent to modern 'transpire'.
37. *restive*] inactive; or refractory, intractable (*OED* 3).
39. *discharge a reckoning*] pay a bill.
40. chiragra] hand-gout (Gk); cf. *DA*, 3.3.79.
41. *purge*] be purged, (with an emetic or an enema, or perhaps both). Cf. *discharge* (l. 39).
44. *sweat, purge and phlebotomy*] chief methods of cure, as in Burton, *Anatomy*, 1.2.2.4 (Peck).
phlebotomy] cutting a vein to release blood, Burton, *Anatomy*, 1.2.2.4: but Burton has reservations about the practice.
47. *dice or cards*] All the following self-indulgences are practised by Rut himself; cf. l. 60.
48. *let blood*] release blood by opening a vein, but metaphorical here for parting with money.
49. *vein*] pun on (1) blood vessel; (2) frame of mind.
50. *ounces*] liquids could be measured by weight as well as by volume.
53. *habit*] custom and practice.
54. *diet*] provision of food.

          Unto the tother: it is good for the eyes.
          But feed you on one dish still, ha' your diet-drink,
          Ever in bottles ready, which must come
          From the King's Head: I will prescribe you nothing
          But what I'll take before you mine own self: 60
          That is my course with all my patients.
Palate. Very methodical, *secundum artem*.
Bias. And very safe pro *captu recipientis*.
Polish. All errant learned men, how they 'spute Latin!
Rut. I had it of a Jew, and a great rabbi,   65
          Who every morning cast his cup of white wine
          With sugar, and by the residence i' the bottom,
          Would make report of any chronic malady,
          Such as Sir Moth's is, being an oppilation
          In that you call the neck o'the money bladder   70
          Most anatomical, and by dissection.

                        Enter NURSE.

Keep. O, Master Doctor, and his pothecary!
          Good Master Item, and my Mistress Polish!
          We need you all above. She's fallen again
          In a worse fit than ever.

---

56. eyes.] *H&S;* eyes, *F.*   65. rabbi] bi *slipped down in some copies of F.*
71.1] *In right margin, F.*

---

57. *diet-drink*] medicinally effective drink for his diet, but it will come
from the inn.
    59. *King's Head*] on Fish Street Hill (Chalfant, p. 115).
    60. *take before you*] Rut will test the food to prove its value.
    62. secundum artem] according to the art.
    63. pro captu recipientis] for the pleasing of the recipient.
    64. *errant*] Presumably a Polish malapropism: it raises a play upon
genuine (*OED* arrant 4) and errant meaning rascally.
    'spute] dispute, but perhaps pun on 'spout' which is a variant spelling in
OED.
    66. *cast*] mix (*OED* 68, first in 1825).
    67. *residence*] residue.
    68. *chronic*] lasting.
    69. *oppilation*] obstruction; cf. *Volp.*, 2.2.66, and Burton, *Anatomy,*
1.2.3.15.
    71. *anatomical . . . dissection*] These two words mean virtually the same
thing: analysis by cutting up. The line gives Rut's approval of the Rabbi's
analysis.

Polish.   Who?
Keep.   Your charge.   75
Polish. Come away, gentlemen.
Interest.   This fit with the doctor
  Hath mended me past expectation.
                              [*Exeunt all but* BIAS.]

                    ACT 3 SCENE 6

          [*Enter*] COMPASS, DIAPHANOUS [*and*] PRACTICE.

Compass. O, Sir Diaphanous, ha' you done?
Diaphanous.   I ha' brought it.
  That's well.
Compass.   But who shall carry it now?
Diaphanous.   A friend:
  I'll find a friend to carry it; Master Bias here
  Will not deny me that.
Bias.   What is't?
Diaphanous.   To carry
  A challenge I have writ unto the captain.   5
Bias. Faith, but I will, sir, you shall pardon me
  For a twi-reason of state. I'll bear no challenges:
  I will not hazard my lord's favour so;
  Or forfeit mine own judgement with his honour,
  To turn a ruffian. I have to commend me   10
  Naught but his lordship's good opinion;
  And to't my calligraphy, a fair hand,

77.1] G.

3.6] *H&S;* ACT III. SCENE V. *F.*

─────────────────────────────

76. *fit*] painful experience (*OED* sb²).
77. *mended*] cured.

2. *friend*] one acting as a second in the duel.
7. *twi-reason*] double reason.
8. *hazard*] risk.
9. *forfeit . . . honour*] give up my own reputation with his lordship.
10. *ruffian*] one engaged in violence, possibly criminal.
12. *to't my calligraphy*] and in addition my (beautiful) handwriting.

Fit for a secretary. Now you know, a man's hand
Being his executing part in fight,
Is more obnoxious to the common peril—   15
Diaphanous. You shall not fight, sir, you shall only search
My antagonist; commit us fairly there
Upo' the ground on equal terms.
Bias.   O sir,
But if my lord should hear I stood at end
Of any quarrel, 'twere an end of me   20
In a state course! I ha' read the politics;
And heard th'opinions of our best divines.
Compass. The gentleman has reason! Where was first
The birth of your acquaintance? Or the cradle
Of your strict friendship made?
Diaphanous.   We met in France, sir.   25
Compass. In France! That garden of humanity,
The very seed-plot of all courtesies!
I wonder that your friendship sucked that aliment,
The milk of France; and see this sour effect
It doth produce 'gainst all the sweets of travel.   30
There, every gentleman professing arms,
Thinks he is bound in honour to embrace
The bearing of a challenge for another,
Without or questioning the cause, or asking

---

13. *Fit . . . secretary*] fit for a professional writer (*OED* 2a); but it may also suggest pretentions to being a minister of state (*OED* 3a).
15. *obnoxious to*] liable to be affected by (*OED* 4).
16. *search*] probe.
17–18. *commit . . . terms*] establish fairly the place of duelling, and the even terms (as at 3.4.44).
19. *at end*] with a remote link.
21. *state course*] career in state affairs.
politics] political authors.
26. *humanity*] mental cultivation (*OED* 4, *humanitas* Lat.).
27. *seed-plot*] ground for nurturing seeds.
28. *aliment*] sustenance.
30. *'gainst . . . travel*] in contrast to all the benefits of travelling. There is a play on sour/sweet, a proverbial contrast. Cf. 'Speak sweetly, man, although thy looks be sour', *R2*, 3.2.193.
31. *professing*] skilled in.
32. *embrace*] welcome.
34. *or . . . or*] either . . . or.

Least colour of a reason. There's no cowardice,   35
No poltroonery like urging why? wherefore?
But carry a challenge, die, and do the thing.
Bias. Why hear you, Master Compass, I but crave
Your ear in private!
[*Aside to Compass*] I would carry his challenge
If I but hoped your captain angry enough   40
To kill him: for, to tell you truth, this knight
Is an impertinent in Court (we think him),
And troubles my lord's lodgings and his table
With frequent and unnecessary visits,
Which we, the better sort of servants, like not,   45
Being his fellows in all other places,
But at our master's board; and we disdain
To do those servile offices, oft times,
His foolish pride and empire will exact
Against the heart or humour of a gentleman.   50
Compass. Truth, Master Bias, I'd not ha' you think
I speak to flatter you: but you are one
O'the deepest politics I ever met,
And the most subtly rational. I admire you.
But do not you conceive in such a case   55
That you are accessory to his death

---

39. private!] *This ed.;* private? *F.*   S.D.] *This ed.; takes him aside G.*   51.
I'd] *Wha;* I'ld *F.*   56. accessory] *Wi (as l. 60 in F);* accessary *F.*

35. *colour*] show, pretext (*OED* 12).
36. *poltroonery*] cowardice.
like] such as.
40. *If . . . hoped*] if only I hoped.
42. *impertinent*] one who is incongruous; cf. *OED* adj, 3: first as noun in
1635.
45. *sort*] group, kind.
46. *fellows*] equals.
47. *board*] table: Bias and his fellows do not sit to eat with their master.
48. *servile offices*] unworthy services.
49. *empire*] false exercise of authority or tyranny: cf. *DA*, 3.3.45.
51. *Truth*] In truth.
53. *politics*] politicians.
55. *do . . . conceive*] you should not think.
56. *accessory*] criminally implicated; cf. l. 60.

From whom you carry a challenge with such purpose?
Bias. Sir, the corruption of one thing in nature
     Is held the generation of another;
     And therefore I had as lief be accessory   60
     Unto his death as to his life.
Compass.   A new
     Moral philosophy too! You'll carry't then?
Bias. If I were sure 'twould not incense his choler
     To beat the messenger.
Compass.   O, I'll secure you;
     You shall deliver it in my lodging safely,   65
     And do your friend a service worthy thanks.
Bias. I'll venture it upon so good induction
     To rid the Court of an impediment,
     This baggage knight.

                    Enter IRONSIDE.

Ironside.   Peace to you all, gentlemen,
     Save to this mushroom; who I hear is menacing   70
     Me with a challenge: which I come to anticipate
     And save the law a labour. Will you fight, sir?
Diaphanous. Yes, in my shirt.

---

57. purpose?] *Wha;* purpose. *F.*   64. O,] *Wha;* O' *F.*   65. lodging]
This ed.; lodging; *F.*   69. S.D.] *in right margin, F.*

57.] If you carry such a challenge from him [intending to bring about his
death].
58–9. *corruption . . . generation*] 'what is corrupt in nature in one thing
causes another corruption to grow'. Proverbial; Tilley C667: 'The corruption
of one is the generation of another', cites this.
60. *lief*] rather.
63. *incense his choler*] make him, the recipient, Ironside, so angry.
64. *secure*] make safe (*OED* 2a).
67. *induction*] initial step (*OED* 3c).
68. *baggage*] worthless (*OED* baggage B.3). Sir Thomas Bodley was not
keen to collect plays for his library at Oxford, calling them 'baggage books'
(letter of 15 January 1612).
70. *mushroom*] upstart (*OED* 2); cf. *EMO*, 1.2.162, and *SW*, 2.4.153. *H&S*
cite Plautus, *Bacchides*, ll. 820–1.
72. *save . . . labour*] by settling for a duel he will not have to trouble the
law.
73. *in my shirt*] Costard proposes fighting Armado in his shirt, but
Armado is not wearing one, *LLL*, 5.2.691–704.

Ironside.   O, that's to save your doublet;
     I know it, a Court trick! You had rather have
     An ulcer in your body than a pink   75
     More i' your clothes.
Diaphanous.   Captain, you are a coward
     If you not fight i'your shirt.
Ironside.   Sir, I not mean
     To put it off for that, nor yet my doublet:
     You've cause to call me coward, that more fear
     The stroke of the common and life-giving air   80
     Than all your fury and the panoply.
Practice. Which is at best but a thin linen armour.
     I think a cup of generous wine were better
     Than fighting i' your shirts.
Diaphanous.   Sir, sir, my valour,
     It is a valour of another nature   85
     Than to be mended by a cup of wine.
Compass. I should be glad to hear of any valours
     Differing in kind; who have known hitherto
     Only one virtue, they call fortitude,
     Worthy the name of valour.
Ironside.   Which who hath not   90
     Is justly thought a coward: and he is such.
Diaphanous. O, you ha' read the play there, *The New Inn*,

---

80. life-giving] *H&S;* life giving *F.*

75. *pink*] decorative hole in clothes (*OED* sb³ cites this).

76. *clothes*] John Earle, describing a Gallant writes: 'His first care is for his dress, the next his body . . .', *Microcosmographie*, no. 18.

77. *not mean*] do not intend.

79. *cause*] Ironside claims that by not taking off his doublet he gives Diaphanous the ironic excuse to call him coward he requires (ll. 76–7), even though Ironside is more afraid of fresh air than of the fury and armour of any opponent, including Diaphanous.

81. *panoply*] complete suit of armour.

83. *generous*] of good quality (*OED* 5, *vinum generosum* from Horace).

84. *valour*] possibly a play on 'value'.

89. *virtue*] i.e. *virtus* (Lat.), valour.

91. *he*] Diaphanous.

92–4. New Inn . . . *public*] Cf. Lovel's defence of true valour as against false, which 'respects not truth or public honesty' (*NI*, 4.4.88–95).

Of Jonson's, that decries all other valour
But what is for the public.
Ironside.   I do that too,
But did not learn it there; I think no valour   95
Lies for a private cause.
Diaphanous.   Sir, I'll redargue you
By disputation.
Compass.   O, let's hear this!
I long to hear a man dispute in his shirt
Of valour, and his sword drawn in his hand.
Practice. His valour will take cold: put on your doublet.   100
Compass. His valour will keep cold, you are deceived;
And relish much the sweeter in our ears.
It may be too i'the ordinance of nature
Their valours are not yet so combatant
Or truly antagonistic as to fight;   105
But may admit to hear of some divisions
Of fortitude may put 'em off their quarrel.
Diaphanous. I would have no man think me so ungoverned
Or subject to my passion, but I can
Read him a lecture 'twixt my undertakings   110
And executions: I do know all kinds
Of doing the business, which the town calls valour.
Compass. Yes, he has read the town, Towntop's his author.
Your first?

---

103. nature] *Wi;* nature. *F.*

---

93. *decries*] denies the value of (*OED*, usually of money).
96. *Lies*] exists.
redargue] confute (*OED* 2).
100. *His ... your*] Practice switches from a general remark about Diaphanous to direct address to him.
take cold] catch cold, i.e. slacken.
101. *keep*] remain.
102. *relish*] please: the cold valour of Diaphanous will generate excuses all the more pleasing to listen to.
103. *ordinance of nature*] the way nature arranged things.
106. *divisions*] different kinds: perhaps by disputing about fortitude they may not be brave enough to fight.
110–11. *twixt ... executions*] between my undertaking to do things and actually doing them.
113. *Towntop*] a whipping-top, bought for exercise in the parish: participation encouraged gossip, and Diaphanous has been listening to it.

Diaphanous.   Is a rash headlong unexperience.
Compass. Which is in children, fools, or your street gallants   115
    O' the first head.
Practice.   A pretty kind of valour!
Compass. Commend him, he will spin it out in's shirt,
    Fine as that thread.
Diaphanous.   The next, an indiscreet
    Presumption, grounded upon often scapes.
Compass. Or th'insufficiency of adversaries,   120
    And this is in your common fighting brothers,
    Your old perdus, who, after a time, do think
    The one, that they are shot-free; the other, sword-free.
    Your third?
Diaphanous.   Is naught but an excess of choler,
    That reigns in testy old men—
Compass.   Noblemen's porters   125
    And self-conceited poets.
Diaphanoous.   And is rather
    A peevishness than any part of valour.
Practice. He but rehearses, he concludes no valour.
Compass. A history of distempers, as they are practised,
    His harangue undertaketh and no more.   130
    Your next?

---

123. other,] *Fc;* other *Fu.*   free.] *Fc;* free, *Fu.*

---

114. *unexperience*] lack of experience, not in *OED*.
116. *O'. . . head*] of the first kind or section of argument.
118. *thread*] Perhaps a concealed stage direction: Compass to point to or pluck a thread from the shirt of Diaphanous.
119. *often scapes*] frequent escapes: 'often' was commonly adjectival in the seventeenth century: cf. 'an often courtier', *Poet.*, 4.2.13.
120. *insufficiency*] lack.
122. *perdus*] soldiers placed in an extremely hazardous position: cf. *Lear*, 4.7.34.
123. *shot-free . . . sword-free*] beyond the effect of pistols or sword.
125. *testy*] irascible.
126. *self-conceited*] thinking too highly of oneself.
127. *peevishness*] perverse ill-temper.
128. *rehearses . . . concludes*] Talks about valour without finally demonstrating it.
129. *distempers*] disturbances of mind.
130. *harangue*] formal speech addressed to an audience.

Diaphanous.   Is a dull, desperate resolving.

Compass. In case of some necessitous misery, or
   Incumbent mischief.

Practice.   Narrowness of mind,
   Or ignorance being the root of it.

Diaphanous. Which you shall find in gamesters, quite blown
       up.   135

Compass. Bankrupt merchants, undiscovered traitors.

Practice. Or your exemplified malefactors
   That have survived their infamy and punishment.

Compass. One that hath lost his ears, by a just sentence
   O'the Star Chamber, a right valiant knave—   140
   And is a histrionical contempt
   Of what a man fears most; it being a mischief
   In his own apprehension unavoidable.

Practice. Which is in cowards wounded mortally
   Or thieves adjudged to die.

Compass.   This is a valour   145
   I should desire much to see encouraged
   As being a special entertainment
   For our rogue people; and make oft good sport
   Unto 'em, from the gallows to the ground.

---

135. you] *Wha;* shou *F.*   136. Bankrupt] *Wha;* Banckrupt *F;* Or banckrupt *H&S.*   139. hath] h ath *F.*

---

132. *resolving*] act of the will.
133. *Incumbent*] threatening.
135. *blown up*] enlarged.
136. *undiscovered*] unrevealed, hidden.
137. *exemplified malefactors*] notorious criminals made an example of
(*H&S*).
139–40. *One . . . Star Chamber*] Probably refers to Alexander Gill with
whom Jonson quarrelled and who, he thought, was justly sentenced by the
Star Chamber in 1628, though he was granted a royal pardon. In his Reply
to Alexander Gill's *Upon Ben Jonson's Magnetick Lady*, Jonson mentions his
'want of ears', *Misc.*, 122.4: see Appendix 1.
141. *histrionical contempt*] one showing deceitful disrespect in a theatrical
or extravagant manner: cf. *OED* contempt 4.
142. *mischief*] misfortune.
143. *apprehension*] comprehension, estimation.
144. *is*] is found.
148. *rogue people*] refers to attendance at public executions.
149. *ground*] from where the people are watching the hanging.

Diaphanous. But mine is a judicial resolving   150
 Or liberal undertaking of a danger—
Compass. That might be avoided.
Diaphanous.   Ay, and with assurance
 That it is found in noblemen and gentlemen
 Of the best sheaf.
Compass.   Who having lives to lose
 Like private men, have yet a world of honour   155
 And public reputation to defend—
Diaphanous. Which in the brave historifièd Greeks
 And Romans you shall read of.
Compass.   And, no doubt,
 May in our aldermen meet it, and their deputies,
 The soldiers of the city, valiant blades,   160
 Who, rather than their houses should be ransacked,
 Would fight it out like so many wild beasts:
 Not for the fury they are commonly armed with,
 But the close manner of their fight, and custom
 Of joining head to head, and foot to foot.   165
Ironside. And which of these so well-pressed resolutions
 Am I to encounter now? For commonly
 Men that have so much choice before 'em have
 Some trouble to resolve of any one.
Bias. There are three valours yet, which Sir Diaphanous   170
 Hath, with his leave, not touched.
Diaphanous.   Yea? Which are those?

---

151. *liberal . . . danger*] noble facing up to a risk.

154. *sheaf*] class: heraldic term; see *OED*, and *EMO*, 2.1.85.

154–6. *Who . . . defend*] Who are mortal, like ordinary men, and yet they must defend their public reputation.

157. *historifièd*] celebrated in history.

164–5. *close . . . foot*] Refers to soldiers fighting tightly packed, side by side, in close order, and goes back via *Aeneid*, 10.361 to Homer, *Iliad*, 16.214–17: 'They stood so close together, shield to shield, helmet to helmet, man to man, that when they moved their heads the glittering peaks of their plumed helmets met' (E. V. Rieu).

166. *well-pressed*] thoroughly urged.

169. *resolve of*] settle upon.

171. *with his leave*] if he will permit me to say so.

Practice. He perks at that!
Compass.   Nay, he does more, he chatters.
Bias. A philosophical contempt of death
 Is one; then an infused kind of valour
 Wrought in us by our genii or good spirits   175
 Of which the gallant ethnics had deep sense,
 Who generally held that no great statesman,
 Scholar or soldier e'er did anything
 Sine divino aliquo afflatu.
Practice. But there's a Christian valour 'bove these too.   180
Bias. Which is a quiet, patient toleration
 Of whatsoever the malicious world
 With injury doth unto you, and consists
 In passion more than action, Sir Diaphanous.
Diaphanous. Sure, I do take mine to be Christian valour—   185
Compass. You may mistake though. Can you justify
 On any cause this seeking to deface
 The divine image in a man?
Bias.   O, sir,
 Let 'em alone: is not Diaphanous
 As much a divine image as is Ironside?   190
 Let images fight, if they will fight, a' God's name.

---

172. *perks*] looks interested.
chatters] shivers, shakes (*OED* 3).
174. *infused*] instilled.
175. *genii*] attendant spirits (*OED* 1). Classical in origin; cf. Horace, *Epistles*, 2.2.187–9.
176. *ethnics*] heathens, *ethnikos* (Gk).
179. Sine . . . afflatu] 'without some portion of divine inspiration', Cicero, *De natura deorum*, 2.167 (*H&S*).
181. *patient toleration*] Christian virtue of patience or suffering, which is a greater fortitude than physical valour: cf. 'the better fortitude of patience', Milton, *Paradise Lost*, 9.31.
184. *passion*] enduring, suffering: cf. 'fortitude did consist *magis patiendo quam faciendo* [rather in suffering than in doing]', *SW*, 4.5.263. The Latin source has not been traced. This passive form of the virtue now appeals strongly to Diaphanous.
188. *divine image*] 'Let us make man in our image and likeness', Genesis, 1: 26.
191. *images*] Diaphanous and Ironside who are images of God.

ACT 3   SCENE 7

[Enter] to them KEEP, *intervening.*

Keep. Where's Master Needle? Saw you Master Needle?
    We are undone.
Compass.   What ails the frantic nurse?
Keep. My mistress is undone: she's crying out!
    Where is this man, trow? Master Needle!

[Enter NEEDLE.]

Needle.   Here.
Keep. Run for the party, Mistress Chair, the midwife.   5
    Nay, look how the man stands as he were gucked!
    She's lost if you not haste away the party.
Needle. Where is the Doctor?
Keep.   Where a scoffing man is,
    And his apothecary little better:
    They laugh and jeer at all. Will you dispatch?   10
    And fetch the party quickly to our mistress:
    We are all undone! The tympany will out else.
                    [Exeunt NEEDLE *and* KEEP.]

[Enter INTEREST.]

Interest. News, news, good news, better than buttered news!

3.7] *H&S;* ACT III. SCENE VI. *F.*   3.7.0.1] *In right margin:* To them inter-
vening. *Centred: Keepe. Needle. Interest. F.*   4. Needle!] *This ed.; Needle? F.*
S.D.] *G.*   6. gucked] *Wi;* gok't *F.*   7. haste . . . party.] *F;* haste. Away!
The Party! *suggested by Honigmann.*   12.1] *G adds both stage directions.*

0.1. *intervening*] interrupting.
2. *frantic*] lunatic.
4. *trow*] do you think? (*OED* v 4b and 4c).
5. *party*] the person in question: cf. 2.5.50.
6. *gucked*] foolish. All the *OED* citations are Scottish.
7. *if . . . party*] Elliptic: if you do not hurry to fetch the midwife.
8. *scoffing*] dismissing or deriding. Keep means that Rut has wrongly
dismissed Placentia's predicament. The sense of eating excessively does
not arise until the nineteenth century: see *OED* v².
12. *tympany*] swelling. *H&S* quote a Star Chamber case of 1632 in which
Joan Lane, married for two months, claimed a tympany: the Bishop of
London thought it was 'a tympany with two heels'.
13. *buttered*] apparently palatable, or pleasing; chosen for jingle (better
. . . butter). Possibly a hit at Nathaniel Butter, who collected and published
news; cf. *Staple*, 1.4.13 (*H&S*).

My niece is found with child, the Doctor tells me,
And fallen in labour.
Compass.   How?   [*Exit.*]
Interest.   The portion's paid!   15
        The portion—O, the captain! Is he here?   *Exit.*
Practice. He'has spied your swords out! Put 'em up, put up,
        You've driven him hence; and yet your quarrel's ended.
Ironside. In a most strange discovery.
Practice.   Of light gold.
Diaphanous. And cracked within the ring. I take the omen   20
        As a good omen.
Practice.   Then put up your sword,
        And on your doublet. Give the captain thanks.
Diaphanous. I had been slurred else. Thank you, noble
            captain:
        Your quarrelling caused all this.
Ironside.   Where's Compass?
Practice,   Gone,
        Shrunk hence; contracted to his centre, I fear.   25
Ironside. The slip is his then.
Diaphanous.   I had like t'have been
        Abused i'the business, had the slip slurred on me—

---

15. S.D.] *G.*   16. O, the] *This ed.;* o'the *F.*   16.1] *in left margin, standing
between l. 15 and l. 16 in F. It could refer to either Compass or Interest.*   17.
He'has] *This ed.;* H'has *F.*   23. captain:] *Fc;* Captaine! *Fu.*   25. hence;]
Fc; hence,! *Fu.*

---

    19. *discovery*] revelation.
    light gold] gold below the standard or legal weight (*OED a*[1].1b): cf. light
(*OED* light 14b, wanton, unchaste).
    20. *cracked . . . ring*] proverbial (Dent R130.1: 'to be cracked in the ring');
deriving from the invalidity of a coin if it were cracked to within the ring
around the king's head (*H&S*). There is also an allusion to the breaking of
the hymen: cf. *OED* crack 13, and Partridge, who cites 'think her bond of
chastity quite crackt', *Cym.*, 5.5.206–7.
    22. *on*] put on.
    23. *slurred*] stained: punning on (1) his doublet dirtied and (2) his honour
tainted.
    26. *slip*] counterfeit coin made, for example, of brass covered with silver
or gilded copper (*OED* sb[4]): cf. *EMI*, 2.5.146, and *Und.*, 45.17. There is an
additional sense of a sexual slip.
    I . . . been] I could easily have been.
    27–8. *had . . . counterfeit*] if the false person, a counterfeit, had dishon-
oured me.

A counterfeit!

Bias.   Sir, we are all abused:
As many as were brought on to be suitors;
And we will join in thanks, all to the captain,   30
And to his fortune that so brought us off.   [*Exeunt.*]

[3] CHORUS

[DAMPLAY, BOY *and* PROBEE.]

Damplay. This was a pitiful poor shift o'your poet, Boy, to
make his prime woman with child, and fall in labour, just
to compose a quarrel.

Boy. With whose borrowed ears have you heard, sir, all this
while, that you can mistake the current of our scene so?   5
The stream of the argument threatened her being with
child from the very beginning, for it presented her in the
first of the second Act with some apparent note of infir-
mity or defect: from knowledge of which the auditory
were rightly to be suspended by the author, till the   10
quarrel, which was but the accidental cause, hastened on
the discovery of it, in occasioning her affright; which
made her fall into her throes presently, and within that
compass of time allowed to the comedy, wherein the poet
expressed his prime artifice, rather than any error, that   15

31.1] *G.*

3 CHORUS] *This ed.; Chorus. F.*   0.1] *This ed.*

---

31. *fortune*] Elliptical: to the good fortune resulting from his action.
brought . . . off] saved.

1. *shift*] trick.
2. *prime woman*] chief woman's role: but this 'leading lady' is not the real
heroine, and Damplay has not the right thread, as the Boy explains.
3. *compose*] settle (*OED* 9).
5. *current*] direction.
6. *argument*] main theme or subject.
9. *auditory*] audience.
10. *suspended*] in suspense.
11. *accidental*] by chance.
hastened on] brought on more quickly.
14. *compass . . . comedy*] limits of time proper to the comedy, i.e. the unity
of time which Jonson observes: cf. Introduction, p. 10.
15. *prime artifice*] supreme skill.

the detection of her being with child should determine
the quarrel which had produced it.

Probee. The Boy is too hard for you, Brother Damplay: best
mark the play, and let him alone.

Damplay. I care not for marking the play: I'll damn it, talk,
and do that I come for. I will not have gentlemen lose   20
their privilege, nor I myself my prerogative, for ne'er an
overgrown or superannuated poet of 'em all. He shall not
give me the law; I will censure, and be witty, and take my
tobacco, and enjoy my Magna Carta of reprehension, as
my predecessors have done before me.   25

Boy. Even to licence and absurdity.

Probee. Not now, because the gentlewoman is in travail: and
the midwife may come on the sooner to put her and us
out of our pain.

Damplay. Well, look to your business afterward, Boy, that all   30
things be clear, and come properly forth, suited and set
together; for I will search what follows severely and to the
nail.

---

18. you, Brother Damplay:] *Wha;* you. Brother *Damplay, F.*

---

16. *determine*] bring to an end.

21. *privilege*] literally, a 'private law': he claims that gentlemen could
criticise the play because of their special status.

prerogative] exclusive right.

22. *overgrown*] Cf. 1.2.34.

superannuated] incapacitated by age (*OED*). The sense of receiving a
pension is not recorded before 1740 (*OED* 3; and cf. superannuate v.1b which
has a citation for 1692).

23. *censure*] give my opinion.

24. *tobacco*] A habit already censured by King James in his *Counterblast to
Tobacco* (1604): cf. 'The taking of tobacco with which the Devil / Is so
delighted', *DA*, 5.8.71-2; censured by Burton, *Anatomy*, 2.4.2.1.

Magna Charta] agreement of 1215 giving barons right of free speech. A.
Tricomi notes here an intrusion of parliamentary ideas, *Anti-court Drama in
England 1603-42* (Charlottesville, Va., 1989), p. 151.

reprehension] reproof, criticising.

26. *licence*] being beyond control.

27. *travail*] labour.

28. *come on*] come on stage.

31. *suited*] set in due order (*OED* 8).

32-3. *to the nail*] punctiliously, to the point of perfection, as in *ad unguem*,
Horace, *Satires*, 1.5.32 (*OED* 3c). The sculptor would pass his fingernail over
the marble to test for flaws or joins (Loeb, p. 66n).

Boy. Let your nail run smooth then, and not scratch, lest the
    author be bold to pare it to the quick, and make it smart: 35
    you'll find him as severe as yourself.
Damplay. A shrewd boy, and has me everywhere. The midwife
    is come; she has made haste.

---

35. *pare . . . quick*] cut away to reveal the sensitive core.

37. *shrewd*] cunning, usually uncomplimentary at this time, even suggesting 'accursed'.

    has me] has me cornered.

Act 4

[*Enter*] CHAIR [*and*] NEEDLE.

Chair. Stay, Master Needle, you do prick too fast
  Upo' the business: I must take some breath.
  Lend me my stool. You ha' drawn a stitch upon me,
  In faith, son Needle, with your haste.
Needle.   Good mother,
  Piece up this breach; I'll gi' you a new gown,   5
  A new silk-grogoran gown. I'll do't, mother.

[*Enter* KEEP.]

Keep. What'll you do? You ha' done too much already
  With your prick-seam and through-stitch, Master
    Needle.
  I pray you sit not fabling here old tales,
  Good Mother Chair, the midwife, but come up.   10
                    [*Exeunt* CHAIR *and* NEEDLE.]

4.1] ACT IIII. SCENE I. (*l*) *Chaire. Needle. Keepe. F.*   4. Good mother]
H&S; in line 5, F.   6. do't] *F;* do it *Wha.*   6.1] *G.*   8. stitch, Master
Needle.] *G;* stitch. Mr. Needle, *F.*   10.1] *G.*

1–2. *prick . . . Upo'*] approach too close (*OED* 12).
  3. *stitch*] sharp pain from being out of breath (*OED* 2), with punning
reference to Needle.
  4. *mother*] term of address for elderly woman of lower class (*OED* 4a).
  5. *Piece up*] repair, or patch up (*OED* II.8).
  6. *silk-grogoran*] coarse silk fabric: cf. *EMI*, 2.1.9, and Stubbes, *Abuses*,
p. 56.
  8. *prick-seam*] stitch used in glove-making (*OED* first here).
  through-stitch] stitch drawn right through, suggesting thoroughness (*OED*
thorough-stitch).

ACT 4   SCENE 2

[Enter] COMPASS *[and]* PRACTICE.

Compass. How now, nurse, where's my lady?
Keep.   In her chamber
Locked up, I think: she'll speak with nobody.
Compass. Knows she o'this accident?
Keep.   Alas, sir, no.
Would she might never know it.   *[Exit.]*
Practice.   I think her ladyship
Too virtuous and too nobly innocent   5
To have a hand in so ill-formed a business.
Compass. Your thought, sir, is a brave thought, and a safe one:
The child now to be born is not more free
From the aspersion of all spot than she.
She have her hand in plot 'gainst Master Practice,   10
If there were nothing else, whom she so loves?
Cries up and values? Knows to be a man
Marked out for a chief justice in his cradle?
Or a lord paramount, the head o'the Hall?
The top or the top-gallant of our law?   15
Assure yourself, she could not so deprave
The rectitude of her judgement to wish you
Unto a wife might prove your infamy,
Whom she esteemed that part o'the commonwealth
And had cried up for honour to her blood.   20

---

4. S.D.] *G.*   9. she.] *Wha;* she? *F.*   10. Practice,] *Wha;* Practise. *F.*
20. cried] *conj. H&S; not in F.*

---

6. *ill-formed*] badly conceived (*OED* B, first in 1704).
7. *brave*] admirable (*OED* 3).
9. *aspersion*] staining.
spot] stain.
10–11.] Would she be plotting against Practice whom she loves so much, setting aside all other reasons [which are subsequently enumerated] for favouring him?
12. *Cries up*] speaks well of.
14. *paramount*] having supreme authority.
head o'the Hall] Master of an Inn of Court.
15. *top . . . top-gallant*] in full career, from sails at the top of the rigging (*OED* top 9c): proverbial (Dent T437: '-top and topgallant'). Cf. *BF*, 4.5.47.
16. *deprave*] impair.
18. *might . . . infamy*] who might bring dishonour to you.

Practice. I must confess a great beholdingness
         Unto her ladyship's offer and good wishes.
         But the truth is I never had affection
         Or any liking to this niece of hers.
Compass. You foresaw somewhat then?
Practice.   I had my notes   25
         And my prognostics.
Compass.   You read almanacs,
         And study 'em to some purpose, I believe?
Practice. I do confess, I do believe, and pray too:
         According to the planets, at some times.
Compass. And do observe the sign in making love?   30
Practice. As in phlebotomy.
Compass.   And choose your mistress
         By the good days, and leave her by the bad?
Practice. I do, and I do not.
Compass.   A little more
         Would fetch all his astronomy from Allestree.
Practice. I tell you, Master Compass, as my friend,   35
         And under seal, I cast mine eye long since
         Upo' the other wench, my lady's woman,
         Another manner of piece for handsomeness

---

29. some times] *Wha;* sometimes *F.*

---

21. *beholdingness*] obligation.
23. *affection*] inclination.
26. *prognostics*] foreknowledge.
   almanacs] These are attacked on Protestant grounds by Stubbes, *Abuses*,
1.2.1. pp. 56–7.
30. *sign*] of the zodiac.
31. *phlebotomy*] opening a vein to allow bleeding. Common practice in
medieval and early modern times required medicine and surgery to follow
astrological indications: cf. Chaucer, *Gen. Prol.*, ll. 415–16.
32. *good . . . bad*] Cf. 'cross out my ill-days', *Alc.*, 1.3.95.
33. *and . . . not*] Perhaps Compass, pressing hard, interrupts Practice.
34. *Allestree*] Richard Allestree of Derby, almanac maker 1624–43 (*H&S*),
maliciously described as a Homer to Jonson by Alexander Gill in *Upon Ben
Jonson's Magnetick Lady*, l. 36: see Appendix I.
36. *under seal*] sealed, in confidence.
37. *Upo'*] The elision is not necesary for the rhythm; perhaps racy or
fashionable speech.
38. *Another manner*] of quite a different order: cf. *BF*, 1.4.87.
   piece] 'a woman regarded sexually', Partridge; cf. *OED* 9b.

Than is the niece. But that is *sub sigillo*
And as I give it you, in hope o'your aid   40
And counsel in the business.
Compass.   You need counsel?
The only famous counsel o' the kingdom
And in all courts? That is a jeer in faith
Worthy your name and your profession too,
Sharp Master Practice.
Practice.   No, upo' my law,   45
As I am a Bencher and now Double Reader,
I meant in mere simplicity of request.
Compass. If you meant so, th'affairs are now perplexed
And full of trouble, give 'em breath and settling;
I'll do my best. But in mean time do you   50
Prepare the parson. I am glad to know
This; for myself liked the young maid before,
And loved her too. Ha' you a licence?
Practice.   No;
But I can fetch one straight.
Compass.   Do, do, and mind
The parson's pint t'engage him—the business;   55
A knitting cup there must be.
Practice.   I shall do it.   [*Exit.*]

51–3. I . . . too] *in parenthesis, F, probably as an aside.*   55. him—] *F;* him
in *Wha;* him i' *H&S.*   56.1] *G.*

_____

39. *sub sigillo*] in secret: cf. 36n.
41–2. *counsel . . . counsel*] pun on (1) advice, and (2) lawyer.
43. *jeer*] joke (not in *OED* in this sense).
46. *Bencher*] title for a Reader (or lecturer) in law at an Inn of Court after
fifteen or sixteen years.
Double Reader] title for Reader in law at an Inn of Court with twenty-three
years' standing (*H&S*).
47. *mere*] pure: he denies making a joke about it.
48. *If . . . so*] If you did really mean this [which I doubt].
perplexed] confused (*OED* 2).
49. *settling*] opportunity of becoming quiet and composed (*OED* 5).
52. *This*] that Practice prefers Pleasance. He speaks aside here.
54. *straight*] immediately (*OED* C 2).
55. *pint*] the pint of ale, given as a bribe. The earliest citation in this sense
in *OED* (c) is 1767.
him—] The *F* reading is retained here as Compass breaks his sentence in
haste and urges attention to the matter in hand.
56. *knitting cup*] a cup handed round at weddings (*OED* cites this): cf.
bride cup, *NI*, 5.4.29.

ACT 4   SCENE 3

[*Enter*] BIAS [*and*] INTEREST.

Bias. 'Tis an affront from you, sir; you here brought me
　　Unto my lady's, and to woo a wife,
　　Which since is proved a cracked commodity;
　　She hath broke bulk too soon.
Interest.　　　　　　　　　　　No fault of mine,
　　If she be cracked in pieces or broke round;　　　　　5
　　It was my sister's fault, that owns the house
　　Where she hath got her clap, makes all this noise.
　　I keep her portion safe, that is not scattered:
　　The moneys rattle not; nor are they thrown
　　To make a muss, yet, 'mong the gamesome suitors.　　10
Compass. Can you endure that flout, close Master Bias,
　　And have been so bred in the politics?
　　The injury is done you, and by him only;
　　He lent you impressed money, and upbraids it:
　　Furnished you for the wooing, and now waives you.　　15
Bias. That makes me to expostulate the wrong
　　So with him, and resent it as I do.
Compass. But do it home then.
Bias.　　　　　　　　　Sir, my lord shall know it.

---

1. 'Tis] *Wha;* Tis *F.*　9. moneys] *Wi;* money's *F.*

---

　　3. *cracked commodity*] damaged merchandise: in line with mercantile
discourse about women and marriage.
　　4. *bulk*] pun on (1) cargo of a ship and (2) the human body.
　　5. *cracked*] Cf. 3.7.20.
broke round] broken round the edges like a clipped coin.
　　7. *clap*] misfortune (*OED* 6): cf. *Alc.*, 4.6.3.
makes] who makes.
　　10. *muss*] scramble, a form of game (Cotgrave) as at *BF*, 4.2.33: cf. next.
gamesome] merry.
　　11. *flout*] insult.
close] secretive (*OED* 7).
　　12. *And have*] i.e. who have.
　　14. *impressed*] paid in advance (*OED* v³, first in 1665).
upbraids it] makes it the basis for complaint.
　　15. *Furnished you*] provided you with money.
waives] disregards (*OED* 8).
　　16. *expostulate*] complain about.
　　18. *do it home*] carry it to a conclusion.

Compass. And all the lords o'the Court too.
Bias.   What a moth
    You are, Sir Interest!
Interest.   Wherein, I entreat you,   20
    Sweet Master Bias?
Compass.   To draw in young statesmen
    And heirs of policy into the noose
    Of an infamous matrimony.
Bias.   Yes,
    Infamous, *quasi in communem famam*:
    And matrimony, *quasi* matter of money,   25
Compass. Learnedly urged, my cunning Master Bias.
Bias. With his lewd, known, and prostituted niece.
Interest. My known and prostitute—! How you mistake
    And run upon a false ground, Master Bias.
    Your lords will do me right. Now she is prostitute   30
    And that I know it—please you understand me—
    I mean to keep the portion in my hands:
    And pay no moneys.
Compass.   Mark you that, Don Bias?
    And you shall still remain in bonds to him
    For wooing furniture and impressed charges.   35
Interest. Good Master Compass, for the sums he has had
    Of me I do acquit him: they are his own.
    Here, before you, I do release him.

21. statesmen] *Wha;* States-men *F.*   33. that,] *Wha;* that *F.*

19. *moth*] play upon his name. The sense is strained: he draws others like moths to his candle, the portion.
    22. *heirs of policy*] those likely to inherit political power.
    23. *infamous*] shameful.
    24. quasi in communem famam] as if [to draw him] into a low public reputation (*fama*, Lat. ill fame).
    25. *matrimony . . . money*] The pun appears in H. Parrot, *The Mastive*, C4: '*Nuptiae post Nummae*', 'marriage for the sake of money' (*H&S*).
    27. *lewd*] Pun on (1) evil, (2) unchaste (cf. prostituted), and (3) ignorant (opposite of learned).
    28. *known*] Interest protests that she was not known to be false up to now, but now that her error is known he will act upon it.
    29. *run . . . ground*] imagery from bowling.
    33. *Don*] complimentary and derogatory.
    35. *For wooing furniture*] for whatever you needed to carry out your attempt at marriage.
    impressed] Cf. 4.3.14n.

Compass.   Good!

Bias. O, sir.

Compass.   'Slid take it: I do witness it:
      He cannot hurl away his money better.   40

Interest. He shall get so much, sir, by my acquaintance
      To be my friend: and now report to his lords
      As I deserve, no otherwise.

Compass.   But well:
      And I will witness it, and to the value;
      Four hundred is the price, if I mistake not,   45
      Of your true friend in Court. Take hands, you ha'
         bought him,
      And bought him cheap.

Bias.   I am his worship's servant.

Compass. And you his slave, Sir Moth. Sealed and delivered.
      Ha' you not studied the Court compliment?

                          [*Exit* BIAS *and* INTEREST.]

      Here are a pair of humours, reconciled now,   50
      That money held at distance; or their thoughts,
      Baser than money.

                   ACT 4   SCENE 4

              [*Enter*] POLISH [*and*] KEEP.

Polish.   Out, thou caitiff witch!

49.1] *This ed., following* G.   4.4.0.1.] *This ed.; after* out *(l. 5)* G.

―――――――――――――――――――――――――――――――――――――――

   39. *'Slid*] by God's eyelid.
   41-2. *He . . . friend*] He will receive this much money through his
knowing me in order that he be made my true friend.
   44. *to the value*] to the previously agreed amount.
   46. *Take hands*] Shake hands.
   49. *compliment*] ceremony: ironic for the process of buying court
influence.
   50. *pair . . . reconciled now*] The two humours characters, Bias and
Interest, are now reconciled, echoing the subtitle of the play.
   51. *held at distance*] forced to remain far apart.
   51-2. *thoughts . . . money*] thoughts which are even more evil than those
about money.

   1.] The action is continuous, and this line completes metrically the last
line of 4.3.
   caitiff] base.

  Bawd, beggar, gipsy: anything indeed
  But honest woman.
Keep.   What you please, Dame Polish,
  My lady's stroker.
Compass. (Aside) What is here to do?
  The gossips out!
Polish.   Thou art a traitor to me,   5
  An Eve, the apple, and the serpent too:
  A viper, that hast eat a passage through me,
  Through mine own bowels, by thy retchlessness.
Compass. What frantic fit is this? I'll step aside
  And hearken to it.
Polish.   Did I trust thee, wretch,   10
  With such a secret of that consequence,
  Did so concern me and my child, our livelihood
  And reputation? And hast thou undone us
  By thy connivance, nodding in a corner
  And suffering her be got with child so basely?   15
  Sleepy, unlucky hag! Thou bird of night
  And all mischance to me.
Keep.   Good lady empress,
  Had I the keeping of your daughter's clicket
  In charge? Was that committed to my trust?

---

6. apple] *Wha;* Apul *F.* 13. us] *This ed.;* us? *F.* 15. be got] *F3;* begot
F.

---

  2. *gipsy*] thought to be deceitful.
  4. *stroker*] flatterer: cf. stroke *Ep.*, 61.2, perhaps derived from *palpator*,
Plautus, *Menaechmi*, 260 (*H&S*).
  5. *The gossips out*] The two gossips have fallen out.
  6. *Eve . . . apple . . . serpent*] Genesis, 3:1–7.
  7. *viper*] The young were thought to feed on their mother's flesh: Pliny,
Natural History, 10.82.170: cf. *Poet.*, 5.3.327, and *Per.*, 1.1.64.
  8. *retchlessness*] Obsolete form of recklessness.
  9. *frantic*] foolish.
  fit] outburst.
  14. *connivance*] conniving (with malefactors) (Cotgrave).
  nodding] dozing off.
  16. *bird of night*] owl, bird of ill-omen.
  17. *empress*] ironic: cf. *SW*, 4.4.32–3.
  18. *clicket*] Pun on (1) latch-key, and (2) copulation, used of foxes in
Fletcher and Massinger, *Humorous Lieutenant* (1619), 2.4.173 (*H&S*).

Compass. Her daughter?

Polish.   Softly, devil, not so loud.   20
    You'd ha' the house hear and be witness, would you?

Keep. Let all the world be witness. Afore I'll
    Endure the tyranny of such a tongue—
    And such a pride—

Polish.   What will you do?

Keep.   Tell truth
    And shame the she-man-devil in puffed sleeves;   25
    Run any hazard by revealing all
    Unto my lady: how you changed the cradles
    And changed the children in 'em.

Polish.   Not so high!

Keep. Calling your daughter Pleasance there, Placentia,
    And my true mistress by the name of Pleasance.   30

Compass. A horrid secret, this. Worth the discovery!

Polish. And must you be thus loud?

Keep.   I will be louder
    And cry it through the house, through every room
    And every office of the laundry-maids
    Till it be borne hot to my lady's ears.   35
    Ere I will live in such a slavery
    I'll do away myself.

Polish.   Didst thou not swear
    To keep it secret? And upon what book?
    I do remember now: *The Practice of Piety.*

Keep. It was a practice of impiety   40
    Out of your wicked forge, I know it now,

---

31. discovery!] *H&S;* discovery; *F.*

24–5. *Tell . . . she-man-devil*] proverbial (Dent T566: 'speak the truth and
shame the devil'): cf. *DA*, 5.8.142–3.

    she-man-devil] Cf. she-friend, *SW*, 2.2.102, and She-man, Overbury, *A
Wife* (*OED* 10b).

    25. *puffed sleeves*] condemned by Stubbes, *Abuses.*

    28. *high*] loud.

    31. *horrid*] revolting.

    discovery] revelation.

    34. *office*] part of a house devoted to household work (*OED* 9).

    39. The Practice of Piety] A popular book of Christian instruction
published by Lewes Bayly, Bishop of Bangor, in 1612.

    41. *forge*] making.

My conscience tells me. First against the infants
To rob them o' their names and their true parents;
T'abuse the neighbourhood, keep them in error;
But most my lady; she has the main wrong: 45
And I will let her know it instantly.
Repentance, if it be true, ne'er comes too late.   [*Exit.*]
Polish. What have I done? Conjured a spirit up
I sha' not lay again? Drawn on a danger
And ruin on myself thus by provoking   50
A peevish fool, whom nothing will pray off
Or satisfy, I fear? Her patience stirred
Is turned to fury. I have run my bark
On a sweet rock, by mine own arts and trust:
And must get off again, or dash in pieces.   [*Exit.*]   55
Compass. This was a business worth the listening after.

ACT 4   SCENE 5

[*Enter*] PLEASANCE.

Pleasance. O, Master Compass, did you see my mother?
Mistress Placentia, my lady's niece,
Is newly brought to bed o'the bravest boy!
Will you go see it?
Compass.   First, I'll know the father
Ere I approach these hazards.
Pleasance.   Mistress midwife   5

47.1] G.   55.1] G.

---

47. *Repentance . . . late*] proverbial (Tilley R80 cites this: originally Aesop, *Fables*, 'The Tortoise and the Eagle').

48–9. *Conjured . . . lay*] summoned a spirit whom I shall not be able to dismiss: possibly bawdy as at *NI*, 3.2.250.

lay] drive away.

48–55.] Polish is trapped by her own device here as Sir Moth is later over the dowry, the 'double break', 5.10.112.

51. *peevish*] malignant (*OED* 2).

pray off] persuade to desist.

53. *bark*] ship.

54. *sweet*] pleasant, used ironically.

3. *bravest*] Cf. 4.2.7n.

Has promised to find out a father for it
If there be need.
Compass.   She may the safelier do't
By virtue of her place. But, pretty Pleasance,
I have a news for you I think will please you.
Pleasance. What is't, Master Compass?
Compass.   Stay, you must   10
Deserve it ere you know it. Where's my lady?
Pleasance. Retired unto her chamber, and shut up.
Compass. She hears o' none o' this yet? Well, do you
Command the coach; and fit yourself to travel
A little way with me.
Pleasance.   Whither, for God's sake?   15
Compass. Where I'll entreat you not to your loss, believe it,
If you dare trust yourself.
Pleasance.   With you the world o'er.
Compass. The news will well requite the pains, I assure you.
And i' this tumult you will not be missed.
Command the coach: it is an instant business   20
Wu' not be done without you.   [*Exit* PLEASANCE.]

[*Enter* PALATE.]

Parson Palate,
Most opportunely met! Step to my chamber:
I'll come to you presently. There is a friend
Or two will entertain you.   [*Exit* PALATE.]

[*Enter* PRACTICE.]

Master Practice,
Ha' you the licence?   25

7. do't] *Wha;* do'r *F.*   14. travel] *Fc;* travell? *Fu.*   15. sake?] *Fc;* sake.
Fu.   21. S.Ds.] *G.*   22. met! Step] *This ed.;* met, step *F.*   24. you.
Master Practice,] *Fc;* you, Mr. *Practice. Fu.*   24. S.Ds.] *G.*

---

6. *find . . . father*] produce a father (not necessarily the true one).
7–8.] The midwife's trade will enable her better to discover the father, or
even conjure one up; see Introduction, p. 32.
9. *a news*] a piece of news; cf. *OED* news 2 and 3.
11. *Deserve it*] earn it.
16. *entreat*] beg you to come.
20. *instant*] urgent.
21. *Wu'*] will.
24. *entertain*] receive (*OED* 12).

ACT 4   SCENE 6

Practice.   Here it is.
Compass.   Let's see it:
   Your name's not in't.
Practice.   I'll fill that presently;
   It has the seal, which is the main; and registered.
   The clerk knows me, and trusts me.
Compass.   Ha' you the parson?
Practice. They say he's here; he 'pointed to come hither.   5
Compass. I would not have him seen here for a world,
   To breed suspicion. Do you intercept him,
   And prevent that. But take your licence with you
   And fill the blank: or leave it here with me;
   I'll do it for you. Stay you for us at his church   10
   Behind the Old Exchange; we'll come i'th' coach
   And meet you there within this quarter at least.
Practice. I am much bound unto you, Master Compass;
   You have all the law, and parts of Squire Practice
   For ever at your use. I'll tell you news too.   15
   Sir, your reversion's fallen: Thinwit's dead,
   Surveyor of the projects general.
Compass. When died he?
Practice.   E'en this morning. I received it
   From a right hand.

4.6] *Practise. Compasse. Pleasance. Palate. F.*   3. registered] *Wi;* resgistred
Fu; registred *Fc.*   7. suspicion] *Wha;* supition *F.*   8. take] *Fc;* trke. *Fu.*
10. you.] *This ed.;* you, *F.*   for us] *Wha;* with us *F.*   11. i'th'] *Wha;* i'th
F.   18. E'en] *This ed.;* Eene *F.*

1.] The action is continuous and this line completes the last line of 4.5
metrically.
   3. *the main*] the most important thing.
   5. *'pointed*] appointed.
   10. *Stay you*] wait (imperative).
   11. *Old Exchange*] The Royal Exchange between Cornhill and Threadneedle Street was superseded in 1609 by the New Exchange: cf. *DA*, 2.1.21.
The *church* was probably St Bartholemew (Chalfant, p. 75).
   12. *quarter*] of an hour.
   14. *parts*] abilities.
   16. *reversion*] right of succeeding to an office: cf. 'the reversion of some
great man's place', Webster, *The Duchess of Malfi*, 3.1.14.
   17. *projects*] monopolies; cf. projector, *DA*, 1.7.5n.
   19. *a right hand*] an indispensable aide (*OED* 1c): cf. *Staple*, 3.2.83.

Compass.   Conceal it, Master Practice,
And mind the main affair you are in hand with.   20
                                    [*Exit* PRACTICE.]

                    [*Enter* PLEASANCE.]

Pleasance. The coach is ready, sir.
Compass.   'Tis well, fair Pleasance,
Though now we shall not use it; bid the coachman
Drive to the parish church, and stay about there,
Till Master Practice come to him and employ him.
                                    [*Exit* PLEASANCE.]
I have a licence now which must have entry   25
Before my lawyer's.

                    [*Enter* PALATE.]

                            Noble Parson Palate,
Thou shalt be a mark advanced: here's a piece
And do a feat for me.
Palate.   What, Master Compass?
Compass. But run the words of matrimony over
My head and Mistress Pleasance's in my chamber.   30
There's Captain Ironside to be a witness:
And here's a licence to secure thee. Parson,
What do you stick at?
Palate.   It is afternoon, sir,
Directly against the canon of the church.
You know it, Master Compass; and beside   35
I am engaged unto our worshipful friend,
The learned Master Practice, in that business.

20.1] *Both G.*   24.1] *G.*   26. S.D.] *G.*   32. Parson,] *G; Parson! F.*

20. *mind*] remember.
in hand with] actively concerned with.
25–6. *which . . . lawyer's*] which must be registered before my lawyer's
licence.
26–7.] Play upon values of coins: perhaps a hit at Palate's mercenary
nature. 1 *noble* (6s 8d) + 1 *mark* (13s 4d) = 1 *piece* (£1).
28. *a feat*] some business.
29. *run*] speak.
34. *canon*] formal law: perhaps a hit at Archbishop Laud's strict regime.

Compass. Come on, engage yourself: who shall be able
　　To say you married us but i' the morning,
　　The most canonical minute o' the day   40
　　If you affirm it? That's a spiced excuse,
　　And shows you have set the common law before
　　Any profession else of love or friendship.

　　　　　　　　　　[*Enter* PLEASANCE.]

　　Come, Mistress Pleasance, we cannot prevail
　　With th'rigid parson here; but sir, I'll keep you   45
　　Locked in my lodging till't be done elsewhere
　　And under fear of Ironside.
Palate.   Do you hear, sir?
Compass. No, no, it matters not.
Palate.   Can you think, sir,
　　I would deny you anything? Not to loss
　　Of both my livings: I will do it for you.   50
　　Ha' you a wedding ring?
Compass.   Ay, and a posy:
　　Annulus hic nobis, quod scit uterque, dabit.
Palate.   Good!
　　'This ring will give you what you both desire.'
　　I'll make the whole house chant it, and the parish.

---

42. common] *F;* canon *F3.*   43.1] *G.*   46. till't] *This ed.;* 'till't *F.*

38. *engage yourelf*] commit yourself, playing upon Palate's 'engaged'
(l. 36).
38–9. *who . . . morning*] who will be able to tell that you did not marry us
in the morning?
40. *most canonical*] the most legal, ecclesiatically speaking.
41. *spiced*] over-scrupulous: cf. *BF*, 1.3.121, and Chaucer, *Gen. Prol.*, 526.
42. *common law*] Compass means that Palate is using false scruples to
prefer the law, in the person of Practice, before love and friendship, his true
spiritual obligations.
43. *profession*] religious vow.
49. *Not to loss*] not [even if it amounts] to the loss.
50. *livings*] Apparently he is the incumbent of two livings simultaneously.
51. *posy*] a motto engraved on the ring: cf. 'the poesie of a ring', *Ham.*,
3.2.162.
52–4.] The translation by Compass does not fit the (untraced) Latin
closely: 'This ring will give to us what each knows'; it may suggest ironically
that they each do not know the other's identity.
54. *chant*] possibly a reference to Laudian church music.

Compass. Why, well said, parson. Now to you my news   55
    That comprehend my reasons, Mistress Pleasance.
                                           [*Exeunt.*]

ACT 4   SCENE 7

[*Enter*] CHAIR, NEEDLE, POLISH [*and*] KEEP.

Chair. Go, get a nurse; procure her at what rate
    You can: and out o'th' house with it, son Needle.
    It is a bad commodity.
Needle.   Good mother,
    I know it, but the best would now be made on't.
Chair. And shall.   [*Exit* NEEDLE.]
         You should not fret so, Mistress Polish,   5
    Nor you, Dame Keep: my daughter shall do well
    When she has ta'en my caudle. I ha' known
    Twenty such breaches pieced up, and made whole
    Without a bum of noise. You two fall out?
    And tear up one another?
Polish.   Blessèd woman!   10
    'Blest be the peacemaker.'

56.1] *G.*

0.1] *Enter Mother Chair with a child . . . G; not in F.*   5. S.D.] *This ed.; Exit
with the child.: G adds at l. 4, for Needle: see Notes 4.7.2.*   10. another?] *Fc;*
another. *Fu.*   11. Blest . . . peacemaker] *italics, F.*

---

56. *comprehend*] contain: the 'news' (his discovery about her parentage)
will include the reasons for action.

2. *it*] The baby. *F* does not show that the baby was actually on stage: *G*
modified 4.7.0.1, and 4.7.5 SD to do so.

3. *commodity*] piece of goods; cf. 4.3.3n.

4. *best . . . on't*] proverbial (Tilley B326: 'Make the best of a bad bargain').
would] should.
on't] of it.

7. *caudle*] warm, spiced potion of gruel and wine, used for women in
child-bed (*OED*): cf. E. Blackfriars, ll. 88–9.

8. *pieced up*] mended: cf. 3.1.14n. Possibly physical repairs are in mind to
'restore' Placentia's innocence.

9. *bum*] hum: not in *OED* except as v^2 to hum loudly, to boom. *H&S*
suggest 'explosion' (unsupported). There is also a play upon breaches/
breeches (l. 8) and bum: and Chair has 'needle' in mind.

11. *Blest . . . peacemaker*] proverbial (Dent P155: 'blessed are the peace-

Keep.   The pease-dresser!
I'll hear no peace from her. I have been wronged,
So has my lady, my good lady's worship,
And I will right her, hoping she'll right me.

Polish. Good gentle Keep, I pray thee, Mistress Nurse,   15
Pardon my passion, I was misadvised;
Be thou yet better by this grave, sage woman
Who is the mother of matrons and great persons,
And knows the world.

Keep.   I do confess she knows
Something—and I know something—

Polish.   Put your somethings   20
Together then.

Chair.   Ay, here's a chance fallen out
You cannot help; less can this gentlewoman;
I can and will, for both. First, I have sent
By-chop away; the cause gone, the fame ceaseth.
Then by my caudle, and my cullise, I set   25
My daughter on her feet, about the house here:
She's young, and must stir somewhat for necessity.
Her youth will bear it out. She shall pretend
T'have had a fit o'the mother: there is all.

---

makers', from the Sermon on the Mount, Matthew, 5: 9).

11–12. *peacemaker . . . peace*] Pun on (1) peace and (2) peas; see next.

12. *pease-dresser*] one who prepares peas for cooking.

14. *I . . . her*] I will see she (Lady Loadstone) is treated fairly.

16. *misadvised*] wrongly advised.

24. *By-chop*] bastard (*OED*, first here), on the analogy of by-blow (*chop*, blow).

cause . . . ceaseth] Once remove the cause the talk about it will disappear.

fame] common talk, public report.

25. *cullise*] strong meat broth: cf. coulis (Cotgrave).

26. *My*] Placentia is not her real daughter, but Chair's authority is extensive: cf. oracle (l. 16), and 'my dear mother' (Polish, l. 47).

27. *stir*] rouse herself (*OED* 2).

28. *Her . . . out*] Being young she is strong enough to do it.

29. *mother*] hysteria (derived from *uterus*, in that the womb was considered to be the source of uncontrollable behaviour in women): cf. 'They do use for the accident [occasion] of the mother to burn feathers: and by those ill smells the rising of the mother is put down', Bacon, *Sylva* (quoted *OED* 11b). For a further application, see 5.1.12.

If you have but a secretary laundress   30
To blanch the linen—Take the former counsels
Into you; keep them safe i' your own breasts;
And make your market of 'em at the highest.
Will you go peach, and cry yourself a fool
At Grannam's Cross? Be laughed at and despised?   35
Betray a purpose, which the deputy
Of a double ward, or scarce his alderman
With twelve of the wisest questmen could find out,
Employed by the authority of the city?
Come, come, be friends, and keep these women-matters   40
Smock-secrets to ourselves, in our own verge.
We shall mar all, if once we ope the mysteries
O'the tiring house, and tell what's done within:
No theatres are more cheated with appearances
Or these shop-lights than th'age is, and folk in them,   45

---

44. appearances] apparences *F.*   45. than th'age is] *This ed.;* then th'Ages
F. See Notes.

---

30. *secretary*] secret, one who keeps confidences or secrets: cf. 'secretary
Pru', *NI*, 1.6.25.

33. *make . . . highest*] sell at the best price available.

34. *peach*] turn informer (*OED* cites this).
cry] proclaim.

35. *Grannam's Cross*] a public place such as a market cross: cf. Weeping
Cross, *CR*, 5.11.147.

36. *deputy*] member of Common Council of London who acted on behalf
of an alderman: cf. *2H4*, 2.4.92.

37. *scarce*] even.

38. *questmen*] elected officials of London Wards charged with investigat-
ing misdemeanours.

41. *Smock-secrets*] women's secrets. *OED*, smock 2b, points out that
'smock-' was very common in seventeenth-century dramatists.

verge] jurisdiction, from Court of the Verge which extended for 12
miles round the King's residence, *EMO*, 4.4.18. It will not have escaped
Jonson that *virga* (Lat.) meant penis, as did the obsolete English *verge* (*OED*
sb¹.1a).

43. *tiring house*] theatre dressing-rooms: cf. *Poet.*, 5.3.577–8.

44. *cheated with appearances*] betrayed by being revealed.

45. *shop-lights*] Darkness in shops to deceive purchasers about goods
on sale: mentioned in Stubbes, *Abuses*, 2.24 (*H&S*). Cf. small windows
allowing poor light into shops (*OED* 9c 1631).

than th'age is] An unexplained textual crux. The whole sentence may mean
that obscure mysteries must be maintained, for to reveal them spoils them:
hence theatres and shop-lights are betrayed if revealed, as would be the whole
truth of the time (age).

That seem most curious.
Polish.   Breath of an oracle!
You shall be my dear mother; wisest woman
That ever tipped her tongue with point of reasons
To turn her hearers! Mistress Keep, relent,
I did abuse thee. I confess to penance,   50
And on my knees ask thee forgiveness.   [*Kneels.*]
Chair.   Rise.
She doth begin to melt, I see it—
Keep.   Nothing
Grieved me so much as when you called me bawd:
Witch did not trouble me, nor gipsy: no,
Nor beggar. But a bawd was such a name!   55
Chair. No more rehearsals; repetitions
Make things the worse. The more we stir—you know
The proverb, and it signifies—a stink . . .
What's done and dead, let it be burièd.
New hours will fit fresh handles to new thoughts.   60
                                        [*Exeunt.*]

ACT 4   SCENE 8

[*Enter*] INTEREST *with his* FOOTBOY.

Interest. Run to the church, sirrah. Get all the drunkards

50. penance,] *G;* pennance: *F.*   51. S.D.] *G.*   53. Grieved] *cw p. 49* ¹e
reversed in some copies of F. Page 50 wrongly numbered 52, in some copies of F.
58. signifies—a stink . . .] *This ed.;* signifies a) stink. *F.*   60. fit] *Wha; sit*
F.   60.1] *G.*

4.8.0.1] *Interest,* with his Foot-boy. To them *Compasse. Ironside. (/) Silkworme.
Palate. Pleasance.* To them the *(/) Lady:* and after *Practise. F, centred. Silkworme
instead of Diaphanous, F.*

48. *tipped . . . reasons*] given her speech persuasive reasons, like arrow tips.
49. *turn*] persuade.
50. *to penance*] as far as to do penance.
55. *such*] such a terrible.
56. *rehearsals*] repeating, going over the same ground.
57–8. *The more . . . stink*] proverbial (Tilley S862: 'The more you stir the
more you stink').
59. *done . . . buried*] perhaps proverbial: cf. 'what's done is done', *Mac.,*
3.2.12.
60. *handles*] In time fresh thoughts will have more power: perhaps proverbial, but usually 'old' thoughts.

To ring the bells, and jangle them for joy.
My niece hath brought an heir unto the house,
A lusty boy.   [*Exit* FOOTBOY.]
          Where's my sister Loadstone?

          [*Enter* LADY LOADSTONE.]

Asleep at afternoons! It is not wholesome;   5
Against all rules of physic, lady sister.
The little doctor will not like it. Our niece
Is new delivered of a chopping child
Can call the father by the name already
If it but ope the mouth round. Master Compass,   10
He is the man, they say, fame gives it out,
Hath done that act of honour to our house
And friendship, to pump out a son and heir
That shall inherit nothing, surely nothing
From me at least.

          [*Enter* COMPASS.]

               I come t'invite your ladyship   15
To be a witness; I will be your partner
And give it a horn spoon and a treen dish,
Bastard, and beggar's badges, with a blanket
For dame the doxy to march round the circuit

---

4. S.D.] *G.*   4.1] *G.*   13. pump] *Wha;* pompe *F.*   15. S.D.] *G.*

5. *at*] during; cf. *OED* at 29.
8. *chopping*] vigorous.
10. *ope . . . round*] drawing a fanciful and malicious link between the
baby's open round mouth and the circle of Compass, allegedly its father.
13. *pump*] conceive, with sexual implications as in *Alc.*, 4.3.44.
14. *inherit*] Illegitimate children inherited virtually nothing.
15. SD] Compass's entry begins the *catastasis*: cf. cheat, 4 Chor.28n.
16. *witness*] Puritan word for godmother: cf. 'they will not be called
godmothers', *BF*, 1.3.127.
partner] as a godparent.
17. *horn spoon*] spoon cheaply made of horn instead of the conventional
two apostle-spoons given as christening gift as at *BF*, 1.3.99–100.
treen dish] bowl made of wood (treen O.E.).
18. *badges*] Vagrants had the letter V fastened on their breasts (Peck).
19. *dame the doxy*] madam slut; cf. *Alc.*, 3.3.23.
march . . . circuit] shamed prostitutes and adultresses were made to walk
or run round the parish behind a cart.

With bag and baggage.

Compass.   Thou malicious knight,   20
Envious Sir Moth, that eats on that which feeds thee
And frets her goodness that sustains thy being;
What company of mankind would own thy brotherhood
But as thou hast a title to her blood
Whom thy ill nature hath chose out t'insult on   25
And vex thus for an accident in her house
As if it were her crime? Good, innocent lady!
Thou show'st thyself a true corroding vermin
Such as thou art.
Interest.   Why, gentle Master Compass?
Because I wish you joy of your young son   30
And heir to the house you ha' sent us?
Compass.   I ha' sent you?
I know not what I shall do. Come in, friends:

    [*Enter* DIAPHANOUS, IRONSIDE, PALATE *and*
                    PLEASANCE.]

Madam, I pray you be pleased to trust yourself
Unto our company.
Lady.   I did that too late
Which brought on this calamity upon me   35

---

27. lady!] *G;* Lady, *F.*   32.1] *G: see Notes.*

---

21. *eats . . . thee*] proverbial (*ODEP*: 'To bite the hand that feeds you', p. 62 (first in 1711)).

22. *frets*] gnaws (*OED* v¹ 2 and 3).

her] Lady Loadstone's.

23. *own*] acknowledge.

brotherhood] state of being a brother to Loadstone.

24. *But as*] Except that.

title] claim, legal right.

25. *insult on*] triumph over.

28. *Thou*] i.e. Interest.

corroding] eating into: but there may be a pun on *corrody*, the right of free quarters from a lord or religious house.

31. *I ha' sent you?*] Interest sustains his bluff.

32.1] This SD follows *G* in naming Pleasance. She does not speak in the scene, but Compass presents her to Lady Loadstone at l. 61.

34. *too late*] too recently.

With all the infamy I hear; your soldier
That swaggering guest.
Compass.   Who is returned here to you,
  Your vowed friend and servant; comes to sup with you
  So we do all; and 'll prove he hath deserved
  That special respect and favour from you   40
  As not your fortunes with yourself to boot
  Cast on a feather-bed and spread o'th' sheets
  Under a brace of your best Persian carpets
  Were scarce a price to thank his happy merit.
Interest. What impudence is this? Can you endure   45
  To hear it, sister?
Compass.   Yes, and you shall hear it,
  Who will endure it worse. What deserves he
  In your opinion, madam, or weighed judgement
  That—things thus hanging, as they do, in doubt,
  Suspended and suspected, all involved,   50
  And wrapped in error—can resolve the knot;
  Redintegrate the fame, first of your house;
  Restore your ladyship's quiet; render then
  Your niece a virgin, and unvitiated;
  And make all plain and perfect, as it was,   55
  A practice to betray you and your name?
Interest. He speaks impossibilities.
Compass.   Here he stands
  Whose fortune hath done this, and you must thank him:

---

49. as ... doubt,] *Wi;* (as they doe in doubt) *F.*   51–4. knot; ... house;
... quiet; ... unvitiated;] *This ed.; all with* (?) *F.*

---

37. *swaggering*] quarrelsome.
41. *yourself*] Compass's forthright sexual imagery anticipates the union
between Loadstone and Ironside: cf. the Boy on 'the stream of the
argument', 3 Chor.6.
to boot] in addition.
43. *Persian carpets*] covers for beds and tables.
47. *Who ... worse*] You [Interest] will suffer worse than Loadstone.
52. *Redintegrate*] restore (Lat.).
53. *render*] restore.
54. *unvitiated*] unspoiled (first in *OED*).
56. *practice*] device.

To what you call his swaggering we owe all this.
And that it may have credit with you, madam,   60
Here is your niece, whom I have married, witness
These gentlemen, the knight, captain and parson,
And this grave politic tell-truth of the Court.
Lady. What's she that I call niece then?
Compass.   Polish's daughter;
Her mother, Goodwy' Polish, hath confessed it   65
To Grannam Keep, the nurse, how they did change
The children in their cradles.
Lady.   To what purpose?
Compass. To get the portion, or some part of it,
Which you must now disburse entire to me, sir,
If I but gain her ladyship's consent.   70
Lady. I bid God give you joy, if this be true.
Compass. As true it is, lady, lady, i'th' song.
The portion's mine, with interest, Sir Moth;
I will not 'bate you a single harrington
Of interest upon interest. In mean time   75
I do commit you to the guard of Ironside,
My brother here, Captain Rudhudibras:
From whom I will expect you or your ransom.
Interest. Sir, you must prove it and the possibility
Ere I believe it.

---

64. daughter] *Wha;* Daughter *F;* Daugh *in some copies of F.*   70. consent]
t *damaged in some copies of F.*

59. *swaggering*] quarrelsomeness.
63. *politic tell-truth*] Bias, who tells the truth politically: cf. 2.6.121–31.
65. *Goodwy'*] Goodwife; a respectful form of address, but ironic here.
70. *If I but*] Providing that.
72. *lady, lady*] Though the song is not precisely known, the refrain 'lady, lady' appears in 'There dwelt a man in Babylon', *TwN*, 2.3.80; and in *Horestes* (1567) and *The Trial of Treasure* (1567): see Peter Happé, *Song in Morality Plays and Interludes* (Lancaster, 1991), pp. 88–9, 92–3.
74. *'bate . . . harrington*] allow you one farthing: proverbial (Dent H178: 'not worth a harrington'). See above, 2.6.101n. Cf. *DA*, 2.1.83.
75. *interest upon interest*] even charging interest upon the interest; but there is also a play on the surnames Harrington (l. 74) and Interest.
78. *ransom*] or a ransom instead. This sustains the mockery of romance.
79. *prove . . . possibility*] you must give evidence and show that what you allege were possible.

Compass.   For the possibility   80
    I leave to trial. Truth shall speak itself.

          [*Enter* PRACTICE.]

    O, Master Practice, did you meet the coach?
Practice. Yes sir, but empty.
Compass.   Why, I sent it for you.
    The business is dispatched here, ere you come;
    Come in, I'll tell you how: you are a man   85
    Will look for satisfaction, and must have it.
All. So do we all, and long to hear the right.   [*Exeunt.*]

          [4] CHORUS

          [DAMPLAY, BOY *and* PROBEE.]

Damplay. Troth, I am one of those that labour with the same
    longing, for it is almost puckered and pulled into that
    knot, by your poet, which I cannot easily, with all the
    strength of my imagination, untie.
Boy. Like enough, nor is it in your office to be troubled or   5
    perplexed with it, but to sit still and expect. The more
    your imagination busies itself, the more it is entangled,
    especially if, as I told in the beginning, you happen on
    the wrong end.
Probee. He hath said sufficient, brother Damplay; our parts   10
    that are the spectators, or should hear a comedy, are to
    await the process and events of things, as the poet pre-
    sents them, not as we would corruptly fashion them. We
    come here to behold plays, and censure them, as they are

81.1] G.   87.1] G.

4 CHORUS] *This ed.; Chorus.* F.   0.1] *This ed.*

---

86. *satisfaction*] the atoning for damage to his honour in a duel (*OED* 4).
87. *the right*] rightful outcome.

1–2. *same longing*] for 'right' as in 4.8.87. There is a link between labour
and longing via pregnancy.
    puckered] wrinkled: cf. pucker (Ind.128), and the concept of the plot there.
    6. *perplexed*] confused.
    8–9. *as I told . . . wrong end*] Cf. Ind.133.
    12. *events*] outcome.
    14. *censure*] judge.

made, and fitted for us; not to beslaver our own thoughts,   15
with censorious spittle tempering the poet's clay, as we
were to mould every scene anew: that were a mere plastic
or potter's ambition, most unbecoming the name of a
gentleman. No, let us mark and not lose the business on
foot, by talking. Follow the right thread, or find it.   20

Damplay. Why here his play might have ended if he would ha'
let it; and have spared us the vexation of a fifth Act yet
to come, which everyone here knows the issue of already,
or may in part conjecture.

Boy. That conjecture is a kind of figure-flinging, or throwing   25
the dice for a meaning was never in the poet's purpose
perhaps. Stay, and see his last Act, his *catastrophe*, how he
will perplex that, or spring some fresh cheat to entertain
the spectators with a convenient delight till some unex-
pected and new encounter break out to rectify all, and   30
make good the conclusion.

Probee. Which, ending here, would have shown dull, flat, and
unpointed; without any shape or sharpness, brother
Damplay.

Damplay. Well, let us expect then: and wit be with us o'the   35
poet's part.

---

15. beslaver] *H&S;* beslave *F.*

15. *fitted for*] prepared for.
15–16. *beslaver . . . spittle*] The figure suggests that the audience should
not contaminate the poet's intention by becoming involved in changing the
scenes to make them closer to their own presuppostions.
17. *plastic*] modelling in clay or wax.
20. *thread*] Cf. Ind.130–2.
22. *fifth Act*] Damplay's stricture on the fifth Act is directly opposite to
Jonson's theory and practice concerning surprises in it: cf. Introduction,
pp. 13–15. Donaldson suggests that Jonson was nervous about spectators
leaving before the fifth Act, and that this is a countermeasure (pp. 107–8).
25. *figure-flinging*] astrological calculating.
26. *was*] that was.
27. catastrophe] final turn of events, not necessarily disastrous (from Gk
'overturn').
28. *cheat*] some twist of events against expectation (*catastasis*): cf. 4.8.15n,
and see Introduction, p. 14.
33. *unpointed*] without clear purpose.
35–6. *wit . . . part*] and let the poet's wit help us.

Act 5

[*Enter*] NEEDLE [*and*] ITEM.

Needle. Troth, Master Item, here's a house divided,   4 humours
    And quartered into parts by your doctor's engine.
    H'has cast out such aspersions on my lady's
    Niece here of having had a child, as hardly
    Will be wiped off, I doubt.
Item.   Why, is't not true?   5
Needle. True! Did you think it?
Item.   Was she not in labour?
    The midwife sent for?
Needle.   There's your error now!
    Yo'ha' drunk o' the same water.
Item.   I believed it
    And gave it out too.
Needle.   More you wronged the party;
    She had no such thing about her, innocent creature!   10
Item. What had she then?
Needle.   Only a fit o'the mother!
    They burnt old shoes, goose feathers, *asafoetida*

---

7. *Needle*] *Wha; Ite.* F.   11. *Item*] *Ite. Wha; Iem* F.   *Needle*] *Wha; not
in* F.

---

2. *engine*] F 'ingine', ingenuity.
3. *aspersions*] false insinuations (*OED* 6).
6. *True!*] Though the audience is in no doubt about the baby's existence
Jonson has some characters exploit the uncertainty of others: cf. 5.4.1–11,
and 5.5.33–5.
8. *drunk . . . same water*] of the same state of mind: proverbial (Tilley
W98, and Stevenson 2465.1: 'Let no one say "I will not drink of this
water"', Cervantes, 1615).
9. *gave it out*] reported it.
12. *feathers*] Cf. 4.7.29n.
asafoetida] strong-smelling gum used as antispasmodic; cf. John
Heywood, *Four PP*, l. 620.

A few horn shavings, with a bone or two,
And she is well again, about the house—
Item. Is't possible?
Needle.   See it, and then report it.   15
Item. Our doctor's urinal-judgement is half cracked then.
Needle. Cracked i'the case, most hugely, with my lady
     And sad Sir Moth, her brother; who is now
     Under a cloud a little.
Item.   Of what? Disgrace?
Needle. He is committed to Rudhudibras,   20
     The Captain Ironside, upon displeasure,
     From Master Compass, but it will blow off.
Item. The doctor shall reverse this instantly
     And set all right again, if you'll assist
     But in a toy, Squire Needle, comes i'my noddle now.   25
Needle. Good—Needle and noddle! What may't be? I long
          for't.
Item. Why but to go to bed, feign a distemper
     Of walking i' your sleep, or talking in't
     A little idly, but so much as on't
     The doctor may have ground to raise a cure   30
     For's reputation.
Needle.   Anything to serve
     The worship o' the man I love and honour.   [*Exeunt.*]

---

23. this] *G; his F.*   25. toy,] *F3;* toy; *F.*   29. on't] *This ed.;* on'it *F.*
32.1] *G.*

---

16. *urinal-judgement*] diagnosis by examining urine in a glass vessel.
cracked] Pun on (1) shattered glass and (2) insane (*OED* cracked 5).
17. *case*] Pun on (1) glass container and (2) the patient as a medical case.
19. *Under a cloud*] proverbial (Tilley C441: 'To be under a cloud', 1662, but derived from 1 Corinthians, 10: 1).
20. *committed to*] in the custody of.
25. *toy*] trifling matter.
comes] which comes.
noddle] head (jocular).
27. *distemper*] disorder; associated with being 'out of humour', in former medical terminology (*OED* sb¹, 3 and 4).
29. *idly*] pointlessly.
30–1. *cure . . . reputation*] bring in a cure which will help his reputation, with play on 'cure' the pretended illness.
32. *worship*] good name.

ACT 5   SCENE 2

[Enter] POLISH *[and]* PLEASANCE.

Polish. O! Gi' you joy, Madamoiselle Compass!
　　You are his whirlpool now: all-to-bemarried
　　Against your mother's leave, and without counsel.
　　H'has fished fair and caught a frog, I fear it.
　　What fortune ha' you to bring him in dower?　　　　　5
　　You can tell stories now: you know a world
　　Of secrets to discover.
Pleasance.　　　　　　　I know nothing
　　But what is told me; nor can I discover
　　Anything.
Polish.　　　No, you shall not, I'll take order.
　　Go, get you in there.　　　　　*[Exit* PLEASANCE.]
　　　　　　　　　It is Ember week!　　　　　10
　　I'll keep you fasting from his flesh a while.

[Enter CHAIR, KEEP *with* PLACENTIA.]

Chair. See, who's here? She'has been with my lady
　　Who kissed her, all-to-kissed her, twice or thrice.

---

10. S.D.] *G.*　　11.1] *G.*　　12, 13.] *Verse Wha; prose F.*

---

1. *Gi' you joy*] Appropriate saying to newly married people (*H&S*). Cf. 5.10.23.
　　Madamoiselle] This apparently polite title is not entirely respectful here.
　　2. *whirlpool*] draws all into itself (*OED* Fuller, 1642). Pleasance will draw Compass to her, no doubt with play on circularity, possibly sexual.
　　all-to-bemarried] thoroughly married (*OED* all 15): cf. all-to-be qualify *CR*, 4.3.16. See also l. 13n.
　　3. *Against . . . leave*] Polish knows of the marriage, and she also knows she is not Pleasance's mother. Her chief interest is to hide Placentia's baby; cf. 5.10.23.
　　4. *fished . . . frog*] made a poor catch: proverbial (Dent F767: 'you fish fair and catch a frog'). Cf. *EH*, 4.2.115.
　　5. *dower*] money or property given by the wife to the husband on marriage.
　　7. *discover*] reveal. At this point Polish does not know Compass has discovered her own deception over the infants (in 4.4), but the audience does.
　　9. *take order*] make arrangements to prevent it (*OED* order, 14).
　　10. *Ember week*] There was one week in each season in which the Church ordained fasting on Wednesday, Friday and Saturday: used with sexual implication here: cf. flesh, l. 11.
　　13. *all-to-kissed*] thoroughly kissed: cf. l. 2n.

Needle. And called her niece again, and viewed her linen.

Polish. You ha' done a miracle, Mother Chair.

Chair.   Not I,   15
    My caudle has done it. Thank my caudle heartily.

Polish. It shall be thanked, and you too, wisest mother;
    You shall have a new, brave, four-pound beaver hat
    Set with enamelled studs, as mine is here:
    And a right pair of crystal spectacles   20
    Crystal o'th' rock, thou mighty mother of dames,
    Hung in an ivory case, at a gold belt,
    And silver bells to jingle, as you pace
    Before your fifty daughters in procession
    To church, or from the church.

Chair.   Thanks, Mistress Polish.   25

Keep. She does deserve as many pensions
    As there be pieces in a—maidenhead;
    Were I a prince to give 'em.

Polish.   Come, sweet charge,
    You shall present yourself about the house;
    Be confident and bear up: you shall be seen.   [*Exeunt.*]   30

---

14. viewed her linen] *Italics, F.*   29, 30.] *Prose in F.*   30.1] *G.*

---

14. *viewed her linen*] seen her as again eligible for marriage by inspecting her trousseau: italics in *F.*

18. *four-pound beaver hat*] hat made from beaver fur, like the Merchant's in Chaucer, *Gen. Prol.*, l. 272. *H&S* read 'pound' as money, and cite a hat costing £4 5s (1661); but it may be weight, as in the Wife of Bath's 'coverchiefs' which weighed ten pounds, l. 454.

20. *right*] genuine (*OED* 17c).

21. *Crystal . . . rock*] transparent mineral like ice (actually quartz), once thought to have been permanently congealed ice; cf. 'Though heat dissolve the ice again, / The Crystal solid does remain', Cowley (1647) (*OED* crystal 2).

24. *fifty*] A reference to her professional productivity.

25. *To church*] Perhaps suggested by the Wife of Bath's going to church, *Gen. Prol.*, ll. 449–50.

27. *pieces*] Pun on (1) fragments (2) coins worth £1.

maidenhead] pun on (1) virginity and (2) first fruits which were notionally plentiful (*OED* 1 and 2).

28. *charge*] Placentia: cf. 2.2.1n.

30.1] The stage is cleared here.

ACT 5   SCENE 3

[*Enter*] COMPASS, IRONSIDE [*and*] PRACTICE.

Compass. What? I can make you amends, my learned counsel,
 And satisfy a greater injury
  To chafed Master Practice. Who would think
  That you could be thus testy?
Ironside.   A grave head!
 Gi'n over to the study of our laws.   5
Compass. And the prime honours of the commonwealth.
Ironside. And you to mind a wife.
Compass.   What should you do
 With such a toy as a wife that might distract you
 Or hinder you i'your course?
Ironside.   He shall not think on't.
Compass. I will make over to you my possession   10
 Of that same place is fallen, you know, to satisfy,
 Surveyor of the projects general.
Ironside. And that's an office you know how to stir in.
Compass. And make your profits of.
Ironside.   Which are, indeed,
 The ends of a gowned man: show your activity 15
 And how you are built for business.
Practice.   I accept it
 As a possession, be't but a reversion.
Compass. You first told me 'twas a possession.
Practice.   Ay,
 I told you that I heard so.

---

18. possession] *Wha; P ssession in all copies seen.* 18–19. Ay, / I] *G;* I, *(/)*
I *F.*

---

 3. *chafed*] irritated: cf. *Shrew,* 2.1.243.
 4. *testy*] Cf. 3.6.125n.
 7. *mind*] intend (*OED* 6b).
 10–11. *make . . . fallen*] transfer to you my legal right to the reversion
which has become enforceable.
 13. *stir*] be busy.
 15. *ends*] objectives.
 gowned man] lawyer.
 17. *possession . . . reversion*] Even if Thinwit really is not yet dead, he won't
be long; and Practice will treat the right as established.

Ironside.   All is one;
He'll make reversion a possession quickly.   20
Compass. But I must have a general release from you.
Practice. Do one; I'll do the other.
Compass.   It's a match
Before my brother Ironside.
Practice.   'Tis done.
Compass. We two are reconciled then.
Ironside.   To a lawyer
That can make use of a place, any half title   25
Is better than a wife.
Compass.   And will save charges
Of coaches, vellute gowns, and cut-work smocks.
Ironside. He is to occupy an office wholly.
Compass. True, I must talk with you nearer, Master Practice,
About recovery o'my wife's portion,   30
What way I were best to take.
Practice.   The plainest way.
Compass. What's that, for plainness?
Practice.   Sue him at common law:
Arrest him on an action of choke-bail,

---

30. wife's] *Wha;* wives *F.*

21. *release*] legal declaration that the restraining conditions no longer apply.

22. *one . . . other*] the possession (l. 10), and the release (l. 21).

23. *Before . . . Ironside*] as witness.

'Tis done] concealed stage direction for a handshake.

24. *reconciled*] in accordance with the play's subtitle.

25. *place*] office or position of influence.

half title] half a claim, which can be exploited legally.

27. *vellute*] velvet.

cut-work smocks] gowns with fashionable open-work embroidery (*OED* cut-work 2b); cf. Burton, *Anatomy*, 2.2.4.

28. *He . . . wholly*] He will be entirely and solely concerned with the office.

29. *nearer*] more closely.

33. *choke-bail*] legal device for preventing bail being allowed by demanding the deposit of an impossibly large sum (*OED*, choke- 2, first here; possibly a Jonson coinage). Such demands were one of the ways of avoiding *Habeas Corpus*, and this matter was of concern to Chief Justice Coke under James I. The abuse caused much wrangling through the seventeenth century and eventually it was restrained in the Bill of Rights (1689).

Five hundred thousand pound; it will affright him
And all his sureties. You can prove your marriage?
Compass.   Yes.   35
We'll talk of it within, and hear my lady.   [*Exeunt.*]

ACT 5 SCENE 4

[*Enter*] INTEREST [*and*] LADY [LOADSTONE].

Interest. I'm sure the vogue o'the house went all that way;
       She was with child, and Master Compass got it.
Lady. Why that you see is manifestly false,
       H'has married the other, our true niece, he says.
       He would not woo 'em both: he is not such   5
       A stallion to leap all. Again, no child
       Appears that I can find with all my search
       And strictest way of enquiry I have made
       Through all my family. A fit o'the mother
       The women say she had, which the midwife cured   10
       With burning bones and feathers.

Enter DOCTOR [RUT].

                              Here's the doctor.
Interest. O, noble doctor, did not you and your Item
       Tell me our niece was in labour?
Rut.   If I did
       What follows?
Interest.   And that Mother Midnight
       Was sent for?
Rut.   So she was; and is i'the house still.   15

---

1. I'm] *Wha;* I'am *F.*   vogue] *Wha;* Rogue *F.*   11. S.D.] *in right margin,*
F.

---

35. *sureties*] those who support him with a deposit, but would fear that
they would lose their money.

1. *vogue*] current belief (*OED* 5b).
6. *leap*] copulate with: cf. *DA*, 3.3.31.
Again] on the other hand.
9. *A fit . . . mother*] a fit of hysteria; cf. 4.7.29n. Pun on (1) female parent;
and (2) hysteria.
14. *Mother Midnight*] Midwife, often a bawd (*H&S*).

Interest. But here has a noise been since: she was delivered
　Of a brave boy, and Master Compass's getting.
Rut. I know no rattle of gossips, nor their noises.　*[handwritten: Where's the baby?]*
　I hope you take not me for a pimp errant
　To deal in smock affairs? Where's the patient?　　　　　20
　The infirm man I was sent for, Squire Needle?
Lady. Is Needle sick?
Rut.　　　　　　My 'pothecary tells me
　He is in danger.

　　　　　　　Enter TIM.

　　　　How is't Tim? Where is he?
Item. I cannot hold him down. He's up, and walks,
　And talks in his perfect sleep, with his eyes shut,　　　25
　As sensibly as he were broad awake.
Rut. See, here he comes. He's fast asleep, observe him.

　　　　　　ACT 5   SCENE 5

　　　[Enter] NEEDLE, POLISH, CHAIR, KEEP *[and]*
　　　　　　　PLACENTIA.

Rut. He'll tell us wonders. What do these women here?
　Hunting a man half naked? You are fine beagles!
　You'd have his doucets.
Needle.　　　　　　I ha' linen breeks on.

23. S.D.] *in right margin, F. (Always* Item *elsewhere, as in l. 24.)*

5.5] *H&S; scene begins at line 2 in F. G has continuous action, with the entry after 5.4.27.*

―――――――――――――――――――――――――

　16. *noise*] rumour: more likely than simply loud sound in view of l. 18.
　18. *gossips*] godparents, or those who gossip.
　19. *pimp errant*] wandering pimp, but errant puns on (1) doing wrong, and (2) wandering like an amorous, heroic knight.
　20. *smock affairs*] matters concerning women: cf. 4.7.41n.
　21. *infirm*] sick.
　25. *perfect*] sound.
　26. *sensibly*] as though in control of his senses.

　2. *fine beagles*] hounds noted for skill in scent and resonant voices: cf. *TwN*, 2.3.179.
　3. *doucets*] testicles of a deer; cf. *SS*, 1.6.7, and Beaumont and Fletcher, *Philaster*, 4.2.13.
　breeks] breeches.

Rut. He hears, but he sees nothing.

Needle.   Yes, I see
   Who hides the treasure yonder.

Interest.   Ha? What treasure?   5

Rut. If you ask questions, he 'wakes presently:
   And then you'll hear no more till his next fit.

Needle. And whom she hides it for.

Rut.   Do you mark, sir? List.

Needle. A fine she spirit it is, an Indian magpie.
   She was an alderman's widow, and fell in love   10
   With our Sir Moth, my lady's brother.

Rut.   Hear you?

Needle. And she has hid an alderman's estate;
   Dropped through her bill in little holes i'the garden
   And scrapes earth over 'em, where none can spy
   But I, who see all by the glow-worm's light   15
   That creeps before.

Polish.   I knew the gentlewoman,
   Alderman Parrot's widow, a fine speaker
   As any was i'the clothing or the bevy;
   She did become her scarlet, and black velvet,
   Her green and purple—
      [*Exeunt* NEEDLE, CHAIR, KEEP *and* PLACENTIA.]

Rut.   Save thy colours, rainbow,   20
   Or she will run thee over, and all thy lights.

11. Hear you?] *in parenthesis,* F.   20. S.D.] *Wi. This stage direction after before (l. 16) G.*

---

4. *He . . . nothing*] He can hear but not see: Needle contradicts.

6. *presently*] at once.

9. *Indian magpie*] hoarding magpie, referring to acquisitive colonial traders.

11. *Hear you*] in parenthesis in *F* as an aside.

13. *bill*] as though a bird: perhaps a magpie, l. 9, or a parrot, l. 17.

15. *glow-worm's*] contrary to the Ghost's reference in *Ham.*, 1.5.89, only the female emits a glow.

18. *clothing*] livery of a Company (*OED* 2d): cf. *Alc.*, 1.3.36.

bevy] company of maidens or ladies: cf. *H8*, 1.4.4.

19. *scarlet*] originally a rich cloth which could be in several colours besides bright red; used for ceremonial dress.

21. *run thee over*] obscure: perhaps go over quickly (*OED* 67b) and dismiss as trifling, using the idea of the rainbow as being above or over everything.

lights] pun on (1) lungs and (2) opinions (*OED* lights, and light 6b, the latter ironic here).

Polish. She dwelt in Doolittle Lane, atop o'the hill there,
　　I'the round cage was after Sir Chime Squirrel's.
　　She would eat naught but almonds, I assure you.
Rut. Would thou hadst a dose of pills, a double dose　　　25
　　O'the best purge, to make thee turn tale tother way.
Polish. You are a foul-mouthed, purging, absurd doctor;
　　I tell you true, and I did long to tell it you.
　　You ha' spread a scandal i' my lady's house here
　　On her sweet niece you never can take off　　　　　30
　　With all your purges, or your plaster of oaths;
　　Though you distil your damn-me, drop by drop
　　I' your defence. That she hath had a child
　　Here she doth spit upon thee, and defy thee,
　　Or I do't for her.
Rut.　　　　　　　Madam, pray you bind her　　　35
　　To her behaviour. Tie your gossip up
　　Or send her unto Bedlam.
Polish.　　　　　　　Go thou thither
　　That better hast deserved it, shame of doctors:
　　Where could she be delivered? By what charm?
　　Restored to her strength so soon? Who is the father?　　40

---

39. charm?] *F;* charm, *Wha.*

---

22. *Doolittle Lane*] small passage off Knightrider Street and Carter Lane, south of St Paul's (Chalfant, p. 68).

23. *after*] in the style of.
Sir Chime Squirrel's] From a type of cage for squirrels with chiming bells.

24. *almonds*] Cf. 5.7.42.

26. *tale*] pun on (1) tale, Polish's chattering narrative and (2) tail for posterior—hence 'foul-mouthed, purging', l. 27.

31. *plaster of oaths*] remedies which depended upon oaths sworn to the contrary.

32. *distil*] extract by heating and condensing for medical purposes. Polish means, fancifully, that even the purest oath (such as 'damn me') sworn by Rut against Placentia will not do.

33-5. *That . . . her*] Here, in her place, I spit upon you in defiance of your accusation that she has had a child.

34. *spit . . . defy*] Perhaps proverbial: cf. 'I do defy him, and I spit at him', *R2*, 1.1.60, and 'as she spit in his face, so she defied him', *Meas.*, 2.1.84.

35. *bind*] constrain.

37. *Bedlam*] a hospital for the insane in the parish of Bishopsgate Without on the north-eastern edge of the City of London.

> Or where the infant? Ask your oracle
> That walks and talks in his sleep.

Rut.   Where is he? Gone?
> You ha' lost a fortune listening to her tabor.
> Good madam, lock her up.

Lady.   You must give losers
> Their leave to speak, good doctor.

Rut.   Follow his footing   45
> Before he get to his bed: the rest is lost else.

> > [*Exit with* INTEREST.]

ACT 5   SCENE 6

[*Enter*] COMPASS, PRACTICE [*and*] IRONSIDE.

Compass. Where is my wife? What ha' you done with my wife,
> Gossip o'the counsels?

Polish.   I, sweet Master Compass?
> I honour you, and your wife.

Compass.   Well, do so still.
> I will not call you mother though, but Polish.
> Good Gossip Polish, where ha' you hid my wife?   5

Polish. I hide your wife?

Compass.   Or she's run away.

Lady. That would make all suspected, sir, afresh.
> Come we will find her, if she be i'the house.

Polish. Why should I hide your wife, good Master Compass?

Compass. I know no cause but that you are goody Polish,   10

43. to her] *Wha;* to her, to her *F.*   46.1] *Wi.*

2. counsels?] Counsels. *Fu;* Counsels? *Fc.*   10. goody] *Wha;* goo'dy *F.*

---

41. *oracle*] i.e. Needle.
43. *tabor*] drum, but here figuratively for 'tongue'.
44–5. *losers . . . speak*] proverbial (Tilley L458: 'Give losers leave to speak'). Cf. *SW*, 2.4.39–40n.
45. *his footing*] Needle's track (*OED* 2).

2. *Gossip . . . counsels*] companion of those 'in the know'.
4. *I will . . . though*] A reminder that Polish is not Pleasance's mother, or Compass's mother-in-law.

That's good at malice; good at mischief; all
That can perplex or trouble a business throughly.
Polish. You may say what you will: you're Master Compass,
And carry a large sweep, sir, i' your circle.
Lady. I'll sweep all corners, gossip, to spring this,   15
If't be above ground. I will have her cried
By the common crier, through all the ward,
But I will find her.
Ironside.   It will be an act
Worthy your justice, madam.
Practice.   And become
The integrity and worship of her name.   [*Exeunt.*]   20

ACT 5   SCENE 7

[*Enter*] RUT [*and*] INTEREST.

Rut. 'Tis such a fly, this gossip, with her buzz,
She blows on everything, in every place!
Interest. A busy woman is a fearful grievance!
Will he not sleep again?
Rut.   Yes, instantly
As soon as he is warm. It is the nature   5
Of the disease, and all these cold dry fumes
That are melancholic, to work at first
Slow, and insensibly in their ascent,

---

15. this,] *Wha;* this. *F.*   16. ground.] *Wha;* ground, *F.*   20.1] *G.*

12. *throughly*] thoroughly.
14. *sweep*] scope, from movement of the compass.
15. *spring*] cause to appear from cover: *OED* 18 notes figurative use in *BF*, 5.6.21.
16. *cried*] initiate a hue and cry; cf. 'raise hue and cry i'the Hundred', *T of T*, 2.1.94.
17. *common crier*] town official who made announcements.
ward] district of London under the jurisdiction of an alderman.
20. *integrity*] innocence.

2. *blows*] lays eggs, as a fly.
3. *busy*] meddlesome, prying (*OED* 5).
grievance] cause of suffering: cf. *RJ*, 1.1.163.
8. *ascent*] It was believed fumes rose from the stomach into the brain (Peck); see Burton, *Anatomy*, 1.3.3.1.

Till being got up, and then distilling down
Upo' the brain; they have a pricking quality   10
That breeds this restless rest, which we, the sons
Of physic, call a walking in the sleep,
And telling mysteries that must be heard
Softly, with art, as we were sewing pillows
Under the patient's elbows, else they'd fly   15
Into a frenzy, run into the woods
Where there are noises, huntings, shoutings, hallowings
Amidst the brakes and furzes, over bridges;
Fall into waters; scratch their flesh; sometimes
Drop down a precipice, and there be lost.   20

Enter ITEM.

How now! What does he?
Item.   He is up again,
And 'gins to talk.
Interest.   O' the former matter, Item?
Item. The treasure and the lady: that's his argument.
Interest. O me, happy man! He cannot off it.
     I shall know all then.
Rut.   With what appetite   25

---

13. heard] *Wha;* heard. *F.*   18. bridges;] *This ed.;* bridges, *F.*   19.
waters; scratch] *This ed.;* waters: Scratch *F.*   flesh;] *This ed.;* flesh: *F.*
20.1] *in right margin Fc; not in Fu.*   21. he] *Wha;* her *F.*   24. happy] *F;*
most happy *G.*

---

10. *pricking*] used for the sting of an insect (*OED* 3).
     11–12. *sons / Of physic*] followers of the art of medicine. The pompous
title is neatly set off by the enjambment.
     13. *telling mysteries*] The 'quality' (l. 10) breeds (l. 11) the faculty of
revealing mysterious truths.
     must be heard] are so authoritative that they must be considered true.
     14. *as*] as if.
     sewing pillows] requiring great stealth: proverbial (Tilley P329, citing this:
'To sew pillows under one's elbows'). Cf. Ezekiel, 13: 18.
     18. *brakes*] bracken.
     23. *argument*] theme, subject.
     24. *happy*] fortunate to me.
     He . . . it] He is incapable of leaving the subject alone.
     25. *appetite*] craving (*OED* 4b).

Our own desires delude us! Hear you, Tim?
Let no man interrupt us.
Item.   Sir Diaphanous
And Master Bias, his Court friend, desire
To kiss his niece's hands, and gratulate
The firm recovery of her good fame   30
And honour—
Interest.   Good, say to 'em, Master Item,
My niece is on my lady's side: they'll find her there.
I pray to be but spared for half an hour:
I'll see 'em presently.
Rut.   Do, put 'em off, Tim.
And tell 'em the importance of the business.   35

[*Enter* NEEDLE.]

Here, he is come! Sooth, and have all out of him.
Needle. How do you, ladybird? So hard at work still?
What's that you say? Do you bid me walk, sweet bird?
And tell our knight? I will. How? Walk, knave, walk?
I think you're angry with me, Pol. Fine Pol!   40
Pol's a fine bird! O fine Lady Pol!
Almond for parrot; parrot's a brave bird:
Three hundred thousand pieces ha' you stuck
Edge-long into the ground, within the garden?
O, bounteous bird!
Interest.   And me, most happy creature.   45

---

28. friend] *H&S, noting* 5.8.1; *friend's F.*   32. is] *Fc*; is, *Fu.*   35.1] *G.*
45. O,] *H&S*; O' *F.*

29. *gratulate*] rejoice in: cf. *Sej.*, 4.514.

32. *on . . . side*] with my lady.

34. *presently*] in a little while: unusually the meaning here is closer to modern usage.

36. *Sooth*] in truth.

37. *ladybird*] sweetheart: cf. *RJ*, 1.3.3.

39. *Walk, knave, walk*] proverbial: Heywood, *Dial. Provs*, 2.6, Giv, and Tilley K140.

42. *Almond . . . parrot*] proverbial (Tilley A220 cites this). Cf. 5.5.24.
brave] Cf. 2.1.11n.

44. *Edge-long*] on the edge (Cotgrave): a fantasy in which the parrot puts some coins into the ground one by one.

Rut. Smother your joy.

Needle.   How? And dropped twice so many—

Interest. Ha! Where?

Rut.   Contain yourself.

Needle.   I'the old well?

Interest. I cannot: I am a man of flesh and blood.
    Who can contain himself to hear the ghost
    Of a dead lady do such works as these?   50
    And a city lady too, o'the straight waist?

Rut. He's gone.

Needle.   I will go try the truth of it.   [*Exit* NEEDLE.]

Rut. Follow him, Tim: see what he does. If he bring you
    Assay of it now—   [*Exit* ITEM.]

Interest.   I'll say he's a rare fellow,
    And has a rare disease.

Rut.   And I will work   55
    As rare a cure upon him.

Interest.   How, good doctor?

Rut. When he hath uttered all that you would know of him
    I'll cleanse him with a pill, as small as a pease,
    And stop his mouth: for there his issue lies
    Between the muscles o' the tongue.

               [*Enter* ITEM.]

Item.   He's come.   60

Rut. What did he, Item?

Item.   The first step he stepped
    Into the garden he pulled these five pieces

52.1] *G.*   53. see] *Wha; See F.*   does.] *G; does; F.*   54. Assay] *This ed.; A 'ssay F.*   now—] *This ed.; now. F.*   S.D.] *This ed.*   60. S.D.] *Wi, following G.*

---

51. *o'the straight waist*] narrow-fitting corset: cf. 'straight bodied city attire', *Poet.*, 4.1.4.

52. *try*] test.

54. *Assay*] test, proving the truth.

54–6. *rare*] precious, valuable.

58. *pease*] pea (earlier form).

59. *issue*] cause of irritation: cf. *OED* 4.

62. *pieces*] worth £1, as at 4.6.26–7n.

  Up, in a finger's breadth one of another.
  The dirt sticks on 'em still.
Item.   I know enough.
  Doctor, proceed with your cure; I'll make thee famous, 65
  Famous among the sons of the physicians,
  Machaon, Podalirius, Aesculapius.
  Thou shalt have a golden beard as well as he had;
  And thy Tim Item here have one of silver:
  A livery beard. And all thy 'pothecaries 70
  Belong to thee. Where's Squire Needle? Gone?
Item. He's pricked away now he has done the work.
Rut. Prepare his pill, and gi'it him afore supper.
            [*Exit* ITEM.]
Interest. I'll send for a dozen o'labourers tomorrow
  To turn the surface o' the garden up. 75
Rut. In mould? Bruise every clod?
Interest.   And have all sifted;
  For I'll not lose a piece o'the bird's bounty
  And take an inventory of all.
Rut.   And then
  I would go down into the well—
Interest.   Myself—
  No trusting other hands: six hundred thousand 80
  To the first three; nine hundred thousand pound—

73.1] G.

63. *in . . . another*] so close you could not insert a finger between them.

67. *Machaon, Podalirius*] sons of Aesculapius, Greek physicians who fought at Troy (*Iliad*, 2.731–2).

Aesculapius] Roman God of medicine, son of Apollo.

68. *golden beard*] Dionysius ordered that Aesculapius should be suitably endowed with *barbam auream*, Valerius Maximus, *Factorum dictorumque memorabilium*, cap. I, 'De religione', Exempla no. 3 (ed. A. J. Valpy, 3 vols (London, 1823), 1.137).

70. *livery*] a badge which expresses membership of a Company. Later (1778) it means liver-coloured. There is also a play on silver, l. 69.

72. *pricked*] ridden quickly (*OED* 11).

76. *In mould?*] Rut anticipates that the digging will be so vigorous that the earth will be turned into a fine texture suitable for growing.

81. *To . . . three*] Three hundred thousand (l. 43), with twice as much added (l. 46).

Rut. 'Twill purchase the whole bench of aldermanity
    Stripped to their shirts.
Interest.   There never did accrue
    So great a gift to man, and from a lady
    I never saw but once; now I remember   85
    We met at Merchant Tailors Hall at dinner
    In Threadneedle Street—
Rut.   Which was a sign Squire Needle
    Should have the threading of this thread.
Interest.   'Tis true;
    I shall love parrots better, while I know him.
Rut. I'd have her statue cut now in white marble.   90
Interest. And have it painted in most orient colours.
Rut. That's right! All city statues must be painted:
    Else they be worth naught i' their subtle judgements.

ACT 5   SCENE 8

[*Enter*] BIAS.

Interest. My truest friend in Court, dear Master Bias;
    You hear o'the recovery of our niece
    In fame and credit?
Bias.   Yes, I have been with her,
    And gratulated to her; but I am sorry

---

86. Merchant] *Wha;* Merchants *F.*   87. Street—] *This ed.;* street, *F.*
90. I'd] *Wha;* II'd *F.*

---

82. *aldermanity*] the body of aldermen (*OED* 2 cites this): possibly a
Jonson coinage, though he uses the word differently at *Staple,* 3.Int.9.
    83. *Stripped*] Besides corrupting all the aldermen, the amount will buy all
their fancy clothes.
    86. *Merchant Tailors Hall*] The Hall of this guild in Threadneedle Street
at the heart of the City was used for prestigious entertainment, such as for
James I (Chalfant, p. 126).
    87–8. *Needle . . . thread*] Rut's astrology depends upon this pun on
Threadneedle Street.
    91. *orient*] brilliant as the rising of the sun.
    92. *painted*] The painting of statues was deplored by Sir Henry Wotton,
The Elements of Architecture (1624), p. 89 (*H&S*).

    3. *credit*] reputation.
    4. *gratulated to her*] rejoiced with her.

To find the author o' the foul aspersion　　　5
Here i'your company, this insolent doctor.
Interest. You do mistake him: he is clear got off on't.
A gossip's jealousy first gave the hint.
He drives another way now, as I would have him.
He's a rare man, the doctor, in his way.　　　10
H'has done the noblest cure here, i' the house,
On a poor squire, my sister's tailor, Needle,
That talked in's sleep; would walk to Saint John's Wood
And Waltham Forest, scape by all the ponds
And pits i'the way; run over two-inch bridges;　　　15
With his eyes fast, and i' the dead of night!
I'll ha' you better acquainted with him. Doctor,
Here is my dear, dear, dearest friend in Court,
Wise, powerful Master Bias: pray you salute
Each other, not as strangers, but true friends.　　　20
Rut. This is the gentleman you brought today,
A suitor to your niece?
Interest.　　　　　　　Yes.
Rut.　　　　　　　　　You were
Agreed, I heard; the writings drawn between you?
Interest. And sealed.
Rut.　　　　　　What broke you off?
Interest.　　　　　　　　　　This rumour of her?
Was it not, Master Bias?
Bias.　　　　　　　Which I find　　　25

---

25. not,] *Wha;* not *F.*

---

6. *insolent*] 'offensively contemptuous of the rights and feelings' (*OED* 1, close to Latin).

7. *he . . . on't*] He has been found to be not responsible for it.

9. *drives*] proceeds, tends (*OED* 27).

13–14. *Saint . . . Forest*] Chalfant points out that a walk from Loadstone's house in the City to St John's Wood to the north-west and on to Waltham Forest in Hertfordshire would be about 25 miles (p. 191).

15. *two-inch bridges*] Unexplained: perhaps an exaggeration for very narrow bridges.

16. *fast*] tight shut: not in *OED*, but cf. fast asleep (fast 1d).

23. *writings*] written agreement.

drawn] were drawn (elliptical).

Now false, and therefore come to make amends.
I' the first place I stand to the old conditions.
Rut. Faith give 'em him, Sir Moth, whate'er they were.
    You have a brave occasion now to cross
    The flaunting Master Compass, who pretends   30
    Right to the portion, by th'other entail.
Interest. And claims it. You do hear he's married?
Bias. We hear his wife is run away from him
    Within: she is not to be found i'the house
    With all the hue and cry is made for her   35
    Through every room; the larders ha' been searched,
    The bakehouses and boulting tub, the ovens,
    Washhouse, and brewhouse, nay the very furnace
    And yet she is not heard of.
Interest.   Be she ne'er heard of
    The safety of Great Britain lies not on't.   40
    You are content with the ten thousand pound
    Defalking the four hundred garnish money?
    That's the condition here, afore the doctor
    And your demand, friend Bias.
Bias.   It is, Sir Moth.

Enter PALATE.

Rut. Here comes the parson then shall make all sure.   45
Interest. Go you with my friend Bias, Parson Palate,
    Unto my niece; assure them we are agreed.
Palate. And Mistress Compass too is found within.

26–7. amends . . . place] *This ed.;* amends *(no stop)* . . . place. *(with stop) F.*
28. whate'er] *Wha;* what ere *F.*   30. flaunting] *Wi;* flanting *F (for* slant-
ing*?)*   37. bakehouses] *Wi;* bake-houses *Wha;* Bak-houses *F.*   tub,] *Fc;*
tub. *Fu.*   44.1] *in right margin, F.*

---

    26. *Now false*] Jonson here has Interest and Bias sustain the pretence that
there was no baby.
    30. *flaunting*] showing off.
    31. *entail*] settlement of right to an inheritance (*OED* 2a).
    37. *boulting tub*] where bran was sifted from corn.
    42. *Defalking*] cutting off a part.
    garnish money] money for extra expenses (*OED* garnish 7 cites this
without explanation).

Interest. Where was she hid?

Palate.   In an old bottle-house
    Where they scraped trenchers; there her mother had
        thrust her.   50

Rut. You shall have time, sir, to triumph on him
    When this fine feat is done, and his Rud-Ironside.

                                            [*Exeunt.*]

                   ACT 5   SCENE 9

        [*Enter*] COMPASS, POLISH, LADY [LOADSTONE],
           PLEASANCE, KEEP, CHAIR [*and*] PRACTICE.

Compass. Was ever any gentlewoman used
    So barbarously by a malicious gossip,
    Pretending to be mother to her too?

Polish. Pretending! Sir, I am her mother, and challenge
    A right and power for what I have done.

Compass.   Out, hag.   5
    Thou that hast put all nature off, and woman,
    For sordid gain; betrayed the trust committed
    Unto thee by the dead, as from the living;
    Changed the poor innocent infants in their cradles;
    Defrauded them o'their parents, changed their names,   10
    Calling Placentia, Pleasance; Pleasance, Placentia.

52.1] *G.*

5.9] *This ed.; Compasse. Pleasance. Lady. Ironside. Practise. (/) Polish. Chaire.*
Keepe. &c. F. (Ironside enters at 5.10.7.1.)

───

    49. *bottle-house*] place for making bottles (*OED*, first in 1875); but the
sense may depend upon *OED* bottle sb³, a bundle of hay or straw.
    50. *trenchers*] wooden plates.
    51. *him*] Compass.
    52. *Rud-Ironside*] This is presumably a shortened form for the full name
used or attributed by Rut at 3.3.11: see note.

    3. *Pretending*] claiming.
    5. *power*] legal authority (*OED* 5).
    6. *put . . . off*] behaved unnaturally.
    7. *sordid*] foul, corrupt (Cotgrave).
    8. *as . . . living*] as also the trust you had from the living.

Polish. How knows he this?

Compass.   Abused the neighbourhood;
    But most this lady. Didst enforce an oath
    To this poor woman, on a pious book,
    To keep close thy impiety.

Polish.   Ha' you told this?   15

Keep. I told it? No, he knows it, and much more,
    As he's a cunning man.

Polish.   A cunning fool,
    If that be all.

Compass.   But now to your true daughter
    That had the child and is the proper Pleasance:
    We must have an account of that too, gossip.   20

Polish. This's like all the rest of Master Compass.

ACT 5   SCENE 10

Enter to them running, RUT.

Rut. Help! Help! for charity: Sir Moth Interest
    Is fallen into the well.

Lady.   Where? Where?

Rut.   I'the garden.
    A rope to save his life!

Compass.   How came he there?

Rut. He thought to take possession of a fortune

20. gossip.] *Wha;* Gossip; *F.*

5.10] *This ed.; in right margin, with -Rut. added after Interest F. See Notes. F*
has Silkworme for Diaphanous for the whole scene: see Introduction, p. 49.
Ironside is included in the scene heading for 5.9 in F in spite of the entry
marked at 5.10.7.1.

    12. *Abused*] Did wrong to.
    15. *keep close*] keep secret.
    impiety] duty towards her child; cf. *pius* (Lat.): frequently used for family
obligations.
    you] Polish turns on Keep.
    17. *cunning man*] See 2.2.41n.
    18. *If . . . all*] As far as that is concerned.
    21. *all the rest*] Perhaps she is cut off here by Rut's entrance, but the sense
seems to be that Compass knows too much.

There newly dropped him, and the old chain broke,   5
And down fell he i'the bucket.
Compass.   Is it deep?
Rut. We cannot tell. A rope: help with a rope!

> *Enter* DIAPHANOUS, IRONSIDE, ITEM, NEEDLE *and*
> INTEREST.

Diaphanous. He is got out again. The knight is saved.
Ironside. A little soused i'the water: Needle saved him.
Item. The water saved him, 'twas a fair escape.   10
Needle. Ha' you no hurt?
Interest.   A little wet.
Needle.   That's nothing.
Rut. I wished you stay, sir, till tomorrow: and told you
It was no lucky hour: since six o'clock
All stars were retrograde.
Lady.   I'the name
Of fate or folly, how came you i'the bucket?   15
Interest. That is a *quaere* of another time, sister;
The doctor will resolve you, who hath done
The admirablest cure upon your Needle.
Gi' me thy hand, good Needle: thou cam'st timely.
Take off my hood and coat. And let me shake   20
Myself a little. I have a world of business.
Where is my nephew Bias? And his wife?

> [*Enter*] BIAS, PLACENTIA [*and*] PALATE.

---

13. o'clock] *G*; a Clock *F.*   14.] *Lady.* in *right margin, F, presumably a
mistaken entry: cf. l. 2, and Introduction, p. 51.*   15. folly,] *F3;*folly *F.*   22.1]
This ed.; Bias. Placentia. Palate. in *right margin, opposite ll. 21–3, F.*

---

9. *soused*] drenched.
10. *saved*] he was saved because the water broke his fall.
fair] fortunate.
12. *stay*] (to) delay.
14. *retrograde*] acting against the normal astrological order.
16. quaere] query, something to be asked (Lat.): cf. *NI*, 2.5.125.
of another time] to be answered at a more suitable time.
21. *world of*] a vast quantity of.
22. *wife*] Placentia: though she is not yet married to Bias and will not be.

Who bids God gi' 'em joy? Here they both stand
As sure affianced as the parson or words
Can tie 'em.
Rut.   We all wish' 'em joy and happiness.   25
Diaphanous. I saw the contract, and can witness it.
Interest. He shall receive ten thousand pounds tomorrow.
You looked for't, Compass, or a greater sum,
But 'tis disposed of, this, another way.
I have but one niece, verily, Compass.   30
Compass. I'll find another.

[Enter] VARLET.

Varlet, do your office.
Varlet. I do arrest your body, Sir Moth Interest,
In the King's name, at suit of Master Compass
And Dame Placentia, his wife. The action's entered
Five hundred thousand pound.
Interest.   Hear you this, sister?   35
And hath your house the ears to hear it too?
And to resound the affront?
Lady.   I cannot stop
The laws, or hinder justice. I can be
Your bail, if't may be taken.
Compass.   With the captain's,
I ask no better.
Rut.   Here are better men   40
Will give their bail.
Compass.   But yours will not be taken,
Worshipful doctor; you are good security

---

23. gi' 'em] *This ed.;* gi'hem *F.*   31. S.D.] *This ed.;Varlet. in right margin
opposite ll. 32/3, F.*

---

23. *bids . . . joy*] Cf. 5.2.1n.
27. *ten thousand pounds*] Cf. 5.6.41.
28. *looked for't*] expected it.
31. *Varlet*] minor official of the City of London: cf. *EMI,* 4.8.67, where
one is also called a sergeant.
34. *entered*] legally registered (at).
36–7. *house . . . resound*] mock heroic imagery suggesting tragedy.

For a suit of clothes to th'tailor that dares trust you:
But not for such a sum as is this action.
Varlet, you know my mind.

Varlet.   You must to prison, sir,   45
Unless you can find bail the creditor likes.

Interest. I would fain find it, if you'd show me where.

Diaphanous. It is a terrible action; more indeed
Than many a man is worth. And is called fright-bail.

Ironside. Faith, I will bail him, at mine own apperil.   50
Varlet, be gone: I'll once ha' the reputation
To be security for such a sum.   [*Exit* VARLET.]
Bear up, Sir Moth.

Rut.   He is not worth the buckles
About his belt, and yet this Ironside clashes.

Interest. Peace, lest he hear you, doctor; we'll make use of
him.   55
What doth your brother Compass, Captain Ironside,
Demand of us, by way of challenge, thus?

Ironside. Your niece's portion; in the right of his wife.

Interest. I have assured one portion, to one niece,
And have no more t'account for that I know of: 60
What I may do in charity—if my sister
Will bid an offering for her maid and him
As a benevolence to 'em, after supper—
I'll spit into the basin, and entreat
My friends to do the like.

Compass.   Spit out thy gall   65

52.1] *Wi.*   61. charity—] *Fc;* charity *Fu.*

---

43. *tailor . . . trust*] Conventionally tailors' bills were large and paid last, and tailors had to trust their customers extensively: but even such debts are trifling to this sum.

47. *fain*] willingly.

49. *fright-bail*] Cf. 5.3.33.

50. *apperil*] peril, risk: cf. *T of T*, 2.2.93, and *DA*, 5.4.34.

51. *once*] on this one occasion.

53. *worth . . . buckles*] proverbial (Tilley S382: 'not worth two shoe buckles': first in 1670, but cf. S383: 'We play not for shoe buckles', 1616).

54. *clashes*] in spite of his poverty Ironside is making a loud intervention: cf. talk recklessly (*OED* clash 10; first citation 1697).

62. *bid*] ask for.

64. *spit . . . basin*] cited by *H&S* as a French proverb (*cracher au bassin*) for making an unwilling contribution.

And heart, thou viper; I will now no mercy,
No pity of thee, thy false niece, and Needle;
Bring forth your child, or I appeal you of murder,
You, and this gossip here, and Mother Chair.
Chair. The gentleman's fallen mad!

PLEASANCE steps out.

Pleasance.   No, Mistress Midwife.   70
    I saw the child, and you did give it me,
    And put it i' my arms; by this ill token,
    You wished me such another; and it cried.
Practice. The law is plain: if it were heard to cry,
    And you produce it not, he may indict   75
    All that conceal't of felony and murder.
Compass. And I will take the boldness, sir, to do it:
    Beginning with Sir Moth here, and his doctor.
Diaphanous. Good faith, this same is like to turn a business.
Palate. And a shrewd business, marry: they all start at't.   80
Compass. I ha' the right thread now, and I will keep it.

---

70. SD] *in left margin, F.*

    66. *will*] will show (elliptical).
    68. *appeal*] will accuse (*OED* 1c): cf. *R2*, 1.1.9.
    69. *You . . . gossip*] refers to Polish, and then Keep.
    70. *fallen mad*] Chair still pretends there is no baby even though it was she who undertook to conceal it; cf. 4.7.23–4.
    72. *ill token*] evil symbol or gesture, wishing I too would have (or be?) an illegitimate child.
    74. *The . . . plain*] The crying of the child is a presumptive element in the law. Killing infants was of some concern: cf. 'If the child be born alive and dieth of the potion, battery or other cause, this is murder: for in law it is accounted a reasonable creature, *in rerum natura*, when it is born alive', Sir Edward Coke, *The Third Part of the Institutes of the Laws of England* (1628; reprinted New York, 1979), p. 50. As he had many legal friends, including Selden and Bacon, Jonson will have been aware of the enactment of 1623 (21 Jas.I, c. 27): this was incorporated into the Offences against the Person Act of 1861, still in force today. See Stephen James Fitzjames, *A History of the Criminal Law in England* (London, 1883), 3.118.
    76. *felony*] serious crime punishable by forfeiture of goods (*OED* 4b).
    79. *turn a business*] turn into a complicated or serious matter.
    80. *shrewd*] dangerous (*OED* 4).
    start at't] show apprehension about it.
    81. *right thread*] follow the right scent: recalls 'the right end', Ind.131.

You, goody Keep, confess the truth to my lady,
The truth, the whole truth, nothing but the truth.
Polish. I scorn to be prevented of my glories.
I plotted the deceit, and I will own it.   85
Love to my child, and lucre of the portion
Provoked me; wherein though th'event hath failed
In part, I will make use of the best side.
This is my daughter, [*Points to Placentia*] and she hath
      had a child
This day—unto her shame I now profess it—   90
By this mere false-stick Squire Needle, but
Since this wise knight hath thought it good to change
The foolish father of it, by assuring
Her to his dear friend, Master Bias; and him
Again to her, by clapping of him on   95
With his free promise of ten thousand pound
Afore so many witnesses—
Diaphanous.   Whereof I
      Am one.
Palate.   And I another.
Polish.   I should be unnatural
To my own flesh and blood would I not thank him.

---

85. I will] I *faint in most copies seen,* F.   87. me;] e *obscured by* (;).   89.
S.D.] *G.*   90. unto . . . it] *This ed.; in parenthesis,* F.   92. knight] *Wha;*
Knight, *F.*   change] *Fc;* change, *Fu.*   98. unnatural] *Wha;* unrurall
Fu; unnaturall *Fc.*

---

82. *goody*] for goodwife; see 4.8.65n.
83. *truth . . . truth*] legal formula and proverb (Dent T590: 'the truth, the
whole truth, and nothing but the truth'). Cf. *T of T*, 2.6.31–2, and below, ll.
102, 106.
84. *prevented of*] deprived of (*OED* 6).
glories] glorious achievements.
85. *own*] pun on (1) admit and (2) keep possession (cf. l. 84).
86. *lucre*] gain derived from (*OED* 2a cites this).
87. *event*] outcome.
90. *profess*] acknowledge (*OED* 2c, Massinger, *The Roman Actor*,
Dedication).
91. *mere false-stick*] pure cheat (not in *OED*).
93. *assuring*] making certain: cf. 5.8.47.
94–5. *him . . . her*] [assuring] that Bias will respond by taking her [which
he does not].
95. *clapping . . . on*] making a bargain (*OED* 7).

I thank you, sir: and I have reason for it.   100
For here your true niece stands, fine Mistress Compass.
I'll tell you truth, you have deserved it from me.
To whom you are by bond engaged to pay
The sixteen thousand pound, which is her portion
Due to her husband on her marriage-day.   105
I speak the truth, and nothing but the truth.

Ironside. You'll pay it now, Sir Moth, with interest?
You see the truth breaks out on every side of you.

Interest. Into what nets of coz'nage am I cast
On ev'ry side? Each thread is grown a noose,   110
A very mesh: I have run myself into
A double break of paying twice the money.

Bias. You shall be released of paying me a penny
With these conditions.

Polish.   Will you leave her then?

Bias. Yes, and the sum twice told, ere take a wife   115
To pick out Monsieur Needle's basting threads.

Compass. Gossip, you are paid: though he be a fit nature
Worthy to have a whore justly put on him,
He is not bad enough to take your daughter
On such a cheat. Will you yet pay the portion?   120

Interest. What will you 'bate?

Compass.   No penny the law gives.

Interest. Yes, Bias's money.

Compass.   What, your friend in Court?
I will not rob you of him, nor the purchase,

---

100. have] *Fc; reversed e Fu.*   103. pay] *Fc; pay, Fu.*   109. coz'nage]
This ed.; cous'nage *F.*   110. noose] noofe *F;* Noof *F3.*

---

103. *whom*] Mrs Compass.
106. *truth*] Cf. ll. 83, 102.
109. *coz'nage*] trickery.
112. *break*] trap (*OED,* brake 6).
116. *pick out*] unpick.
    basting] loosely sewed (*OED* v¹): cf. basted *MAdo,* 1.1.289.
120. *cheat*] trick.
    yet] now.
121. *'bate*] reduce.
    No . . . gives] nothing of what is allowed to me by law.
123.] I will not take away (rob) from you the right to pay him, nor will I
take (rob) the money from the amount agreed.
    purchase] plunder (*OED* 8): cf. *Alc.,* 4.7.122.

Nor your dear doctor here; stand all together,
Birds of a nature all, and of a feather.   125
Lady. Well, we are all now reconciled to truth.
There rests yet a gratuity from me,
To be conferred upon this gentleman,
Who, as my nephew Compass says, was cause
First of th'offence, but since of all th'amends.   130
The quarrel caused th'affright; that fright brought on
The travail, which made peace; the peace drew on
This new discovery, which endeth all
In reconcilement.
Compass.   When the portion
Is tendered and received.
Interest.   Well, you must have it   135
As good at first as last.
Lady.   'Tis well said, brother.
And I, if this good captain will accept me,
Give him myself, endow him with my estate,
And make him lord of me, and all my fortunes:
He that hath saved my honour, though by chance,   140
I'll really study his, and how to thank him.
Ironside. And I embrace you, lady, and your goodness,
And vow to quit all thought of war hereafter,
Save what is fought under your colours, madam.
Palate. More work then for the parson; I shall cap   145
The Loadstone with an Ironside, I see.

---

124. here;] *Wha;* here, *F.*   all together,] *Wha;* altogether. *F.*   130.
amends.] *Wha;* amends, *F.*   132. peace;] (;) *damaged in some copies of F.*
136. *Lady*] *F3; not in F.*   140. honour] *1716, Wha;* houre *F.*

---

125. *Birds . . . feather*] proverbial (Dent B393: 'birds of a feather will flock
together').
126. *reconciled*] sustains the subtitle.
127. *gratuity*] wages; cf. *Und.,* 76.10.
130. *amends*] reparation: cf. Leviticus, 5: 16.
135. *tendered*] offered. Compass points out that the money has yet to
change hands.
136. *As good . . . last*] proverbial (Dent F294: 'As good do it first as last').
141. *study his*] seek to improve his fortunes.
144. *colours*] flag or patronage, suggesting chivalry.
145. *cap*] cover, with metaphorical significance from magnetism, and also
from sexual covering.

Ironside. And take in these, the forlorn couple, with us,
    Needle and 's Thread, whose portion I will think on,
    As being a business waiting on my bounty:
    Thus I do take possession of you, madam,   150
    My true magnetic mistress and my lady.   [*Exeunt.*]

The end.

CHORUS
Changed into an EPILOGUE:
To the KING

Well, gentlemen, I now must under seal
    And th'author's charge, waive you, and make my'appeal
To the supremest power, my Lord, the King;
    Who best can judge of what we humbly bring.
He knows our weakness, and the poet's faults;   5
    Where he doth stand upright, go firm, or halts;
And he will doom him. To which voice he stands,
    And prefers that, 'fore all the people's hands.

[FINIS.]

151.1] *G.*   152.] *in right margin, F.*

147. *forlorn*] wretched; ruined.
148. *Thread*] i.e. Placentia.
151. *magnetic*] playing upon attractive (*OED* 1c, from 1667).

Changed] In substituting this Chorus Jonson possibly suppressed
concluding business between Probee, Damplay and the Boy.
1. *under seal*] Cf. 4.2.36 and 39.
2. *waive you*] put you aside.
5. *our*] the actors'.
6. *he*] the poet.
halts] limps.
7. *he . . . him*] i.e. the king . . . the poet.
doom] judge. The theme of judgement or discrimination is here sustained
and completed. It is as though Jonson has only one informed spectator in
his audience, the King: hence *stands*, obediently awaiting judgement or
applause (hands). Cf. *OED* stand 76.
To] In deference to.
8. *prefers*] puts before.

Appendix I

ALEXANDER GILL'S VERSES AND JONSON'S REPLY

UPON BEN JONSON'S '*MAGNETIC LADY*'

Parturient Montes Nascetur ridiculus Mus.

Is this your Loadstone, Ben, that must attract
Applause and laughter at each scene and act?
Is this the child of your bedridden wit
And none but the Blackfriars to foster it?
If to the Fortune you had sent your Lady   5
'Mongst prentices and apple-wives it may be
Your rosy fool might have some sport begot
With his strange habit and indefinite knot.
But whenas silks and plush and all the wits
Are called to see and censure as befits,   10
And if your folly take not, they perchance
Must hear themselves styled Gentle Ignorance.
Foh, how it stinks! What general offence
Gives thy profaneness and gross impudence!
O how thy friend Nat Butter 'gan to melt,   15
Whenas the poorness of thy plot he smelt;
And Inigo with laughter there grew fat
That there was nothing worth the laughing at.
And yet thou crazily art confident
Belching out full-mouthed oaths with foul intent,   20
Calling us fools and rogues, unlettered men,

Parturient . . . Mus.] 'The mountains shall give birth and a laughable mouse shall be born', Horace, *De Arte Poetica*, l. 139. Proverbial.

7. *rosy*] in rude health, red-faced: presumably this is meant to be Ironside, and may be allusive to Lowen, as in l. 61n. There may be a pun on his first name as abbreviated to 'Rud' at 5.8.52.

8. *knot*] ornamental bow, or military epaulette (*OED* 2).

17. *fat*] insensible, stupid (*OED 14*).

Poor narrow souls that cannot judge of Ben:
Yet, which is worse, after three shameful foils
The printers must be put to further toils,
Whereas indeed, to vindicate thy fame,   25
Th'hadst better give thy pamphlet to the flame.
O what a strange prodigious year 'twill be
If this thy play come forth in thirty three!
Let Doomsday rather come on New Year's Eve
And of thy paper plague the world bereave.   30
Which plague I fear worse than a sergeant's bit
Worse than the infection or an ague fit,
Worse than astronomers' divining lips
Worse than three suns, a comet or eclipse;
Or if thy learned brother Allestree   35
(Who's Homer unto thee for poetry)
Should tell of rain upon St Swithun's day,
And that should wash the harvest clean away.
As for the press, if thy play must come to't
Let Thomas Purfoot or John Trundell do't   40
In such dull characters as for reliefs
Of fines and wracks we find in begging briefs;
But in cap-paper let it printed be
(Indeed brown paper is too good for thee)
And let it (then) be so apocryphal   45
As not to dare to venture on a stall
Except it be of druggers, grocers, cooks,
Victuallers, tobacco men and sunlike rooks;

---

23. *foils*] times; see Introduction, p. 24.

24. *printers . . . toils*] This implies that printing may have been envisaged by Jonson, perhaps on a parallel with *NI*.

31. *sergeant's bit*] condemnation (bite) of a judge.

35. *Allestree*] almanac-maker: cf. *ML*, 4.2.34.

40. *Thomas . . . Trundell*] Thomas Purfoot 2 (d. ?1640) and John Trundell (d. 1626) were printers and booksellers.

41. *characters*] letters.

42. *wracks*] disasters (*OED* sb^1 2).

begging briefs] legal petitions asking for relief (not in *OED*, but cf. brief, 2c).

43. *cap-paper*] wrapping paper (*OED* 1).

45. *apocryphal*] of doubtful authenticity,

48. *rooks*] abusive name for a traders.

From Bucklersbury let it not be barred,
But think not of Duck Lane or Paul's Churchyard.   50
But to advise thee, Ben, in this strict age,
A brick-hill's fitter for thee than a stage.
Thou better know'st a groundsill how to lay,
Than lay the plot or groundwork of a play,
And better canst direct to cap a chimney   55
Than to converse with Clio or Polyhimny.
Fall then to work in thy old age again,
Take up thy trudge and trowel, gentle Ben,
Let plays alone: or if thou needs wilt write,
And thrust thy feeble muse into the light;   60
Let Lowin cease, and Taylor fear to touch
The loathèd stage, for thou hast made it such.
[Bodleian MS Ashmole 38, p. 15: transcribed in *H&S*,
      11.346.]

49–50. *Bucklersbury . . . Churchyard*] Duck Lane and St Paul's Church-yard are addresses of known printers, but Bucklersbury, off Poultry in the City of London, is not so identified in *STC* vol. 3. John Stow says that 'on both sides throughout [it] is possessed of grocers and apothecaries'; see *A Survey of London* (1603), edited by Charles L. Kingsford, 2 vols (Oxford, 1908), 1.260.

52. *brick-hill's fitter*] The jibe about Jonson's past as a bricklayer went back at least as far as *The Returne from Parnassus* which was acted at St John's College, Cambridge in 1606: see *H&S*, 11.364.

53. *groundsill*] a timber acting as a foundation, usually for wooden structures (*OED* sb²).

56. *Clio*] Muse of History.

Polyhimny] Polyhymnia or Polymnia, Muse who presided over singing and rhetoric.

58. *trudge*] tray or hod for mortar (*OED* trug 2: not this spelling).

61. *Lowin . . . Taylor*] John Lowen (1576–1653) and Joseph Taylor (?1585–1652) were leading actors and managers with the King's Men from the 1620s, acting in *NI* and *ML*. Lowen was large in size and played bluff, 'honest' parts, though he is said to have appeared as Falstaff, Volpone and Sir Epicure Mammon. Taylor was more of a romantic lead, handsome in youth. In 1632 he played Mirabell in *The Wild Goose*, 'a gret defyer of Ladies in way of marriage'; and he is said to have played Hamlet, Truewit (*SW*), Face, and Mosca. See Bentley, 2.499–506, and 590–8.

62. *The loathèd stage*] *MP*, 33.1, Jonson's lament after the failure of *NI*.

BEN JONSON'S ANSWER

Shall the prosperity of a pardon still
Secure thy railing rhymes, infamous Gill,
At libelling? Shall no Star Chamber peers,
Pillory nor whip, nor want of ears,
All which thou has incurred deservedly;   5
Nor degradation from the ministry
To be the Denis of thy father's school,
Keep in thy barking wit, thou bawling fool?
Thinking to stir me, thou hast lost thy end;
I'll laugh at thee, poor wretched tyke; go send   10
Thy blatant muse abroad, and teach it rather
A tune to drown the ballads of thy father:
For thou hast naught in thee to cure his fame,
But tune and noise, the echo of his shame.
A rogue by statute, censured to be whipped,   15
Cropped, branded, slit, neck-stocked: go you are stripped.

(*MP*, 122)

[Another response to Gill in English by Zouch Towneley is printed
in *H&S*, 11.348–9.]

---

7. *Denis . . . school*] Alexander Gill was sentenced to the pillory in 1628,
and to be degraded from his priesthood, but he was later pardoned. His
father was High Master of St Paul's School. Like the tyrant Dionysius of
Syracuse (Denis), Gill kept himself by teaching after his fall.

10. *tyke*] ill-mannered boor.

11. *blatant*] invented by Spenser to describe a thousand-tongued monster
symbolising calumny (*OED*).

16. *branded, slit*] Jonson was branded on the thumb after his plea of
benefit of clergy ensured his pardon for killing Gabriel Spencer in 1598; and
he narrowly escaped having his nose slit when imprisoned over *Eastward Ho*
in 1605–6.

neck-stocked] put in the pillory, which held the neck fast.

Appendix II

THE ANTIPLATONICK

The soldier, that man of iron,
Whom ribs of horror all environ
That's slung with wire instead of veins,
In whose embraces you're in chains
Let a magnetic girl appear   5
Straight he turns Cupid's cuirassier
Love storms his lips and takes the fortress in
For all the bristled turnpikes of his chin.

Since Love's artillery then checks
The breastworks of the firmest sex   10
Come let us in affections riot
Th'are sickly pleasures keep a diet.
Give me a lover bold and free
Not eunuch'd with formality
Like an ambassador that beds a queen   15
With the nice caution of a sword between.

(ll. 33–48)

From *The Poems of John Cleveland*, ed. B. Morris and E. Willington
(Oxford, 1967), pp. 54–6.

[I am grateful to Alastair MacDonald for drawing my attention to
this poem.]

Appendix III

When the Boy tells Mr Damplay that his name is John Trygust and that he is Cornish (1 Chor. 64–5) he raises a question about why Jonson chose this local connection, since he does not use it anywhere else in the play. The simplest suggestion is that Jonson was naming his character to give him a symbolic function, as discussed in the Introduction, and that having thought of Try- he thought of a parallel with the common prefix Tre- for Cornish surnames. But there is a further conjecture which may account for Jonson's choice. It would involve Jonson's starting with the knowledge that the person he had in mind was Cornish and inventing the name and significance accordingly.

In the first place it seems likely that the Boy is a fictional version of Richard Brome (?1590–?1652), who had been Jonson's servant and apprentice and who, by the time of the composition of *The Magnetic Lady*, was over forty years old, and had established a reputation as a dramatist which was in some ways rivalling Jonson's. The Boy speaks as though he is trusted by Jonson and says some things which in the theatrical code of the play convey the urgency and seriousness of Jonson's views of comedy. The fiction, though, is obliquely developed, because the Boy says he had learned about Terence in the third form at Westminster School. There is no reason to suppose that Brome did, but every reason to think that this is what had happened to Jonson himself. Outside the play, Jonson praises Brome's grasp of the principles of comedy. Though there had been some tension between them earlier, it appears that by 1632 fences had been mended when Jonson's commendatory verses were prefixed to Brome's *The Northern Lass* (*H&S*, 8.409). The invention of the Boy as a spokesman for Jonson lies at the heart of Jonson's wish to be present in the theatre—which he could not because of his illness—but the presence needed to be indirect since Jonson did not wish to speak openly in his own voice, but by using the voice of a fictional character.

Virtually nothing has come to light about Brome's birth and

upbringing. He comes into view about 1614 as Jonson's secretary, and he is mentioned by name in *Bartholomew Fair* as being in the playhouse during the performance: 'I am looking lest the poet hear me, or his man, Master Brome, behind the arras' (Ind.7–8).

The possible link with Cornwall is supported by the following scattered references in Brome's plays, as in *The Dramatic Works of Richard Brome Containing Fifteen Comedies*, 3 vols (London, 1873).

1. One of the few surviving specimens of Middle Cornish is found in *The Northern Lass*, in five words spoken by Master Hercules Nonsense, specified as a Cornish Gentleman (3.101), as follows: '*Peden bras, vidne whee bis cregas*' This was corrected to *Pedn bras a vednough why bos creges*, and translated as 'Fat-head, you will be hanged', by Henry Jenner (Some Miscellaneous Scraps of Cornish', in *Annual Reports of the Royal Cornish Polytechnic Society* n.s. 6 (1927–30), pp. 238–55 (pp. 249–50). The rarity of examples of Middle Cornish makes this quite remarkable.

2. Nonsense promises that he will make a stage play when he goes home to Cornwall (3.107).

3. In *The Demoiselle* there is Sir Amphilus, specified as a Cornish Knight, and his servant Trebasco. The former speaks of 'my poor little goonhilly [pony]' carrying him from Penzance to St Columb in one day (1.402).

4. In the same play Canitha Holdup's father 'bore the office of a Commissioner for the Peace in the West Country'. Squelch adds that he lived by the seaside and traded with the pirates and sold them victuals. (3.67–8)

5. Barbara, in *The Antipodes*, says 'Beyond the moone and starres/ Or mount in Cornwall either.' (3.240).

6. The word *skipper* (*Jovial Crew*, 2.2.167), meaning 'barn' has a possible Cornish derivation (*OED* sb3.a).

The name Brome does not appear to be especially Cornish: I have found one instance of it at Redruth in 1545 in T. L. Stoate, *Cornwall Subsidies in the Reign of Henry VIII*, p. 1. It is, however, rather more common in Devon at this time. Equally, I have not been able to identify anything else Cornish in Jonson documentation, though he did possess a Welsh Grammar (*H&S*, 1.258–60).

I am grateful to Brian Murdoch and Oliver Padel for their advice and information about matters Cornish, though the conjecture about Brome is my responsibility. The evidence here assembled does not point conclusively to a Cornish origin for Brome but I think it does establish a possible link. If the supposition is correct it significantly increases the stage effectiveness of the Boy, especially as there is a comic undertone of appreciation, and it is the Boy who so vigorously refutes any idea of specific identification (2 Chor. 18–23).

Appendix IV

[Latin texts printed by H&S, 11.349–50. For the full text of the Latin play and the Commendatory Verses, see *Peter Hausted's 'Senile Odium'*, edited and translated by Laurens J. Mills (Bloomington, Ind., 1949). The play was performed in Queens' College, Cambridge, probably in 1630 or 1631. Edward Kemp and John Rogers both appeared in plays at Queens' at this time: see Alan H. Nelson, *Cambridge*, Records of Early English Drama, 2 vols (Toronto, 1989), pp. 922–3 and 960. I am much indebted to Bella Millett and Alison Samuels for their help in preparing these translations.]

EDWARD KEMP

But what malignant star governs the stage? The same evil destiny afflicts the boards—the triumph of noise and generous lungs. Set aside the verdict of the common herd; away with their scales of judgement. This monster, Jonson, dares to scorn the magnetic power of your comedy, and its lofty 5
rapture. The bankrupt mob has no true appreciation of your worth; it laughs to contemplate the snowy head and grey hairs of the author. Its wilful insolence has hastened the old Laureate's palsy—how he suffers. Lo! You, the great man, are toppling, victim of an enviable slander: your distillations 10
of ancient texts are considered thefts. Because you strive with reverent zeal to emulate Pindar and the poetry of your beloved

---

5. *magnetic*] *ML* was performed in 1632, and *Senile odium* printed in 1633.
6. *bankrupt*] The Latin (*inops*) suggests both financial and moral poverty.
8. *author*] parens in the original suggests both author and father.
10. *enviable*] Jonson is wrongly blamed for what is really the praiseworthy learning displayed in his plays, which ought to be the object of envy: cf. the discussion of comic theory in *ML*.

Horace, Empiricus, a prophet of drunken frenzy, whose
ravings can hardly be stopped, has both branded you with the
disgrace of his charges, and most recently has denounced your   15
verses. Arrogant man, why do you grudge his writings a long
life? Do you, Jonson, think the world was too small, when
Musca spread his fragile wings to your Celia? Lo! Everywhere
pens run foul with copious dysentery, and useless quills are
loaded with drivel! Let the bank of the Thames, more bold,   20
glory in its native swans: but to receive a salary exposes worthless minds. Mechanical talents earn their coppers selling (the
shame of it!) the insipid perfumes and incense of a frigid poesy
to the altar of the Phoenix—if only they brought them as offer-
ings piety would be observed. The billowing flags at the top   25
of the tower summon the guests. A friend provides a more
pleasant show with a company of actors. One man toys with
a silver watch; another amuses himself with the slit in his glove
through which the little gem of his ring gleams; a third . . . but
there is no time: an old duty is upon us: this play will remain   30
a model, a Pattern for the slowly coming ages.

---

13. *Horace*] Kemp's Latin here echoes Horace, *Odes*, 4.2.1.

Empiricus] Probably a personification of ignorant public opinion, though
a now unknown contemporary is possible.

16. *Arrogant man*] Probably Empiricus is meant.

17. *Jonson*] not in original, but there is apparently a change in the person
addressed here.

18. *Musca . . . Celia*] Mosca (fly, Ital.) and Celia are characters in
Jonson's *Volpone* (written in 1605 or 1606, and printed in 1607).

20. *bank . . . Thames*] Where the popular theatres were situated.

22–4. *Mechanical . . . Phoenix*] Possibly a hit at Inigo Jones, whom Jonson,
by this time, regarded as mechanical, uninspired and unjustly prosperous,
and who was closely associated with the Phoenix Theatre in Drury Lane (i.e.
not on Bankside).

25. *flags*] These were flown at the top of theatre towers, but the reference
may be to flags on the tower of Queens' College, Cambridge, where *Senile
odium* was performed. Mills, however, translates *carbasa* as 'sails', suggesting
that merchants climbing to a high place to view approaching ships solicit the
patronage of all comers.

26–7. *more pleasant*] from *gratius*, Mills: *gratus* H&S

30. *duty*] obscure, but in some Colleges, notably Christ's, participation in
plays was a statutory scholastic duty.

J. ROGERS

If Jonson's brimming vessel receives its due,
(though the ignorant mob now declare it empty)
May you be Tricongio, by right of the Hippocrene spring.
Very often have I seen the wonder's of Jonson's drama.
Yours are not less: for by the powers of your poetry   5
HATRED is in love, and OLD AGE scorns to grow old.

---

3. *you*] Hausted.
Tricongio] a drunken bookseller in *Senile odium* whose change of clothes
brings him comic adventures which end happily. Rogers implies an analogue
between two deep drinkers, Jonson and Tricongio.
Hippocrene] 'Fount of the horse': a spring on Mount Helicon, sacred to
the Muses, said to have sprung from Pegasus' hoofprint.

Glossarial Index to the Commentary

An asterisk (*) before an entry indicates that the note contains information about meaning, usage or date which supplements *OED*.

men, cunning, 2.2.41
mended, 3.5.77
mere, 2.5.15, 4.2.47
mind, 4.6.20, 5.3.7
misadvised, 4.7.16
mischief, 3.6.142
money-bawd, *Pers.*17
month's mind, 3.1.23
morsel, 2.4.25
mother (1), 4.1.4
mother (2), 4.7.29
move, 2.4.24
murmurs, 2.6.38
mushroom, 3.6.70
muss, 4.3.10

nail, to the, 3 Chor.32–3
natural, 2.6.71
nearer, 5.3.29
neat, 1.3.36, 2.2.43
neater, 2.1.14
neck-stocked, Appx.I.16
nemo scit, 1.7.76
*nick it, 2.4.34
night-cap, 1.6.21
night-crow, 2.1.16
nodding, 4.4.14
noddle, 5.1.25
noise, 5.4.16

obnoxious to, 3.6.15
*obscene, 1.2.43
'od shield, 1.4.17
office, 4.4.34
open, 2.1.12
oppilation, 3.5.69
orient, 5.7.91
ounces, 3.5.50
over-entreat, 1.1.61
overgrown, 3 Chor.22
own, 4.8.23, 5.10.85

Palate, *Pers.*12
panoply, 3.6.81
parallax, 1.6.39
paramount, 4.2.14
parerga, 1.7.69
parts, 4.6.14
party, 3.7.5
passage, 2.6.152
passion, 3.6.184
pawn, Ind.34
paynims, 1 Chor.20, 3.2.10
peach, 4.7.34
pease, 5.7.58
pease-dresser, 4.7.12
peevish, 4.4.51
peevishness, 3.6.127
perdus, 3.6.122
peremptory, 1 Chor.35
perfect, 5.4.25
perimeter, Ind.103, 3.4.98
perks, 3.6.172
perplexed, 4.2.48, 4 Chor.6
personate, 2 Chor.3
persons, 1.5.24
perstringe, 2 Chor.3
pert, 3.1.32
Pharisees, 1.5.40
phlebotomy, 3.5.44, 4.2.31
piece, 4.2.38
pieced, 3.1.14, 4.7.8
pieces, 5.2.27, 5.7.62
piece up, 4.1.5
pink, 3.6.75
pint, 4.2.55
pissing while, 1 Chor.44
place, 5.3.25
Placentia, *Pers.*6
plastic, 4 Chor.17
pleading, 2.3.48, 2.6.15
plush, Ind.31, 2.1.15

venison, Ind.26
vent, 2.3.12
vents, 1.2.43
verge, 4.7.41
vesica, 3.5.34
vi-politic, *Pers*.18
virtue, 1.1.57, 3.6.89
viscountess, 2.3.60
Vitruvius, Ind.76
vively, 2 Chor.37
vogue, 5.4.1
voluptuary, 1.2.41
votes, 3.4.66
vouchsafe, 1.5.41
vowed to, 3.4.24

waist, straight, 5.7.51
waives, 4.3.15
waive you, Ep.2
ward, 1.2.19, 5.6.17

wardmote quest, 1.2.28
waters, strong, 3.1.37
weapon, 3.3.15
wedges, Ind.29
well-pressed, 3.6.166
Westminster, Ind.42
where, 2.6.90
*whirlpool, 5.2.2
whole, 2.6.58
within, 3.1.3
witness, 4.8.16
wit-work, 1.1.41
work upon, 1.6.19
world of, 5.10.21
worship, 2.2.39, 5.1.32
worshipful, 1.4.20
writings, 5.8.23

yet, 2.4.16, 5.10.120